AN AFRICAN MIRACLE

AN AFRICAN MIRACLE

State and Class Leadership and Colonial Legacy in Botswana Development

Abdi Ismail Samatar

HEINEMANN
Portsmouth, NH

Heinemann
A division of Reed Elsevier Inc.
361 Hanover Street
Portsmouth, NH 03801–3912
www.heinemann.com

ISBN 0–325–00069–7 (Heinemann cloth)
ISBN 0–325–00068–9 (Heinemann paper)

Library of Congress Cataloging-in-Publication Data

Abdi Ismail Samatar
    An African miracle : state and class leadership and colonial legacy in Botswana
development / Abdi Ismail Samatar.
        p.   cm.
    Includes bibliographical references and index.
    ISBN 0–325-00069–7 (alk. paper). —ISBN 0–325–00068–9 (pbk. : alk. paper)
    1. Democracy—Botswana. 2. Political leadership—Botswana. 3. Botswana—Politics
and government—1966– 4. Botswana—Economic conditions—1966– 5. Botswana—
Economic policy. 6. Botswana—Colonial influence. I. Title.
JQ2760.A91A23   1999
338.96883—dc21   98–34820

Cover design by Gaile Ivaska
Paperback cover photo: Parliament house, Gaborone, Botswana. Courtesy of author.
Printed in the United States of America on acid-free paper.
03 02 01 00 99 BB 1 2 3 4 5 6 7 8 9

Copyright Acknowledgments

The author and publisher gratefully acknowledge permission to use the following material:

Excerpts from *Strong Societies and Weak States* by Joel S. Migdal. Copyright © 1989 by Princeton University Press. Reprinted by permission of Princeton University Press.

Excerpts from *Development Planning and the Importance of Democratic Institutions in Botswana: Report 7* by Andreas Danevad. Copyright © 1993. Reprinted by permission of Chr. Michelsen Institute.

To the many decent and committed African public servants, like Hashi Abib, whose noble efforts have been thwarted by political and military elite, and the bureaucratic and intellectual foot soldiers of international finance capital.

To President Aden Abdullah Osman, who in 1967 was the first African president to leave office democratically, and his Prime Minister Abdirazaq H. Hussein.

To the indigenous entrepreneurs who understand the significance of a people's collective project and their role in it.

Finally to my mother, Halimo Abdillahi, and my sister, Amina Ismail.

CONTENTS

ILLUSTRATIONS

TABLES

FIGURES

MAPS

PHOTOGRAPHS

PREFACE

After nearly a decade of field studies in Somalia I decided to change my field site. My last fieldwork in southern Somalia, 1989–90, was an exhausting and a dangerous year as I closely and helplessly watched the Somali elite mindlessly and irresponsibly obliterate what little remained of national moral and political order. It was as if the elite had resolved to commit collective suicide and virtually to squander the lives of hundreds of thousands of human beings and the future of an entire people. I decided to work in a part of the continent that had real promise of a better future and where existential conditions were less dangerous and despairing.

My preliminary explorations of the Botswana political economy convinced me that Botswana was such a place. The consensus in the literature was that the state of Botswana is a unique African institution. Its characteristics seemed a far cry from the predatory Somali state. Moreover, I felt that other features Botswana shared with Somalia, such as the significance of livestock in the economy, their marginality as colonial outposts, and the semiarid and arid climate might provide a sound basis for comparative work. It was immediately apparent that the Botswana state and the Somali state occupied the opposite ends of the political and developmental spectrum. Botswana has a growing economy and liberal democracy while Somalia's stagnant economy and political dictatorship led to the disintegration of polity and society.

I encountered the Botswana bureaucracy when I applied for my first visa to visit the country. I called the embassies of Botswana and an East African country (I will call it Y) in Washington, D.C., and requested visa applications from both. I planned to go to Y for a week to attend a conference. I received the forms from both authorities. I filled out the form for Botswana, attached a check to it and sent it back with my passport to Washington, D.C. In a week's time I received my passport, a visa and a refund check for six dollars from the Embassy for an apparent overpayment. I immediately filled out the application form for Y, attached a fifty-dollar check and posted it to the Embassy. In ten days, I received my passport with a single-entry visa rather than the double-entry visa I had paid for and requested. The charge for the single entry visa was ten dollars; the embassy, however, never reimbursed me the remaining forty dollars. This incident bolstered the image I had of the Botswana bureaucracy as a professional and rule-driven apparatus. Everything seemed orderly upon arrival at Gaborone, the capital. The immigration and customs officials were formal but friendly, and I went through the formalities within fifteen minutes without being harassed by anyone. The rest of my stay in Botswana over the next two years was pleasant.

This research project started out as a comparative one between Botswana and Somalia. However, in the midst of the fieldwork in Botswana I decided to concentrate on writing a book on Botswana first, and then develop a series of comparative articles.[1] I chose to carry out field research in Botswana for six reasons. First, it was possible to conduct research without being harassed by the authorities. Second, I thought that the state of Botswana had positive lessons to offer other African countries since it was able to sustain systematic capitalist development and liberal democracy. Third, it managed its resources relatively well, and its interventions in the economy did not induce stagnation and political degeneration. Fourth, in sharp contrast to Somalia, where conventional Western scholars, media and authorities argued that clan and tribal division destroyed the state and civil society, Botswana's "tribal" and "clan" divisions seemed benign. The innocuous nature of "tribal" division in Botswana reaffirmed an anti-clanist and *nonessentialist* argument several Somali and Somalist scholars have developed regarding the causes of the Somali calamity.[2] Fifth, the experience of the Botswana state since 1966 seemed to go against another grain in the literature. The literature suggests that African states are weak because of the omnipotence of parochial centers of authority outside the state, or because of the anti-developmental nature of African tradition. Finally, Botswana seemed a good place to do research because all government agencies are mandated to produce annual reports. These reports are available to scholars and other interested parties. The well-managed library at the University of Botswana, and particularly its fine Botswana collection, was an added bonus. Moreover, public institutions were accessible and public officials were welcoming and professional rather than being defensive and unnecessarily secretive.

I have learned a great deal about the relationships between development, democracy and African tradition since I wrote this book's proposal six years ago. The first lesson I relearned was that democracy cannot take root in the continent through the unfiltered importation or imposition of blueprints developed in the West; it can take root only through systematic transformation of indigenous political relationships guided by local realities and priorities and informed by global developments. It is through such an exercise that Botswana has been able to avoid political degeneration and consequent economic decline. Critics of *An African Miracle* may point out that this book should have devoted more space to questions of inequality and poverty in Botswana. This is an important concern. However, I deliberately decided to focus on state capacity building, which has not received much attention in the continent. This is by no means to romanticize Botswana's tradition or gloss over the problems in its current political economic order, such as extreme economic inequality and marginalization of the San people. Instead, I argue that only through serious culturally grounded and locally driven political and economic priorities will an appropriate system of accountable and responsive government and development be forged in our continent.

The moral of *An African Miracle* is that reversing horrible recent political economic trends on our continent requires that people's needs determine development. The key to such a project is developing and organically linking autonomous African intellectual capacity with autonomous, embedded, legitimate, and purposeful political authority. African development policy since independence has mainly been informed or even shaped by Western liberal and neoliberal, and/or Soviet/socialist thought and practice. Africans rarely were major players in the conception of development ideas and their translation into practice. In other words, the continent never developed a broad and deep enough intellectual wherewithal to bend and add to those ideas in order to take account of its particular circumstances. Where individuals and small groups with such capacities existed, they have been, at best, marginalized, and the economic malaise of the last twenty years has dealt them a serious blow. The dearth of this autonomy is best exemplified by the commonly known relationship between many Western academics (liberal, conservative or radical) and African scholars, in which the latter are employed as field assistants in the former's "research projects." One of my own experiences in my department confirms some of the attitudes of many North Americans and Europeans toward people of African origin. One of my colleagues, who was absent from campus during my job interview, authoritatively and publicly noted that the "department made an important breakthrough in affirmative action by hiring Samatar." Unfortunately for my colleague, he was informed that I was not an affirmative action hire. That seasoned scholars can make and act on such spurious assumptions is a sign of our times and underscores the task ahead for the peoples of Africa. In other circumstances, African scholars have been compelled by the dull force of the market and weak economy to be the foot soldiers of international interests who do not share local priorities.[3] These conditions have turned the only potential centers of intellectual autonomy into a grotesque parody of what they should have been. The absence of intellectual autonomy and originality and the weak dependent state mutually reinforced each other. This deadly combination critically exposes Africa to the brutal exploits of global capitalism. A reversal of current fortunes demands that these twin engines of development gain undivided attention.

My experience in Botswana enriched my intellectual life in so many ways. I would therefore like to acknowledge the immense generosity of many individuals and institutions who made this experience possible. Since it is not possible to mention everyone by name, I would like to thank all of them for their professional and personal considerations. However, there are several institutions and individuals whose support deserve a special mention. Foremost among these are the four institutions that underwrote my research. The Writing and Research Program of the John D. and Katherine T. MacArthur foundation generously supported nearly half of the research and writing cost. I am grateful for the program's financial generosity and its unobtrusive modus operandi. I also thank the Fulbright Program for supporting nine months of field work. Both the staff at the head office in Washington, D.C., and those at the United States Information Agency in Gaborone gave me excellent professional support. I want to particularly thank Mr. (and Mrs.) Howard Jetter, the former United States Ambassador to Botswana, and Mr. Dudley Simms and his staff at the USIA office in Gaborone for their assistance. The American Council of Learned Societies, the Social Sciences Research Council Africa Program, and the Graduate School of the University of Minnesota supported three more months of fieldwork in Gaborone.

I was fortunate to be affiliated with the University of Botswana and its National Institute for Research, Development and Documentation. Its former director, Professor A. Data, and his associate, Dr. I. Mazonde, were both very helpful. Other scholars and staff at the Institute were equally kind. I am also grateful for the support I received from Dr. Patrick Molutsi of the Sociology Department, and the chair of the Department of Environmental Science (Geography), Dr. R. M. K. Silitshena; and Dr. K. Legesse (currently at the University of Namibia) of Social Studies. The staff of the Botswana Collection of the University Library were most generous and extraordinarily helpful: Mr. J. C. Kufa, Mr. K. N. Rao, Ms. N. Jongman, Mr. T. Maphorisa, and Mr. I. Thothe. My thanks to the two anonymous readers for Heinemann for their suggestions. I am grateful to Cambridge University Press for giving me permission to use parts of my 1995 article in chapter 4 of this book. Thanks to the staff of the cartography laboratory of the University of Minnesota for helping with the maps.

Many professionals, businesspeople and political leaders gave good advice and were generous with their time given their busy schedules. Special thanks goes to Beledzi Gaolathe, former managing director of Debswana, former permanent secretary of the Ministry of Finance and

Development Planning, and current governor of the Bank of Botswana; Mr. Quell Hermans, the former governor of the Bank of Botswana; Mr. David Finlay, the former Executive Chairman of Botswana Meat Commission; Mr. M.P.K. Nwako, the Speaker of the National Assembly; Mr. Phil Steemkamp, the former permanent secretary of the Office of the President; Mr. Lawrence Lekalake, former Permanent Secretary; Ms. Lyanda Lekalake, former special assistant to Governor Hermans; Mr. P. Landel-Mills of the World Bank; Mr. Charles Tibone, former Permanent Secretary and presently a businessman; Mr. Chris Dambe, former head of the Botswana Civil Service Association and currently a businessman; Mr. John Masala, public relations officer of the Botswana Meat Commission; Mr. Paul Ranto, member of Botswana National Front and member of the National Assembly; Mrs. Botimulo Molefhe, public relations officer of Botswana Development Corporation; K. M. Rafifing and James Kgosiemang of BDC; and Mr. M. Molefe, Managing Director of Botswana Development Corporation; Mr. Philipe Bimbo of the Ministry of Agriculture and the late Dr. T. Ditiko, head of Veterinary; Dr.Gladson Kayira, formerly of the MFDP and presently with UNDP; Mr. Modise Modise of MFDP; Mr. Taufila Nyamadzabo, chief economist with MFDP; Mrs. Elizabeth Ditshego of the Ministry of Commerce and Industry, Mr. Phagane Tladi, chief photographer of Botswana Information and Broadcasting, who was generous enough to grant me permission to use some of his photographs in this book; and Ms. Dorcus Monyatsi of the library of the Bank of Botswana.

I want to particularly thank public institutions in Botswana without whose assistance this research would not have been possible. These are the Office of the President of the Republic of Botswana for giving me a research permit, the Botswana Meat Commission, the Botswana Development Corporation, the Ministry of Agriculture, the Ministry of Finance and Development Planning, the Ministry of Commerce and Industry, and the University of Botswana.

I am grateful to the MacArthur Program at the University of Minnesota and its director, Allen Isaacman, and its associate director, Bud Duval, for being wonderful colleagues and for their support. Thanks also to Eric Sheppard, Phil Porter, Richard Skaggs, Jody Larson, Bonnie Williams, and Margaret Rasmussen. Many thanks also to Sophie Oldfield for helping me gather some of the data in chapter 4, and to Ms. J. Loshek for reading the manuscript and giving me good editorial advice. My gratitude to my graduate students, Fracis Y. Owusu, Jim Glassman, Farhana Sultana, Padraig Carmody, Yohannes Gubsa, Chris Sneddon, Joel Weinwright, Sophie Oldfield, Leila Harris and Lencho Boti for challenges and cheers.

I want to register my gratitude to friends who helped me out at various stages of the fieldwork: Mr. Abdirahman Hersi, Maryan Abdallah and family, Dr. M. A. Hassan and Mrs. Sigrid Hassan, Dr. Mohamed Hagos and Nurish, Jama Yussuf and family, Mohamed H. Asker, Mohamed Abdillahi Ogsadey, and to Jim Lafky, who read drafts of all chapters and made important suggestions. Thanks also to my former colleagues and friends Dave and Dierdre Reynolds and Michael and Darlene McNulty. A special appreciation to Michael Watts and to my brother Ahmed and my sister-in-law Marlene for comradeship and support. Finally, a special thanks to Zemzem, my niece, and daughter, for being independent and responsible.

These last few words were written when I joined the Human Sciences Research Council in Pretoria as a senior research fellow. Here the issues of building effective African institutions and autonomous African intellectual centers are at the forefront of strategic planning and daily life. The HSRC was formerly one of the major research centers of the apartheid state and Afrikaner nationalism. As the postapartheid transformations unfold the micropolitics of institutional change here signal the larger concerns in South Africa. The key issues of struggle are the transformation of the intellectual and demographic hue and breaking the old networks embedded in the HSRC culture. It seems that the predominantly white academic and research institutions are not in a hurry to transform although they are eager for legitimacy. But legitimacy without transformation is like taxation without representation and therefore unsustainable. Some of the new leadership of the HSRC are cognizant of the old postcolonial pitfalls of Africanization without concomitant skilling of the formerly disadvantaged people. Their effort is made doubly onerous by apartheid's success in insuring the underdevelopment of professional and skilled African and black labor. This realization that transformation entails new opportunities and *responsibilities* is frustrated by neocolonial petty politics. The struggle over HSRC transformation is symbolic of the continent-wide need for Africans to build intellectual autonomy and institutional capacity. For the opportunity to observe the transformation of the HSRC, I am deeply grateful to Professors Rolf H. Stumpf, Vincent T. Maphai, and Yvonne G. Muthien. Finally, thanks to Jim Lance and Lynn Zelem of Heinemann for their professional support.

NOTES

[1] Among these comparative articles are Abdi Ismail Samatar, "Leadership and Ethnicity in the Making of African State Models: Botswana Versus Somalia," *Third World Quarterly* 18, 4 (1997): 687–707; and Jim Glassman and Abdi Ismail Samatar, "Development Geography and the Third World State," *Progress in Human Geography* 21, 2 (1997): 164–198.

[2] Ahmed Samatar, ed., *The Somali Challenge: From Catastrophe to Renewal?* (Boulder, CO: Lynne Rienner, 1994). For the bankruptcy of the culturalist explanation of

political phenomena see Kwan S. Kim, "The Korean Miracle (1962–80) Revisited: Myths and Realities in Strategies and Development," in H. Stein, ed., *Asian Industrialization and Africa: Studies in Policy Alternatives to Structural Adjustment* (New York: St. Martin's Press, 1995).

[3] On this subject see Thandika Mkandawire, "The Social Sciences in Africa: Breaking Local Barriers and Negotiating International Presence," *African Studies Review* 40, 2 (1997): 1–22.

Dire-Dawa, Ethiopia
Pretoria, South Africa

ACRONYMS

BDC	Botswana Development Corporation
BDP	Botswana Democratic Party
BEDC	Batswana Enterprises Development Company
BEDU	Botswana Enterprise Development Unit
BMC	Botswana Meat Commission
BNF	Botswana National Front
BPP	Botswana People's Party
BTA	Bechuanaland Trading Association
CDC	Colonial Development Corporation
CDW	Colonial Development and Welfare
ECA	Economic Commission for Africa
ECC	Economic Committee of Cabinet
EEC	European Economic Community
EU	European Union
FAP	Financial Assistance Policy
GATT	General Agreements on Tariffs and Trade
GNP	Gross National Product
HDI	Human Development Index
HDR	Human Development Report
IMF	International Monetry Fund
KPP	Keynote Policy Paper
MEMBOT	Microeconomic Model of Botswana
MFDP	Ministry of Finance and Development Planning
MITI	Ministry of International Trade and Industry
MNCS	Multinational Corporations
NDB	National Development Bank
NDP	National Development Plan

NEMIC	National Employment Manpower and Incomes Council
NICs	Newly Industrializing Countries
ODA	Overseas Development Administration
PDSF	Public Debt Service Fund
ROB	Republic of Botswana
RSA	Republic of South Africa
SACU	Southern African Customs Union
TGLP	Tribal Grazing Land Policy
TIPA	Trade and Investment Promotion Agency
UK	United Kingdom
UNDP	United Nations Development Program
UNICEF	United Nations Children's Education Fund
ZA	Zambia
ZIM	Zimbabwe

INTRODUCTION

The last quarter of this century has been extremely unkind to the African people. The devastating famines of the early 1970s graphically exposed the vulnerability of millions of Africans to economic and climatic perturbations. They also foreshadowed the precipitous and persistent decline of the economy and the political degeneration and disintegration in many African societies. Africa did not lose one decade, as the former secretary of the United Nations Economic Commission for Africa (ECA) noted, but nearly three. Much of the social sciences literature in the last two decades has been devoted to explaining the intractability of the African condition. Their approaches rely on a discourse of doom and hopelessness dubbed "*Afro-pessimism.*"

An African Miracle represents an antidote to Afro-pessimism. In sharp contrast to the failures and disappointments that cloud the rest of Africa, Botswana's thirty years of independence have been a time of hope, optimism, and progress. Paradoxically, the departing British colonial authorities were quite pessimistic about Botswana's future prospects. Most African political leaders elsewhere considered it another Bantustan of apartheid. Both Western and African experts looked elsewhere for Africa's development pace setters. Countries like Ghana, Cote d'Ivoire, Nigeria, and Kenya that inherited more developed infrastructure and better resources endowments were thought to have better chances.

Botswana leaders in 1966 were mindful of the enormous obstacles their country faced, but contrary to the prevailing views, refused to accept the prognosis of the pessimists. They acted like people with an attainable mission rather than lumbering along like hopeless victims of colonialism, apartheid, and a harsh climate. A better understanding of the story of Botswana is absolutely essential for not only overcoming the dominance of Afro-pessimism, but also in appreciating what Africans can do for themselves despite

Table I.1 Trends in Economic Development: Botswana Compared to Select African and Asian Countries

Country	HDI*	GNP/1991 Billions $	Total GNP 1980–1991 Annual growth	GNP/Capita Annual Growth Rate 1960–80	1980–91
South Africa	93	102	3.3	3.2	0.7
Egypt	100	33.5	NA	4.2	-0.7
Algeria	109	52.3	NA	4.2	-0.7
Gabon	114	4.7	-0.9	5.6	-4.2
Zimbabwe	122	6.9	3.6	1.7	-0.2
Cameroon	124	10.4	2.1	2.4	-1.0
Kenya	125	8.6	4.1	3.1	-0.3
Ghana	134	6.4	3.1	-0.8	-0.3
I. Coast	136	8.9	0.3	2.8	-4.6
Nigeria	139	33.7	1.4	4.2	-2.3
Zambia	138	3.4	0.7	-1.3	NA
Zaire	140	8.1	1.6	-1.3	NA
Senegal	143	5.6	2.9	-0.5	0.1
Ethiopia	161	6.4	1.5	0.4	-1.6
Guinea	173	2.8	NA	1.3	NA
Botswana	**87**	**3.3**	**9.3**	**9.9**	**5.6**
Seychelles	83	0.4	3.2	4.6	3.2
Mauritius	60	2.6	7.2	3.6	6.1
Indonesia	105	116.6	5.8	5.2	3.9
Malaysia	57	47.3	5.6	4.7	2.9
Thailand	54	88.1	7.8	4.4	5.9
S. Korea	32	297.1	10	7.3	8.7
Hong Kong	24	77.9	6.9	6.2	5.6

Source: United Nations Development Program, *Human Development Report 1994* (New York: Oxford University Press, 1994: 136–137. *HDI = Human Development Index.

the colossal constraints of the world order and the internal legacy of the last three decades.

This book's concerns are as much about Botswana as they are about the ways in which Africans can realistically disprove the prophets of doom. It postulates that a socially responsible and more effective activist African state is essential for the continent's recovery. Thus, an African Miracle is about the broader questions of the African state and its role in development at the end of the twentieth century. This book brings together two issues that have often been artificially separated in the development literature: that is, the simultaneous effects of national and international forces on development

Table I.2   Botswana: Sectoral Growth of the Economy, 1981–1991

Sector	Average Annual Growth
Agriculture	3.1
Mining	9.4
Manufacturing	6.6
Electricity & Water	12.7
Construction	9.7
Commerce	9.8
Transport &Communication	17.2
Finance &Business Services	10.4
Government	14.5
Social & Community Services	11.3

Source: UNDP, UNICEF, and Republic of Botswana, *Planning for People: A Strategy for Accelerated Human Development in Botswana* (Gaborone: Sygma Publishing, 1993): 12.

and performance of the state and the economy. Finally, it sketches an outline of an analytical framework that helps reconceptualize African development to counter prophecies of doom with development strategies that incorporate contingency.

Botswana has meteorically leaped from the ranks of the most impoverished countries in Africa with a GNP/capita of less than $80 a year in 1966 to a dynamic middle-income economy with per capita earning of nearly $1,800 in 1996. Botswana outperformed, in aggregate terms, all countries in Africa and also all the first- and second-generation Asian tigers (except South Korea) of Hong Kong, Thailand, Malaysia, and Indonesia (Table I.1). Botswana's superb and sustained macroeconomic performance was not narrowly grounded. However, the distribution of sectoral growth varied from a low average annual growth of 3.1 percent in agriculture to the astounding rate of 17.2 percent in transport and communication during 1981 to 1991 (Table I.2). Such an economic transformation translated into high formal employment growth, from 25,000 in 1973 to 224,000 in 1992,[1] and also into substantially improved services. For example, primary and secondary school enrollment increased from 62,833 and 1,036 in 1966 to 301,370 and 99,560 in 1994 respectively; the University of Botswana was established and enrollment grew to 4,533 by 1994, and is expected to have more than 10,000 students at the turn of the century.

In addition to this awesome economic and social performance Botswana accumulated tremendous amounts of foreign exchange reserves. It had an import cover of over 28 months in 1994 that was five times those of Singapore and Thailand.[2] Botswana earned these reserves from the sale of its diamond exports (Table I.3). The exploitation of this mineral began in the mid-1970s

Table I.3 Botswana's Foreign Exchange Reserves in Millions of Dollars

Year	Amount
1966	0
1977	0
1987	2,057.08
1989	2,841.11
1991	3,718.66
1992	3,793.42
1993	4,097.34
1994	4,500.00
1995	4,696.00
1996	5,028.00

Source: Bank of Botswana, *Annual Reports* (Gaborone, 1989–1996).

although major new mines came on stream in the early 1980s. New diamond deposits were discovered recently in the western part of the country that will deepen the country's pocket.[3] Despite the rapid growth in revenues from diamonds, Botswana avoided the infamous "Dutch disease" by carefully investing some of its resources in physical and social infrastructure and in productive areas of the economy such as industry. Moreover, the government prudently managed its purse so that the economy was not overwhelmed by mineral revenues that it could not productively absorb. Consequently, Botswana eluded rampant corruption and mismanagement that bedevil Third World states and particularly mineral-rich countries such as Gabon, Nigeria, and Venezuela. These achievements seem incredible given the gloomy predictions made by most authorities about Botswana's future at the time of independence.

Botswana's economic accomplishment is even more astounding given the fact that it has had a genuinely functioning liberal democratic political system since independence while all Asian tigers were (some still are) under brutal authoritarian regimes. It is noteworthy that the political leadership of the country had many "opportunities" to invoke the excuse of "national security," under the real material and military pressures, from racist South Africa and Rhodesia, in order to silence whatever political opposition that existed.[4] This historical context makes Botswana's experience remarkably unique, not only in Africa but in the Third World.

This book explains the making of the miraculous political economic achievements of the Republic of Botswana. It argues that two domestic forces induced the miracle while the colonial legacy and the dominant subimperialist apartheid regime in the region curtailed further economic transformation. The dominant indigenous class and its political leadership, and the state apparatuses that it created have been responsible for the transformation of Botswana from a South African labor reserve to a liberal democratic developing political economy. Thus, discerning the "character" of the dominant class and its particular relationship with the state machinery is key to unlocking the "mystery" of the miracle. An accurate discussion of Botswana will be incomplete if it does not deal with the historic regional and international forces that circumscribe the contemporary context of this experience. A brief discussion of the these key ideas of class and state leadership and colonial legacy is warranted.[5]

CLASS LEADERSHIP

The concept of class has gone out of fashion particularly among those who have been writing in the vein of state versus civil society. I would like to bring class back into the analysis of development issues and the formation of public policy. The pertinence of class and related issues in real-life experience has increased, not lessened in Africa with the rise of neoliberal development policy. Those social classes detrimentally affected by the policy changes of the last two decades remain, however, unorganized and unable to have a meaningful impact on policy formulation.

The mechanical application of the concept of class in African studies in the past has not been very useful to understanding how projects are conceptualized and implemented. We need to focus not so much on the theoretical propensity of a social class, but its lived experiences and practice. To get at that practice, one needs to examine the internal structure of a particular class as well as the quality and consciousness of its leadership. This means that we need to engage existing historical and geographic realities without either abandoning our conceptual apparatus to understand the dynamics of such process or being unduly abstract. Such a conceptually informed historical analysis is akin to the agenda proposed by Bob Jessop's *State Theory*.[6] Jessop's "strategic relational approach" to the study of capitalist states notes that there are multiple and competing capitalist accumulation projects in any country, and the state plays key roles in fashioning them. The agents of these competing projects develop strategies in order to gain support and legitimacy. Those projects that attain ascendancy succeed in dominating a nation's development program. The legitimacy and longevity of their projects depends on how well they provide services to the indigent classes. Such an organic linking of the hegemonic project with the "welfare" of the popular classes is what Jessop calls "one nation strategy." Jean-François Bayart has, in a parallel fashion, recently reintroduced the argument that the problem of African development is largely due to the inability of one leading class or alliances of different classes to successfully impose a hegemonic project on society that attends to some of the basic needs of the population.[7] This failure has produced chaotic political and economic conditions that have undermined systematic accumulation.

The debate pertaining to the role of classes and their relations to the state and capitalist development in Africa is narrated in chapter 1. The Marxist literature of the past 25 years on the state, class, and development in Africa was crafted in such a way that it has not been able to account for the differential performances among states espousing similar development agendas. This has been significantly due to the fact that it paid scant attention to the relationships between internal social dynamics of the dominant class, the quality of its leadership, and how this affected the development and operation of public institutions. This analysis had the effect of concealing vital difference between regimes by treating them as homogeneous capitalist states.

The chapter also critically reviews currently fashionable literature on state and civil society. Two strands of this literature are discussed because of their importance for the debate on the role of the state and class in development. The first thread argues that strong societies often produce weak states.[8] The strong societies of Africa are characterized as those with established local nodes of power, such as chieftainships. This theorem is contradicted by the rise of the strong Botswana state in the midst of strong chiefdoms. The second strand of this literature claims that the problem in Africa is due to the fact that authoritarian states smothered the entrepreneurial energy of civil society. Again, this thesis is contradicted by the experience of the most successful states in the Third World who were/are authoritarian, that is, the Asian tigers. Finally, the chapter goes beyond these established schools of thought and proposes a framework that deals seriously with the agencies of domestic and external forces that condition the ability of African states to fashion and nurture their economies. I propose that this approach is able to explain why some capitalist states perform better than other capitalist states that face relatively similar international contexts. A key force that distinguishes successful from failed states is the social chemistry of the dominant class and the discipline of its leadership.

Members of Botswana's dominant class, at the time of independence, were largely from chiefly families who were among the largest traditional cattle owners;[9] also involved were a handful of educated individuals in the public service. This group was closely affiliated with the colonial administration and a small number of white settlers. This class has been able to dominate public life, imposing a capitalist development strategy on society. Furthermore, they have been able to develop state capacity to guide the affairs of the nation without looting the public purse. The cohesion of the dominant class and its single-minded pursuit of economic growth is one of the features that distinguish this class from their counterparts in the continent. The important question is how and under what conditions have the dominant class and its political leaderships emerged from (pre)colonial chiefly traditions.

The Batswana chiefs and their junior associates were not only the wealthiest class in precolonial and colonial Botswana but also the political leaders of their communities. The poverty of the territory's resource base,[10] the legitimacy of chiefly rule, and the intelligent and persistent exploitation and manipulation of British politics enabled the chiefs to resist changes detrimental to their interest, which were advanced by the colonial authorities. The chiefs retained much of their political authority despite their subjugation to colonial rule. The most important political advantage British colonial rule had for the chiefs was that it brought them together under one umbrella so that they could coordinate their dealings with the colonial authority. This forum sowed the seed of contemporary Botswana national identity. An equally important economic benefit of colonial rule was the modernization of the livestock industry through the establishment of the livestock trade and ultimately the Bechuanaland Meat Commission. The latter created a secure market for all livestock owners and particularly the wealthy class.

The "national" hegemony of the chiefs was not superseded until the middle of the 1960s. Seretse Khama, the young, college-educated chief of the largest "tribe" and the largest cattle owner in the Protectorate, organized a political party (Bechuanaland Democratic Party) that brought together most of the educated Batswana, many of whom were from chiefly families. Khama and his party articulated a modernist capitalist project that preserved a national role for the chiefs without challenging the economic dominance of chiefly families. This organic marriage between the old establishment and modernist elements was facilitated by the fact that the children of the dominant class had greater access to colonial and missionary education. The few who had such opportunities became some of the leading elements of Khama's party. Khama's leadership became an anchor of the modernist group that defended it from the political challenges of the reigning chiefs while giving this group chiefly legitimacy with the population. Finally, the commercialization of livestock, the only source of indigenous wealth, gave the modernist and traditional establishment a common economic base. The capitalist development project adopted by Botswana enhanced the economic unity of the two elements of the dominant class. Thus, the legitimacy of Khama's leadership could not be assailed by members of the dominant class on economic, political, or traditional grounds.

The story of this transformation is told in chapters 2 and 3. Chapter 2 discusses the relationship between the chiefs and the colonial administration and the attempts of the former to maintain their traditional power while taking advantage of whatever opportunities the colonial system provided. The emergence of Seretse Khama and his political party as national leaders are narrated in chapters 2 and 3. Chapter 3 explains the ways in which this leadership used its authority to build a professional and insulated government machinery.

It is impossible to clearly understand how the Botswana miracle was manufactured without appreciating the important function that the political and economic unity of the dominant class played. I go farther and argue that such unity was necessary, but not sufficient to ensure that the development project was nurtured *systematically* under the tutelage of the dominant social class unless its political leadership was disciplined and conscious of the institutional requirements of the project. As such, the miracle is not a product of the mere existence of a united dominant class, but more importantly the presence of a conscious social agency (leadership) that is able to translate structural conditions into purposive institutional capacity. Thus, the united dominant class and its disciplined political leadership led the state in such a way that public affairs were managed professionally.

STATE LEADERSHIP

The role of African states in development has been declining in the last 20 years. Meanwhile their institutional capacity to effectively reverse underdevelopment has vanished. By contrast the role of the Botswana state has remained steady while its capacity has improved significantly. Consequently the public sector in Botswana has been able to play a central role in effectively directing the national economy. The capacity of the state to ably induce economic development and shape the patterns of resource use distinguish developmental states such as Botswana from other Third World states.

The important question is how Botswana's key state institutions and enterprises were developed and able to manage the economy so effectively when their counterparts dismally failed. The foremost factor that shaped the development and nature of these institutions has been the legitimate, stable, and united political leadership. This leadership clearly assumed that the public sector will play a leading role in the development of a capitalist economy in postcolonial Botswana in the absence of dynamic local capital and the danger of being swallowed by racist South Africa. Since Botswana inherited virtually no administrative infrastructure, it had to build everything from scratch. The leadership mainly used two qualities to guide the development and operations of such institutions: skills and merit. These qualities were essential if the bureaucracy was to acquire technical capacity necessary to guide Botswana development. In the absence of sufficient numbers of skilled Batswana, the government chose to use foreigners while it progressively trained its own bureaucratic cadre. This meant that the political leaders had to stem the popular call for quickly promoting African citizens to higher posts in the bureaucracy without much regard for their ability to effectively perform their duties. Moreover, it insured that merit strictly determined promotion and remuneration in the service. The technical capacity of the public institutions has quantitatively and qualitatively expanded in the last three decades as Botswana made tremendous progress in educating and training its population. Many of these young people occupy the vast majority of key positions in the bureaucracy without any need to "lower standards."

The use of skill and merit as the foundation stone of building Botswana's technical capacity was crucial. However, this was not sufficient to transform the "colonial administrative" orientation of public service. The government of Botswana had to (re)invent its institutions in such a way that their primary preoccupation shifted from routine administration to development planning and management. This transformation took several years and its basic structure was firmly in place by the early 1970s. The Ministry of Finance and Development Planning (MFDP) has been the brain trust (comparable to MITI of Japan) of the state's technocratic edifice and has effectively managed and coordinated economic development in Botswana.

Three things collectively distinguish Botswana's public sector management style from most African states. First, the allocations of public sector posts on the basis of education and job training, followed by rewarding those who excel with higher remuneration and promotions, have created professionalism that is rare in Africa and most other Third World countries. Second, the development of professional culture grounded on skill and merit was constantly and consistently reinforced by political leaders who effectively demanded accountability. Third, Botswana is not different from other countries either in expanding educational opportunities for a large number of its population or in promoting trained people to senior positions in government, but by the high degree of professional autonomy political leaders granted to public servants. The professional insulation of the civil service created internal coherence and discipline that enhanced its integrity. Public servants operated within the broad circumference demarcated by political leaders. It is this close professional relationship between the political leaders and the bureaucracy that in essence define the effective capacity of the Botswana state. The power relations and the division of labor between politicians and bureaucrats were compared, by a former minister of Works, Transport and Communications (Chapsen Butale) to that of a "husband and wife that complement one another."[11]

The ethnography of this relationship is told in chapter 3. I use published and unpublished material and extensive oral history to demonstrate the unity of the dominant class and how its conscious and disciplined leaders launched and sustained the Botswana state project. A detailed history of the making of the Ministry of Finance and Development Planning and how it was crafted as the epicenter of the state apparatus show the importance attached to a competent and professional public service. Moreover, this history elucidates how the MFDP manages the economy both in terms of planning and implementing (via sectoral state agencies) development programs.

There is no question that the MFDP directs the country's development program. This highly centralized planning structure is suffused with a decentralized managerial style wherein line ministries and agencies have significant degree of freedom in operating their particular programs within the confines set by government. Thus, management in these ministries and agencies have sufficient professional insulation. It is this intricate multilayered political, managerial relationship that has facilitated state agencies and public enterprises to lead and direct the economy.

Two agencies that lead their respective sectors of the economy and which exemplify how well this planning and management system works are the Botswana Meat Commission (BMC) and the Botswana Development Corporation (BDC). Chapter 4 deals with the BMC and the livestock sector, showing how and why this parastatal has become so successful in developing and managing the industry. The key to unlocking this puzzle is the clearly defined mandate given to the commission, the establishment of a merit- and skill-based labor force, a professionally insulated but accountable management cadre, and a political leadership willing and able to support the institution attain its goals. Furthermore, the "sustained" growth of the livestock industry demonstrates that neither is the traditional sector of the economy allergic to proper management, nor are public enterprises inherently incapable of nurturing economic growth and development. Finally, the successes of this parastatal show how the dominant class can formally and collectively advance its interest through the state and consequently avoid intraclass struggle.

Chapter 5 chronicles Botswana's attempts to induce industrial and commercial development. It evaluates the effectiveness of the institutions and policy instruments responsible for this task. The BDC has been the premier development agency in the urban industrial sector while the Financial Assistance Policy (FAP) has been the chief policy instrument to induce industrial development since 1982. Botswana's BDC- and FAP-guided commercial and industrial sector has been successful in stimulating and nurturing the development of enterprises as well as significantly increasing employment. The achievements of BDC and FAP are even more spectacular since they have not saddled the government with huge debt and unproductive and unprofitable enterprises. Finally, BDC and FAP operate within the framework set by the government for all public enterprises and instruments.

Lest this discussion of public enterprise and state guidance of the economy be misconstrued as a license for an expansive and bloated public sector, it is important to note that the issue is competent state leadership rather than sheer size. Although public enterprises dominate some key sectors of the economy such as housing (Botswana Housing Corporation), the utilities, livestock, and mining, the government retains tight control over their operations in order to avoid mismanagement and corruption.

Several elements in the government's strategy for managing public enterprises made this success possible. First, the government gave a clearly and carefully defined mandate to each enterprise. Second, it insured that there was competent management at the helm of each enterprise with a significant degree of professional freedom. Third, government concentrated its effort on key sectors and therefore avoided overstretching its administrative capacity. Fourth, although government used public enterprises to direct the economy, it insured that most such enterprises operated on a commercial basis. Thus, these enterprises were not expected to replace the market but indeed help develop it. Fifth, the government avoided owning and operating enterprises that private entrepreneurs could easily manage except in strategic sectors such as livestock. This is the principle that has guided the business of the BDC and FAP.

COLONIAL CONTEXT

The indiscipline of the dominant classes and the ineptitude of state managers created a political and administrative environment in most parts of the continent that was not conducive to systematic accumulation. These circumstances *seem* to justify the claims of many that the colonial legacy is not a factor in the reproduction of Africa's underdevelopment. This stance lacks much merit, particularly if it means that colonialism did not significantly shape both the social/human and material infrastructure of the postcolonial era. The significance of the colonial legacy is particularly apparent in situations in which internal forces are developmentally oriented. The Botswana experience makes this obvious. The external forces and legacy affecting Botswana have been the lack of human and material resources development during the colonial century and its economic integration into South Africa. Such a context has frustrated the industrialization program of the effective Botswana state. Although Botswana is overcoming the deficit in skills, it has been unable to loosen South African domination of its economy (chapter 5). Thus, some elements of a colonial legacy are more difficult to overcome than others. Hence colonial legacies remain an important concept in our analytical arsenal to unpack what exactly ails African economies.

The interconnections between the three concepts outlined above form an appropriate framework for analyzing the major forces that circumscribe African development. Liberal analysts focus on internal causes of the African condition, while nationalists and many Marxists often emphasize the centrality of external forces. Such a dichotomy always tells one side of the story. The proposed framework recognizes the relative importance of the dominant local class, its relationship to the state as well as the legacy of colonial and postcolonial external forces. Thus, it helps us capture the collective impact of domestic and external forces on the Botswana experience.

The Botswana miracle is Janus-faced. Botswana's success in building effective public institutions and enterprises and inducing economic growth and employment is indeed a miraculous achievement for a society that was a migrant labor reserve for apartheid South Africa. The accomplishment of the last three decades must be credited to the competent political and technocratic leaders of the state. This aspect of the miracle is worthy of careful study by others in the continent who are eager to find ways of reworking and strengthening state institutions. The second aspect of the miracle often ignored in conventional circles is the "radical inequality" that is part and parcel of the Botswana experience.[12] The increasing gap between the rich and poor in Botswana could have been avoided had the political leaders worked from a different set of assumptions that emphasized growth with equity rather than growth without equity.[13] The value of the miracle would have been greater were the social predisposition of the leadership changed.

Three major lessons can be derived from the Botswana miracle (chapter 6). First, a disciplined and legitimate political leadership of the dominant class is essential in developing state capacity and insuring that public power and resources are not used for personal gain. Second, a purposive and effective state guidance of the economy can lead to sustained growth and development, for example, beef exports and employment growth. The third, and maybe the most important, lesson is that an effective and capable African state can minimize the deleterious effects of the international system while enabling the country to take advantage of whatever opportunities the system offers. The best examples of this are how the government managed its relations with South Africa and how it astutely and gingerly negotiated with De Beers, the multinational diamond giant. These resulted in increased revenues from the Southern African Customs Union as well as greater share of the profits from diamonds. This means that even relatively weak states (in international terms) need not always be at the mercy of global forces if they do their homework. The centrality of domestic initiative and policy autonomy for African political and economic recovery is narrated in chapter 6.

NOTES

[1] Botswana had a total population of 545,105 in 1973 and 1.3 million in 1992. Moreover, total active population in 1973 was 240,000 and 443, 455 in 1992.

[2] See K. R. Jefferies and C. Harvey, "Botswana's Exchange Controls: Abolition or Liberalization," *Development Policy Review* 13, 3 (1995): 277-305.

[3] Human rights groups note that the government is harassing the San people to move out of the area. The San, who are poorest of the poor in Botswana, live in the area where recent diamond deposits were discovered.

[4] The huge investment in a massive military base near Molepolole in the 1990s is worrisome given the liberation of South Africa. Many informed people suggest that Western, particularly American, funding was involved.

[5] I want to thank Ahmed Samatar for his suggestion that I devote some space in the introduction to the concepts embedded in the title of the book.

[6] Bob Jessop, *State Theory: Putting Capitalist States in Their Place* (University Park: Pennsylvania State University Press, 1990), pts. 2 and 4.

[7] Jean-François Bayart, *The State in Africa: The Politics of the Belly* (New York: Longman, 1993). See also Kristian Stokke's "The Postcolonial African State and Development Geography," *Norsk Geografisk Tidsskrift* 48, 123 (1994): 123-131; and his "Authoritarianism in the Age of Market Liberalism in Sri Lanka," *Antipode* (forthcoming). This piece is an application of Jessop's framework to the particular conditions of Sri Lanka.

[8] Joel Migdal, *Strong Societies and Weak States: State and Society Relations and State Capabilities in the Third World* (Princeton, NJ: Princeton University Press, 1988).

[9] The first major enterprise to be taken over by the Botswana state was the Meat Commission. Livestock was the most important sector of the economy, and most traditional and modern leaders had a stake in it. The modernization of the commission and its effective management became a model for other parastatals. Managing BMC professionally for its stake holders eliminated rent seeking and political intervention in professional affairs.

[10] Compare the treatment of African chiefs in South Africa to the Tswana in the Protectorate. The former lost much of their autonomy as their resources were taken away by hungry white settlers and the colonial state. Botswana was too marginal to attract such attention.

[11] Quoted in Roger Charlton, "Bureaucrats and Politicians in Botswana's Policy-making Process: A Reinterpretation," *Journal of Commonwealth & Comparative Politics* 29, 3 (1991): 267.

[12] UNDP, UNICEF, and Republic of Botswana, *Planning for People: A Strategy for Accelerated Human Development in Botswana* (Gaborone: Sygma Publishing, 1993).

[13] The managing director of the Government-De Beers-owned Debswana recently blasted the Botswana leaders for not doing enough to economically empower indigenous citizens. See "Botswana Not Doing Enough to Empower Citizens," *Business Day*, September 22, 1997, 4.

1

CONCEPTUALIZING THE AFRICAN STATE

INTRODUCTION

[E]nhancing state capacity remains a requirement of effective economic policy, including sustained structural adjustment. Pretending otherwise would be a dangerous form of utopianism. Transforming the state from a problem to solution must be a central item on any realistic Third World policy agenda.[1]

For over 25 years, in sharp contrast to the sloth of the colonial period, the Botswana Government has exemplified how rapid growth and domestic accumulation can be achieved by skillful exploitation of limited resources. This has been done in large part through the build-up of a relatively strong state with a capacity for effective, selective, and sustained intervention . . . state intervention has been in part concerned with the reinvestment of available surplus in infrastructure and education, and the wastage of potential investment in prestige, non-productive projects, and through elite and urban consumptionism, has generally been avoided.[2]

There is an agreement in the literature that unaccountable political and professional leaders and excessive and ineffective state involvement in the economy have significantly contributed to the African development disaster. The World Bank has argued that to rejuvenate African economies the states' authority and reach must be substantially retracted and public enterprises must be privatized.[3] This "free-market" and noninterventionist state-based model prescribed for Africa is said to underlie East Asia's development success.[4] Peter Evans notes that the World Bank's extreme neoliberal agenda has passed its zenith. Senior Bank officials recognize the "positive" role the state can play in economic development.[5] The Bank's supposed change of heart is betrayed by its attempt to forcibly fit the Asian experience into its neoliberal strategy.[6]

Botswana is the only African country to sustain growth since independence. A careful study of Botswana's experience shows that an interventionist state is responsible for the country's economic transformation. In Botswana, state agencies dominate major sectors of the economy, such as housing, industrial investment, transport, communication, education, livestock, agriculture, and mining. Moreover, the state sector has grown at the high rate of 14.5 percent per year between 1981 and 1991.[7] The Botswana experience supports recent research in East Asia[8] that reveals the centrality of state leadership in guiding dynamic economies.[9] The Botswana and East Asian experiences suggest that an economy's success or failure is not only due to the size of the government or the degree of its intervention, but essentially the quality of its involvement in the economy.

Botswana's success and the failure of the rest of African economies confirm that the state is a key force in determining the fortunes of an African society. Consequently we need to distinguish between different state types. What kind of state can make a positive difference? How does a society create this state type? What is a successful state's social constitution? What relations does this state have with major groups in society and the outside world? This chapter demonstrates that the literature's examination of these questions does *not* satisfactorily explain Botswana's experience. First, I discuss radical political economy's success in dealing with the state's social makeup and the state's relations to the outside world.[10] However, this analytical framework has not accounted for the differential capacities of similar capitalist or socialist regimes, facing comparable external forces. For example, why has Botswana performed differently than Senegal and Gabon? All three regimes subscribed to the same economic agenda. Next, I show that recent state-civil society literature creates an artificial division between the state and civil-society.[11] This literature also overlooks the important impact of international forces on the state and its capacity to induce development. Neither radical political economy nor the state-civil society literature can successfully explain the dramatic rise of states like Botswana. These states defy the assumptions of this literature.

Two recent contributions supersede this literature. The first strand successfully reformulates state-civil society discourse by identifying local classes and international forces that jointly or separately limit state autonomy. This literature equates state autonomy with state capacity; therefore, it cannot explain why many autonomous Third World states lack the capacity to foster development. The second contribution goes beyond the state versus civil society and the state autonomy debates. It shows that specific types of relations between an autonomous state and select elements of society are key to successful economic development. Finally, I extend this contribution by filling in gaps in the framework.

POLITICAL ECONOMY AND THE
CHARACTER OF THE AFRICAN STATE

Nearly twenty-five years ago Hamza Alavi initiated the now-familiar debate about the role and the nature of the state in postcolonial societies.[12] The debate rages on as the issues central to that discourse have been rediscovered recently in the fashionable state-civil society literature. Alavi's main concern was to map the postcolonial state's strength and role in newly independent countries (Pakistan and Bangladesh). Accordingly, the postcolonial state inherited the colonial state's overdeveloped military-bureaucratic apparatus.[13] The colonial state was designed to subjugate autonomous precapitalist societies.[14] The collapse of formal colonial domination ended direct metropolitan rule, and the state apparatus passed into the hands of nationals. The rulers of the new nation play a pivotal role in the economy in the absence of strong local bourgeoisie. Consequently, the overdeveloped postcolonial state mediated between dominant local social classes and the hegemonic metropolitan bourgeoisie (what Alavi terms neocolonial bourgeoisie). The postcolonial state also had a larger role:

> The relationship between neocolonialist bourgeoisie and the post-colonial state is clearly of a different order from that which existed between the imperialist bourgeoisie and the colonial state. The class basis of the postcolonial state is therefore complex. It is not entirely subordinate to the indigenous bourgeoisie, in view of the power and the influence of the neocolonial bourgeoisie. Nor is it simply an instrument of any of the latter, with the implication that independence is a mere sham. Neither bourgeoisie excludes the influence of the other; and their interest compete. The central proposition which I wish to emphasize is that the state in post-colonial society is not the instrument of a single class. It is *relatively autonomous* and it mediated between the competing interests of the [dominant] classes . . . while at the same time acting on behalf of them all to preserve the social order in which their interests are imbedded, namely the institution of private property and the capitalist mode as the dominant mode of production (italics mine).[15]

The postcolonial state maintains the balance between external and internal forces despite its relative autonomy. As a result, it is unable to transform the postcolonial context. This means that independence was a project that harmonized the interests of metropolitan capital and local propertied classes. Thus, the postcolonial state represents the consummation of such an alliance.[16]

Alavi's issues, such as the state's relative autonomy, the relationship between domestic social classes, foreign capital and the state, and the role played by those who manage the state apparatus, inspired a long and influential debate in African political economy. Broadly speaking, this debate was between dependency theorists and their "Marxist" critics.[17] Dependency theorists claimed that the state and local capitalist classes depended on the metropolitan center. This relationship reinforced the status quo. Critics marshaled enough counter evidence to show that some local capitalists and states challenged metropolitan capital's dominance. Others suggested that the collaboration of African states and the African dominant classes created a rent haven that undermined the economy's capacity to grow in productive and competitive ways.[18]

The theoretical gulf between those who emphasized the international forces' prowess and local groups' subservience (dependency) and those who claimed the postcolonial state's relative autonomy and the native bourgeoisie's growing strength (Marxists) seemed too wide to bridge. Bjorn Beckman attempted to overcome this conceptual impasse by criticizing both camps.[19] He focused his criticisms on the debate's two central issues. The first is the way both sides framed capitalist development in the periphery. On the one hand, dependency theorists claim capitalist development without a national bourgeoisie is an oxymoron. On the other hand, critics note the growth of indigenous capital as a sign of an emerging bourgeoisie and independent capitalist development in Africa.[20] Second, both groups portray the state as the instrument of local capital against the metropolitan bourgeoisie or as a servant of the metropolitan bourgeoisie. Beckman notes the antagonistic relationship between local capital and international capital; the state and local or international capital are all products of theoretical mistakes. These errors are due to the two sides' inability to see the totality of the capital accumulation process:

> While the [African] state serves as an organ both for the penetration of international capital and for the emancipation of the domestic bourgeoisie, it cannot be reduced to either. Nor is it possible to comprehend the significance of either of the two aspects without examining such class functions of the . . . state for which the distinction between foreign and domestic is not relevant. The *primary role of the* [African] *state is to establish, maintain, protect and expand the conditions of capitalist accumulation* in general, without which neither foreign nor [African] capitalists can prosper (italics mine).[21]

The characterization of the state as the guardian of a country's capital accumulation means it has some degree of autonomy from local and international capital. Beckman recognizes the possible conflicts between domestic and international capitalists and within each group. However, his approach does not directly answer two questions. First, how does the state muddle through the irreconcilable conflicts between local and international capital? The African state's primary role may be to insure the reproduction of capitalism within the continent; however, such a task can be accomplished in many ways. One approach is to encourage the development of domestic firms at the expense of international ones, particularly if this will enhance the state's autonomy from international capital. Another approach is when a close collaboration exists among the state, international capital, and some of the factions of local bourgeoisie (the so-called triple alliance[22]). A third scenario is one in which the state acts as a comprador. The second question: why have so many states failed to secure the conditions necessary for capitalist accumulation? Beckman's criticisms of the previous literature is important. However, his analysis, which focuses on the general requirements of capitalist accumulation, cannot tell us exactly how the state resolves conflicts between local and multinational interests. Furthermore, he says little about how states gain capacity to establish the necessary conditions for development.

Beckman's arguments are grounded on three assumptions: (a) The continent's political economies have internalized imperialism; (b) No irresolvable conflicts exist between local and foreign capital; and (c) Dominant politics represent a coalition between local and foreign dominant groups. Such premises lead him to conclude that the state's task is to ensure the general reproduction of capital accumulation. Beckman's scenario of mutuality between dominant domestic and external forces may hold true in the long run. However, in the short and the medium terms, conflicts exist between national and foreign capitalists, and the state is the crucial actor that can tilt the balance in one way or the other.

Furthermore, how do we explain the roles various African capitalist states play and their contrasting capacities to carry out their agenda? Beckman's studies and the literature he criticizes treat African states as homogeneous entities. The contrast between Taiwan and Mexico, Kenya and Zambia, Ghana and Ivory Coast are examples that demonstrate how different Third World and African regimes exploit whatever freedom they have within the global capitalist system. This indicates how these states balance competing international and domestic forces. Conceivably the state can induce conditions suitable to capital accumulation and privilege the bourgeoisie's domestic/nationalist wing. Under these circumstances, the conceptual gulf between those Beckman criticizes and his own thesis disappears.

The synthesis of the seeming theoretical opposites—Beckman, dependency theorists, and Marxists—captures the essence of the role the Botswana state played in all of its efforts to induce development. An excellent illustration of this is the government's actions during its negotiations with De Beers, the multinational diamond giant. The state recognized that it needed De Beers to exploit its mineral wealth. However, the government wanted to gain as much as possible of the profits from this resource (I briefly discuss this in chapter 3). Moreover, it wanted to insure that the mines developed into viable towns rather than closed company towns. It also realized that De Beers needed Botswana to get access to the diamonds to fortify its monopolistic control over the global diamond market. The government found a way to get what it wanted. Botswana's position with De Beers was relatively strong because of the richness of its resources. However, this would not have mattered if disciplined and determined leadership and skilled negotiators had not guided the state. As a result, De Beers ceded to many of the government's conditions. Diamond revenues enabled Botswana to support its development agenda.

The theoretical moral of the Botswana–De Beers story is that the state's strategy was not to nurture capitalism in some abstract way, but to keep the balance sheet minimally in its favour. Thus, the state can be committed to creating and nurturing the conditions for capitalist development in general while favoring domestic interests. Botswana's counterexample is former Zaire. Foreign and local interests looted Zaire's mineral wealth without enhancing systematic capitalist accumulation. The alliance between the dominant local class and international forces did not help the Zairian state insure development. The Botswana and Zaire examples show that some types of domestic and international alliances are not predisposed to promoting productive capitalist development, while others may do so.

CIVIL SOCIETY, STATE CAPACITY
AND CAPITALIST DEVELOPMENT

The [African] state, in both their socialist and capitalist versions, have too often done little of what they could and should do, and too much of what they cannot or should not do, and much of that badly.[23]

The "character of the state" literature says much about the architecture of the alliance between domestic and international forces and the state. However, it says little about state capacity. This lacuna becomes more obvious as the African state, socialist or capitalist, failed to foster dynamic, productive, and sustainable development.[24] The maturing development crisis in the early 1980s marked the disintegration of the postcolonial regime of accumulation.[25] The degeneration of African economies led to the realization that African postcolonial states whether capitalist or socialist, were not adept at fostering productive and articulated accumulation. This realization shifted the nature of the debate about the state's role and the obstacles to African development.

Three theories attempt to explain the African conundrum. The first thesis posits that Africa's involution is due to tension between strong societies and weak states. The second thesis claims that interventionist states dominated civil societies and ruined the continent's economies. The third explanation argues that the African development crisis is a product of dominant class accumulation strategies that put little premium on expanding productive capacity.[26] Moreover, international political economic conditions and forces adversely affected these economies.

The African states' decay and the demise of the region's economies led to another theory about the state. This theory questions whether the state has the strength and capacity to promote and sustain long-term, productive, economic transformation. The discussion centers around the particularity of African state–civil society relations and their implication for economic development. Two historic events significantly inform this debate: the "reemergence" of civil society in authoritarian East Europe and the rise of the Asian tigers.

Although both events are important, the East Asian route is more relevant to Africa especially if the questions are how to induce economic development and the nature of the state's appropriate role in development. The East Asian literature points to the centrality of an effective and autonomous state to the making of the miracle.[27] The East Asian state's autonomy meant that it was free from the many and often-conflicting demands of various civil society groups. The political and military elites' unity and the brutal suppression of decent enhanced the state's autonomy, particularly at the political level. Finally, state leaders used the state's autonomy purposely to build technical capacity that effectively nurtured the miracle.

Four factors facilitated the development of autonomous and effective states in East Asia. These included: (a) massive social upheavals that weakened civil society; (b) the presence of a major military danger from outside; (c) the availability of support from powerful states; and (d) the emergence of Japan as a global industrial power with a regional sphere of influence. Imaginative leaders, anxious to consolidate their grip on the state, used these structural conditions as raw material to thoroughly transform their societies' economies.[28]

In contrast to East Asian societies, African societies are said to be strong. Consequently they prevent the evolution of strong and autonomous states.[29] Joel Migdal notes that the basis for weak states was laid during the colonial reconstruction of these societies:

> while the old foundations of social control withered and old strategies of survival crumbled, colonialism provided the basis for new bonds of dependency. Often, the new social control of a chief far outstripped what he had maintained before. British rulers further strengthened the new bonds by regarding the population as members of social organizations led by chiefs, inefficient as they were, as conduits to the population. In these circumstances, the strategies adopted by most of the population necessarily started with the chief's

organizational base, the tribe. The tribe was a key organizational ally of the
colonial state, . . . Using the tribal organization, the chief controlled key resources . . . received from the state. The tribe catapulted forward as a key
structure in the modern world.[30]

In other words, the development of a market economy under the colonial
umbrella initiated a societal restructuring process that led to the formation
of localized power nodes. These nodes blocked the emergence of strong
states.

Others have debated the origin and the nature of weak African states and
the economic and social consequences of such regimes. Sara Berry, Goran
Hyden, and Richard Sandbrook all concur with the strong society thesis.[31]
One implication of this argument is that capitalist development in Africa
will require a transformed and strengthened state.[32] Building the state's
strength means increasing its relative autonomy from civil society.

The second thread of this Africanist debate contradicts the claim that civil
society derailed development. This literature points to the unhealthy state domination of civil society in postcolonial Africa.[33] Historian John Iliffe noted this
problem more than a decade ago, "African governments have shown that they
can prevent capitalism; they have not shown that they can replace it with anything else that will release their people's energies."[34] Although more recent literature does not use autonomy and strength as critical concepts, it does claim
that the state's monopolistic control of social life, or conversely the absence of
autonomous civil society, has ruined these societies.

Conceivably the growth of associational life and other civil society groups
will enhance the development of a pluralist society and democratic development.[35] However, nurturing and strengthening civil associations goes against
the thrust of this recent literature. This literature contends that a strong civil
society undermines the state's capacity and, consequently, hampers capitalist development.[36] Thus, this literature implicitly concurs with the neoliberal
agenda of a minimalist state.

The strong society thesis and the thesis that blames the state for the African disaster do not explain how the effective Botswana state emerged from
this "strong" traditional society. Chapter 2 shows that Botswana had strong
traditional chiefs. Despite this tradition, the chiefs have not hampered the
postcolonial state's development. Moreover, the state-dominated civil-society thesis fails to elucidate why the highly interventionist and centralized
state of Botswana (see chapters 4 and 5), or for that matter, the Asian tigers,
did not lead to economic and political ruin. We therefore need to look to
other literature to explain which combinations of state, civil society, and
international forces may be development friendly.

The third theoretical framework that anticipated the state-civil society
thesis interlaces rent-seeking theory with Marxist political economy.[37] Parnab

Bardhan's work on the Indian state reformulated Hamza Alavi's earlier contribution about the relationship between the dominant classes (industrial bourgeoisie, rich farmers, and the professionals) and the state.[38] He argues that the conflict between these groups over the distribution of surplus significantly impaired the state's ability to foster capitalist development:

> When diverse elements of the loose and uneasy coalition of the dominant proprietary classes pull in different directions and *when none of them is individually strong enough to dominate the process of resource allocation*, one predictable outcome is the proliferation of subsidies and grants to placate all of them, with the consequent reduction in available surplus for public capital formation.[39] (italics mine)

Thus, the dominant classes, not a homogenized traditional civil society, limit state autonomy and capacity:

> It is in this context of a *lack of political insulation* from conflicting interests, coupled with a strong power base of the white-collar workers in public bureaucracy, that keeps the Indian state, in spite of its pervasive economic presence, largely confined to regulatory function, avoiding the hard choices and politically unpleasant decisions involved in more active developmental functions.[40] (italics mine)

Research in Nigeria, in contrast to Bardhan's India, shows a pattern of state-civil society relation different from India's, but one that results in state inaptitude more damaging to systematic and productive accumulation.[41] Multilateral finance capital and multinationals play a more significant role in Nigeria than in India. Moreover, the three dominant domestic classes that cripple the state in the subcontinent are absent from the Nigerian scene. Instead, the relevant Nigerian groups are a commercial class and the civilian-military oligarchy. These external and internal forces have severely constrained state autonomy and battered the state's capacity to foster productive capitalist development:

> the particular weakness of state robbery in Nigeria is not simply its magnitude but also its consequences; the huge quantity of money drained from the state is not in itself debilitating, but in the Nigerian context its evacuation from the country, its investment in land speculation . . . or simple hoarding all tightly circumscribe the potential productive use of state resources. Finally, while commerce and finance could survive the arbitrariness of patrimonial rule, the massive state *indiscipline* and bureaucratic irrationality that accompany corruption in Nigeria could not provide the groundwork for disciplined industrial or agrarian capitalism.[42] (italics mine)

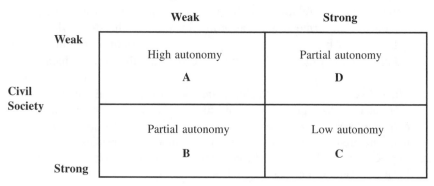

Figure 1.1   Determinants of State Autonomy

Others writing on Nigeria show how a corrupt dominant class and multinationals competing for the state-dominated domestic market fundamentally eroded the state's ability to formulate and affect rational development programs.[43]

The conceptual implications of these writings are that the major forces constraining the state's ability to guide development are internal and external. More specifically, this literature indicates the centrality of dominant domestic classes and international forces for state autonomy. These studies implicitly argue that more autonomous states will better serve capitalist development. The Indian and Nigerian cases are two illustrations of the types of state autonomy that may exist. The axes that determine the latitude of state autonomy are particular forces within civil society and the international environment (Figure 1.1).[44] This heuristic figure proposes four state autonomy conditions, products of the interaction between civil society and international forces. This framework combines two explanations that were heretofore cast in mutually exclusive terms. The following description of the four scenarios shows the merits of simultaneously examining external and internal forces to better understand the state's autonomy in Africa and elsewhere in the underdeveloped world.

In scenario A, civil society and external forces are weak. Theoretically, this gives state actors a great deal of latitude from particularistic civil society interests and international forces. South Korea and Taiwan exemplify these conditions. The Korean and Taiwanese state managers used their autonomy to build state capacity, which they then deployed to create a productive capitalist economy. Political, economic, and strategic conditions—regionally and globally—assisted these states' autonomy, capacity, and interventions.[45] These regional and global circumstances and the state's autonomy led to industrialization and the emergence of vibrant economies. There is no industrially dynamic African counterpart to the Asian Newly Industrializing Countries (NICs). The counterexample to the Asian NICs is Somalia, where civil society and international forces were weak. International forces came in the form of the cold war rivalry between the United States and the Soviet Union. This rivalry gave the state a certain degree of autonomy from the West and the East, but the cold war context, particularly the strategic, militaristic superpower interests circumscribed its latitude. The fragmented and nihilistic conflicts among the dominant class wasted whatever degree of freedom the state had. Thus, the combination of dominant class's fragmentation and the superpowers' conflict in the region mangled the state. In fact, in the end they destroyed it completely. This case clearly shows that autonomy is a necessary but insufficient condition for state-led development.

In scenario B, civil society is strong and external forces are weak. Consequently the state is relatively autonomous from external forces. The exact implication of this scenario on state autonomy depends on the internal social configuration of the society in question. If a united dominant class and other organized and mobilized groups exist, the state may have relatively low autonomy. Under this circumstance, the state may be closely tied to these group's projects. This affiliation is not necessarily bad, provided that the dominant groups discipline the state to create the necessary conditions for the project to take off. The dominant classes' disciplining of the state reverses Alice Amsden's thesis. Amsden's thesis explains how the state disciplines local business, forcing it to toe the line. If, on the other hand, the dominant classes are fragmented, they may paralyze the state so that it is unable to pursue what is in the interest of the collective project. Instead, the state may pander to the particularistic and short-term interests of segments of the dominant class. The Indian case signifies this scenario.[46]

In scenario C, civil society is organized and strong while international forces have a significant presence. The strength of internal and external forces limits state autonomy. The exact effect of this type of constraint on the state will depend on the nature and social composition of these forces. Possibly the dominant local groups may be sufficiently united to balance the external forces' influence. This will be particularly so if the interest of indigenous capital and its local alliance oppose the designs of international capital. Such circumstances can give the state some latitude. By contrast, if the interests of the internal and external forces significantly overlap, the state will have much less freedom. The influence of this type of local-international alliance on the state will be contingent on the nature of the "common" project. If the project requires systematic accumulation, rather than grand robbery or perpetuating neocolonialism, then the alliance can exercise discipline. If on the other hand the converse is the case, then indiscipline, chaos, and a lack of accountability may be the order of the day. Nigeria and Senegal typify two of these situations. External and internal forces' grand looting of public resources and low state autonomy has been Nigeria's fate.[47] In Senegal's case, two factors have significantly limited state autonomy: mourides (traditional Islamic brotherhood) and merchant capitalist organizations and strong French presence.[48]

In scenario D, civil society is weak while external forces are relatively strong. In this situation the state has autonomy from domestic forces while international and regional forces greatly define the state's latitude. This partial autonomy of the state can have multiple consequences, depending on whether the interests of the state and international capital are in conflict. For example, if the state is serious about nurturing the development of local capital that will compete with foreign interests, then it will come under tremendous pressure from these foreign interests to adopt a more congenial strategy. If, on the other hand, their interests are not in fundamental conflict, then they may work out a compromise that harmonizes their claims. This settlement's outcome will depend on what each party brings to the bargaining table as well as each party's determination to protect its particular interest. This scenario helps explain part of Botswana's experience. A weak civil society gave a united dominant class and the state sufficient autonomy from local forces. Moreover, the discovery of huge diamond resources gave the state tremendous leverage with De Beers. The state and De Beers saw their mutual interests and agreed on a compromise which gave the state tremendous revenues from diamond sales. Another example of Botswana's determination to extend its autonomy occurred when it pushed South Africa for the renegotiation of the Southern African Customs Union in 1969. Again, despite the state's weakness it successfully extracted more revenues from South Africa. These instances indicate that a purposive state can minimally expand its maneuvering room in the international system. Despite its substantial financial assets and autonomy from local social forces, the Botswana economy remain trapped in the web of South Africa dominated economy via the Southern African Customs Union. Another example of scenario D is the Ivory Coast.[49]

The aforementioned scenarios of state–civil society–international forces' impact on the state's *relative* autonomy are heuristic devices to explore the complexity of the issues involved. However, what is needed is an explication of the social chemistry of the constituent elements of civil society and international forces and their dynamics.

This discussion indicates the importance of state autonomy. However, it does not illustrate the relationship between state autonomy and the state's capacity for purposive action.[50] A successful autonomous state—in terms of economic development—is a Janus-faced institution. On the one hand, it is relatively autonomous from civil society; its political and technocratic institutions are insulated from "undesirable" society influences. On the other hand, those same institutions selectively link up with segments of civil society whose active involvement in the economy is necessary for productive transformation. Evans labels this type of state-society relation as embedded autonomy:

> . . . the mirror image of the incoherent absolutist domination of the predatory state and constitutes the organizational key to the effectiveness of the developmental state. Embedded autonomy depends on an apparently contradictory combination of Weberian bureaucratic insulation with intense [and selective] immersion in the surrounding social structure. How this contradictory combination is achieved depends, of course, on both the historically determined character of the state apparatus and the nature of the social structure in which it is embedded.[51]

Embedded autonomy raises the possibility of state–civil society relations in which a relatively autonomous state endorses or instigates a particular accumulation strategy and seeks alliances with social groups necessary for the realization of such a program.[52] In addition, embedded autonomy entails the existence or formation of state institutional capacity that can manage the relationship without being drawn into a rentier trap. Thus, autonomous states that can successfully embed with *segments* of civil society are those which have translated their autonomy into capacity or are in the process of doing so.

Embedded autonomy identifies a particular relationship between relatively autonomous state institutions and *particular segments* of civil society. As such, it overcomes two major weaknesses of the political economy and state–civil society literature: the focus on the state's character and the unnecessary conceptual gulf between the state and civil society. Moreover, it links state autonomy and state capacity.

Despite its fundamental contribution, embedded autonomy does not fully bridge the gap in our understanding. The Botswana experience points to four ways that Evans's concept can be extended.[53] First, embedded autonomy implies and assumes but does not explain how autonomous leaders emerge. Nor does it explain their links with the population.[54] The autonomy of the political leadership in Botswana evolved out of an enduring relationship between African traditional authority and its subjects. The colonial state failed to break this bond. Moreover, those who command the postcolonial state are leaders of a small but united dominant class.[55] This new leadership had legitimacy in the country. This leadership was also relatively autonomous from the dominant group and the population. Tradition-based autonomy and the absence of real challenge to the political leadership from the opposition explains the uniquely autonomous and legitimate Botswana state.[56] These characteristics sharply contrast with the East Asian states' (except Japan) authoritarian basis. This Botswana tradition facilitated the establishment of

insulated bureaucracy and liberal democracy in Botswana. The smooth transfer of power from former President Ketumile Masire to President Festus
Mogae in March 1998 adds to Botswana's democratic credentials.

Second, embedded autonomy assumes these autonomous state commanders are conscious of the treacherous nature of protecting the integrity of the
collective project, as they selectively invite particular groups from civil society to join forces with the state. These civil society groups may undermine
the state's purpose by pursuing their short-term interests. Consequently the
question is: how do those who dominate the state become aware of and
define the nature of the collective project? The leaders' definition of the
project will significantly affect how the autonomous institutions of the state
are built and deployed. Knowing how and when particular leaders gain awareness of "what is to be done" is a difficult matter to accurately pinpoint. In
the Botswana case, however, the traditional leaders' long struggle to keep
the colonial state and, more critically, South Africa at bay taught them the
importance of developing skill-based state capacity to undertake projects
competently.

Third, embedded autonomy does not tell us how states create institutions
that sustain the embedded relationship. Examining the history of Botswana's
Ministry of Finance and Development Planning helps fill in this gap. This
organization's history shows how Botswana established the institutional apparatus of the MFDP through trial and error. It also demonstrates how the
state used this institution to create and sustain those agencies responsible
for carrying out different aspects of the development program. This is particularly an important story to tell since many African states have not had
the experience of setting up public institutions with a sustained and successful track record.

Fourth, embedded autonomy does not directly address state-inherited weak
institutions where the entrepreneurial elements in civil society necessary for
consummating the embedded partnership do not exist. However, Evans describes three roles an activist state can play to make up for this deficit.[57]
The state plays the role of *demiurge* when it feels that private entrepreneurs
do not exist or are not up to the task. This means the state becomes directly
involved in production. The Botswana state reluctantly engages in production. The Botswana Meat Commission is the only major enterprise the state
owns and manages. In other cases, such as housing, the state hires private
contractors to build public housing. The state owns most of the urban housing in the country—and other buildings and infrastructure.

The state plays the role of a *midwife* when it assists in developing entrepreneurs or encourages existing ones to move into new areas. The state helps
entrepreneurs by reducing the risk involved in starting or investing in new
business. The Botswana state has primarily played the midwife role. The
Botswana Development Corporation is the principal government mechanism

for attracting investors from overseas and encouraging local entrepreneurs. The BDC conducts feasibility studies to identify profitable avenues for investment. The BDC then recruits investors once it identifies such an avenue. The BDC commits some of its resources to establish ventures. The BDC may create its own company and invest in the venture when investors are not forthcoming. The BDC has invested in over 160 firms, ranging from those it fully owns to others in which it controls minor shares. Botswana's FAP is another version of Botswana's midwife strategy. FAP was initiated in 1982 to diversify the economy away from diamonds and beef. The program involved grants and other incentives to create productive enterprises in industry. Moreover, FAP's main purpose has been to support and encourage local entrepreneurs and entice investors into industrial production. This program has been successful. Chapter 5 narrates the BDC's and FAP's story.

The third role the state plays in promoting development is that of *husbandry*. Husbandry involves nurturing firms spawned through midwifery so they may mature. The BDC and FAP have also been the main tools for midwifing and husbanding firms.

One of British colonialism's major legacies in Botswana has been the dearth of indigenous entrepreneurs. Because of this, the state had to establish its own institutions to plan and implement its development agenda. Consequently, it created its public institutions to nurture local entrepreneurship. Botswana did not want to invite racist white South African businessmen to fill the void colonialism left behind. Botswana, unlike most African countries, insured that most of its public enterprises operated on a commercial basis. This ensured that they remained financially solvent without burdening the state with a constant deficit. Two examples of Botswana's public enterprises, the BMC and BDC, discussed in chapters 4 and 5, illustrate this point.

Finally, although Evans's concept overcomes the state versus civil society straightjacket, it does not *explicitly* deal with the international, regional, and historic forces conditioning and shaping the terrain in which the state has to function. For example, Botswana inherited a weak state, no entrepreneurial class, and an economy dominated by a hostile neighbor. This weakness can be overcome by contextualizing the evolution of the social and political structure of a particular African society, its relationships to colonial forces, and the emergence of conscious human agents that manage development. Figure 1.2 expands the scope of Figure 1.1 by identifying the major forces that affect not only an African state's autonomy but also its capacity to meaningfully induce development. These six major forces include: (a) the traditional political economy; (b) the nature of the colonial project; (c) the formation of (post)colonial state and regional/international context; (d) civil society; dominant classes; (e) and leadership consciousness. The interaction between traditional political economy, the expanding

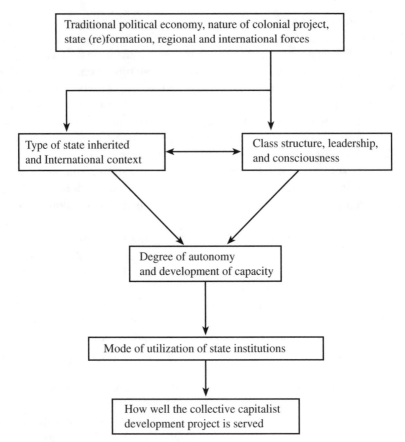

Figure 1.2   The Determinants of State Autonomy and Capacity

world system, and the specific project of the colonizer shaped the nature of the colonial state, its autonomy and capacity, the emerging social and power structure, and the regional/international context of the new colonial society. This interactive process determines whether a society's social structure and its dominant classes are fragmented or united and how restraining is its geographic and historical context. Moreover, this same process conditions the type of leadership that emerges from the ranks of the dominant groups. The fact that these processes circumscribe the kind of leadership that emerges does not mean these processes determine leadership quality. Postcolonial leaders can neither stand out of history and wishfully dream; nor must they follow the beaten path. As such, they must work with products of this historical process such as the apparatus of its colonial predecessor, the dynamics of local social structure, and a country's larger regional context.

If a state inherits a social environment providing a high degree of autonomy, the state still may not be able to translate autonomy into capacity to systematically nurture the collective project. On one hand, the prospects for enhanced state capacity improves tremendously where conscious and disciplined leaders are married to a relatively autonomous state and a friendly international milieu. On the other hand, if an autonomous state is coupled with leaders who fail to grasp the nature of the collective project, then state capacity will not likely develop. In fact, the new dominant class may undermine whatever capacity the postcolonial state inherited. Conscious and disciplined leadership is therefore an essential prerequisite to create an effective state. This leadership is also important in defining the scope of the collective project. The social structure and the leadership's quality determine the (re)development of competent, effective state machinery and whether this nurtures productive, speculative, or renter strategy. Last, the quality of dominant class's leadership distinguishes between the performances of two comparable and relatively autonomous postcolonial states, such as Somalia and Botswana.[58]

The remaining five chapters have three overarching objectives. First, they demonstrate how the dominant class and its leadership emerged out of the transformed precolonial society. Second, they show how this leadership built public institutions and enterprises and then used them to foster a particular kind of capitalist development: tremendous growth and radical inequality.[59] Third, they illustrate the limit imposed on this capable African state by its colonial legacy and the formative and formal articulation of its economy to the white dominated subimperial center of South Africa.

NOTES

[1] Peter Evans, "The State as a Problem and Solution: Predation, Embedded Autonomy, and Structural Change," in S. Haggard and R. Kaufman, eds., *The Politics of Economic Adjustment: International Constraints, Distributive Conflicts and the State* (Princeton, NJ: Princeton University Press, 1992), 139-181.

[2] K. Good, "Interpreting the Exceptionality of Botswana," *Journal of Modern African Studies* 30, 1 (1992): 94.

[3] World Bank, *Accelerated Development in Sub-Saharan Africa: An Agenda for Action* (Washington, DC: World Bank, 1989); World Bank, *Sub-Saharan Africa: From Crisis to Sustainable Growth* (Washington, DC: World Bank, 1989); World Bank, *Adjustment in Africa: Reforms, Results, and the Road Ahead* (New York: Oxford University Press, 1994); Richard Sandbrook, *The Politics of Africa's Economic Recovery* (New York: Cambridge University Press, 1993). Sandbrook argues that dismantling the existing African state is essential. I agree with him on this score, but I do not share his acceptance of the neoliberal agenda as the prescription for accomplishing this task. For a contrary view, see Claude Ake, *Democracy and Development in Africa: Debt Development and Democracy in Africa* (Washington, DC: Brookings Institution, 1996). See

also Fantu Cheru, *The Silent Revolution in Africa: Debt, Development and Democracy in Africa* (London: Zed Books, 1989).

[4] The Bank argues that the developmental success of the East Asian economies would have occurred even if the state had not intervened. World Bank, *The East Asian Miracle: Economic Growth and Public Policy, A World Bank Research Report* (New York: Oxford University Press, 1993). For a contrary interpretation of the East Asian experience and its relevancy for Africa, see Howard Stein, ed., *Asian Industrialization and Africa: Studies in Policy Alternatives to Structural Adjustment* (New York: St. Martin's Press, 1995).

[5] Peter Evans, *Embedded Autonomy: States and Industrial Transformation* (Princeton, NJ: Princeton University Press, 1995), 21.

[6] Alice Amsden, "Why Isn't the Whole World Experimenting with the East Asian Model? Review of the World Bank's *The East Asian Miracle: Economic Growth and Public Policy*," Working Paper Series, no. 47 (New School for Social Research, n.d.). See also Robert Wade, "Japan, the World Bank and the Art of Paradigm Maintenance: The East Asian Miracle in Political Perspective," *New Left Review* 217 (1996): 3-36.

[7] This must not be interpreted as a defense for the bloated and inefficient bureaucracies nor an argument for an expansive public sector. It is an argument against the equally rigid prescription for a minimalist state, no matter what the circumstances.

[8] Neoliberal commentators argue that recent turbulence in financial markets in East Asia underscores problems generated by state involvement in markets. They suggest that further liberalization of those economies will correct the problem. Contrary to this view, it must be noted financial upheavals are not the same as economic crisis. The competitive advantage of the industrial economies of these countries is beyond doubt. In fact Japan announced that its export in November 1997 were nearly double those of a year earlier. In addition, many of the upheavals are a product of speculative drive of firms since the state began to reduce its regulatory reach in the middle and late 1980s.

[9] P. Evans, D. Rueschemeyer, and T. Skocpol, *Bringing the State Back In* (New York: Cambridge University Press, 1985); A. Amsden, *Asia's Next Giant: South Korea and Late Industrialization* (New York: Oxford University Press, 1989); R. Wade, *Governing the Market: Economic Theory and the Role of the Government in East Asian Industrialization* (Princeton, NJ: Princeton University Press, 1990); P. Evans, "Class, State and Dependence in East Asia: Lessons for Latin Americanists," in F. Deyo, ed., *The Political Economy of New Asian Industrialism* (Ithaca, NY: Cornell University Press, 1987), 203-226. For a fuller development of the internal structure of the developmental state, see P. Evans, *Embedded Autonomy*. For a comparative study of the importance of the East Asian experience for Africa, see Stein, ed., *Asian Industrialization and Africa*.

[10] Hamza Alavi, "The State in Post-colonial Societies: Pakistan and Bangladesh," *New Left Review* 74 (1972): 59-82; John Saul, "The State in Post-colonial Societies: Tanzania," *Socialist Register* (1974): 349-372, and his "The Unsteady State: Uganda, Obote and General Amin," *Review of African Political Economy* 5 (1976): 12-28; Issa Shivji, *Class Struggle in Tanzania* (New York: Monthly Review Press, 1976); Mahmood Mamdani, *Politics and Class Formation in Uganda* (New York: Monthly Review Press, 1976); Colin Leys, "The Overdeveloped Post-colonial State: A Revaluation," *Review of African Political Economy* 5 (1976): 39-49, and his "Capital Accumulation, Class Formation and Dependency—The Significance of the Kenyan Case," *Socialist Register* (1978): 241-266; C. Meillassoux, "A Class Analysis of Bureaucratic Process in Mali," *Journal of Development Studies* 6, 2 (1970): 91-110; R. Murray, "Second Thoughts on

Ghana," *New Left Review* 6, 2 (1967): 25-39; Nicola Swainson, "The Rise of a National Bourgeosie in Kenya," *Review of African Political Economy* 4 (1977): 39-55; Swainson, *The Development of Corporate Capitalism in Kenya, 1918-1977* (Berkeley: University of California Press, 1980); Michaela Von Freyhold, *Ujamaa Villages in Tanzania: Analysis of a Social Experiment* (New York: Monthly Review Press, 1979); S. Langdon, "The State and Capitalism in Kenya," *Review of African Political Economy* 8 (1977): 90-97; R. Kaplinsky, "Capitalist Accumulation in the Periphery—The Kenyan Case Re-examined," *Review of African Political Economy* 17 (1980): 83-105; Michael Watts and Thomas Bassett, "Politics, the State and Agrarian Development: A Comparative Study of Nigeria and the Ivory Coast," *Political Geography Quarterly* 5, 2 (1986): 103-125; W. Ziemann and M. Lazendorfer, "The State in Peripheral Societies," *Socialist Register* (1977): 143-177; Harry Galborone, "The Problem of the State in Backward Capitalist Societies," *African Development* 6, 1 (1981): 45-70; Bjorn Beckman, "Imperialism and Capitalist Transformation: Critique of a Kenya Debate," *Review of African Political Economy* 19 (1980): 48-62; B. Beckman, "Imperialism and the National Bourgeoisie," *Review of African Political Economy* 22 (1981): 5-19; B. Beckman, "Whose State? State and Capitalist Transformation in Nigeria," *Review of African Political Economy* 23 (1982): 37-51; B. Beckman, "The Post-colonial State: Crisis and Reconstruction," *IDS Bulletin* 19 (1988): 26-34; Ahmed Samatar, *Socialist Somalia: Rhetoric or Reality?* (London: Zed Books, 1988); Abdi Samatar, *The State and Rural Transformation in Northern Somalia, 1884-1986* (Madison: University of Wisconsin Press, 1989); Craig Charney, "Political Power and Social Classes in the Neocolonial African State," *Review of African Political Economy* 38 (1987): 48-65.

[11] Joel Migdal, *Strong Societies and Weak States: State and Society Relations and State Capabilities in the Third World* (Princeton, NJ: Princeton University Press, 1988); Michael Bratton, "Beyond the State: Civil Society and Associational Life in Africa," *World Politics* 41, 3 (1989): 407-430; J. Barkan, M. McNulty, and P. M. Ayeni, "Hometown Voluntary Associations, Local Development, and the Emergence of Civil Society in Western Nigeria," *Journal of Modern African Studies* 29, 3 (1991): 457-480.

[12] Alavi, "The State in Post-colonial Societies."

[13] Ibid., 60.

[14] Ibid., 61.

[15] Ibid., 63.

[16] Ibid., 76.

[17] For a sample of this long list of contributors see note 9.

[18] David Himbara, *Kenyan Capitalists, the State, and Development* (Boulder, CO: Lynne Rienner Publishers, 1994).

[19] Beckman, "Imperialism and Capitalist Transformation"; "Imperialism and the National Bourgeoisie"; "Whose State?"; and "The Post-colonial State."

[20] Beckman, "Imperialism and Capitalist Transformation," 36.

[21] Beckman, "Whose State?", 45.

[22] For discussions of the triple alliance, see Peter Evans, *Dependent Development: The Alliance of Multinationals, State and Local Capital in Brazil* (Princeton, NJ: Princeton University Press, 1979); and Jonathan Barkar, *Rural Communities Under Stress* (Cambridge: Cambridge University Press, 1989).

[23] Piotr Dukiewics and Gavin Williams, "All the King's Horses and All the King's Men Couldn't Put Humpty-Dumpty Together Again," *IDS Bulletin* 18, 3 (1987): 39-44.

[24] See the perceptive and comparative discussion of Ghana and Ivory Coast in Richard Crook, "State Capacity and Political Institutions in Cote d'Ivoire and Ghana," *IDS Bulletin* 21, 4 (1990): 24-34. See also his "State Capacity and Economic Development: The Case of Cote d'Ivoire," *IDS Bulletin* 19 (1988): 19-24.

[25] See Timothy Shaw for this concept: "Towards a Political Economy of the African Crisis: Diplomacy, Debates and Dialectics," in M. Glantz, ed., *Drought and Hunger in Africa: Denying Famine a Future* (New York: Cambridge University Press, 1987).

[26] Jean-François Bayart, *The State in Africa: The Politics of the Belly* (London: Longman, 1993); Abdi Samatar, *The State and Rural Transformation in Northern Somalia*.

[27] Gordon White, ed., *Developmental States in Asia* (London: Macmillan, 1988); Thomas Gold, *State and Society in the Taiwan Miracle* (Armonk, NY: M. E. Sharpe, 1985); Chalmers Johnson, *MITI and the Japanese Miracle: The Growth of Industrial Policy, 1925-1975* (Palo Alto, CA: Stanford University Press, 1982); Wade, *Governing the Market: Economic Theory and the Role of Government in East Asian Industrialization* (Princeton, NJ: Princeton University Press, 1990).

[28] Joel Migdal, *Strong Societies and Weak States: State and Society Relations and State Capabilities in the Third World* (Princeton, NJ: Princeton University Press, 1988): chapter 8; Bruce Cuming, *The Origins of the Korean War* (Princeton, NJ: Princeton University Press, 1981); Cuming, "The Origins and Development of Northeast Asian Political Economy: Industrial Sectors, Product Cycles, and Political Consequences," in F. Deyo, ed., *The Political Economy of New Asian Industrialism* (Ithaca, NY: Cornell University Press, 1987): 44-83.

[29] Migdal, *Strong Societies,* chapters 3 and 5.

[30] Ibid., 115-116.

[31] In spite of their difference regarding the nature of African social history, these scholars agree that the inability of states to effect positive economic transformation is due to the existence of competing centers of social control outside the purview of the state. Sara Berry, *Fathers Work for Their Sons: Accumulation, Mobility, and Class Formation in an Extended Yoruba Family* (Berkeley: University of California Press, 1983); Goran Hyden, *Beyond Uzamaa in Tanzania: Underdevelopment and an Uncaptured Peasantry* (Berkeley: University of California Press, 1980); Richard Sandbrook, *The Politics of Africa's Economic Stagnation* (New York: Cambridge University Press, 1985).

[32] A. Odhiambo Oyugi, M. Chege, and A. K. Gitonga, ed., *Democratic Theory-Practice in Africa* (London: James Currey, 1988).

[33] D. Rothchild and N. Chazan, ed., *The Precarious Balance: State and Civil Society in Africa* (Boulder, CO: Westview Press, 1988); Bratton, "Beyond the State"; Barkan, McNulty, and Ayeni, "Hometown Voluntary Associations, Local Development, and the Emergence of Civil Society in Western Nigeria."

[34] John Iliffe, *The Emergence of African Capitalism* (London: Macmillan, 1983): 79.

[35] See also Richard Sklar, "Developmental Democracy," *Society for Comparative Study of Society and History* 29, 4 (1987): 686-714.

[36] For a contrasting view, see David Booth, "Alternative in the Restructuring of State-Society Relations: Research Issues for Tropical Africa," *IDS Bulletin* 18, 4 (1987): 23-30. For an incisive, empirically rich, and balanced critique of the dominant literature on civil society and nongovernmental organizations, see Judith Tendler, *Good Government in the Tropics* (Baltimore, MD: Johns Hopkins University Press, 1997).

[37] Parnab Bardhan, *The Political Economy of Development in India* (London: Basil Blackwell, 1984); Michael Watts, ed., *The State, Oil and Agriculture in Nigeria* (Berke-

ley, CA: Institute of International Studies, 1987); M. Watts, "The Agrarian Question in Africa," *Progress in Human Geography* 13 (1989): 1-44. Thandika Mkandawire and Naceur Bourenane, ed., *The State and Agriculture in Africa* (Dakar: CODESRIA Book Series, 1987).

[38] Bardhan, *The Political Economy*, chapters 6 and 7.

[39] Ibid., 61.

[40] Ibid., 74.

[41] M. Watts, *Silent Violence: Food, Famine and Peasantry in Northern Nigeria* (Berkeley: University of California Press, 1983), and Watts, ed., *The State, Oil*; Bjorn Beckman and Gunilla Andrea, *The Wheat Trap: Bread and Underdevelopment in Nigeria* (London: Zed Books, 1985); Bade Onimode, *Imperialism and Underdevelopment in Nigeria* (London: Zed Press, 1982).

[42] Watts, introduction to Watts, ed., *The State, Oil*, 17-18.

[43] Terisa Turner, "Multinational Corporation and the Instability of the Nigerian State," *Review of African Political Economy* 5 (1976): 63-79. See also Beckman and Andrea, *The Wheat Trap*; and Thomas Biersteker, *Multinationals, the State and Control of the Nigerian Economy* (Princeton, NJ: Princeton University Press, 1987).

[44] This author is mindful of the problems involved in capturing dynamic and fluid processes in a matrix such as Figure 1.1. Such a presentation is, however, useful as a mere tool to illustrate the general outline of the context. As the text shows, much will also depend on the texture of the social forces involved in the struggle.

[45] Cuming, "The Origins and Development of Northeast Asian Political Economy."

[46] Bardhan, *The Political Economy*. See also the interesting discussion of the "weak-strong" Indian state in I. Rudolph and S. Rudolph, *In Pursuit of Lakshami: The Political Economy of the Indian State* (Chicago: University of Chicago Press, 1987).

[47] Beckman and Andrea, *The Wheat Trap*; Watts, *The State, Oil*.

[48] M. C. Diop and M. Diouf, *Le Senegal sous Abdou Diouf: Etat et societé* (Paris: Karthala, 1990); M. C. Diop, ed., *Senegal: Essays in Statecraft* (Dakar: CODESRIA, 1993); C. Boone, *Merchant Capital and the Roots of State Power in Senegal* (Cambridge: Cambridge University Press, 1992); D. Cruise O'Brien, *Saints and Politicians: Essays in the Organization of a Senegalese Peasant Society* (Cambridge: Cambridge University Press, 1975).

[49] Crook, "State Capacity and Economic Development."

[50] Evans, "The State as a Problem and Solution"; Crook, "State Capacity and Political Institutions in Cote d'Ivoire and Ghana"; Wade, *Governing the Market*; Alice Amsden, *Asia's Next Giant: South Korea and Late Industrialization* (New York: Oxford University Press, 1989); White, *Developmental States*; Johnson, *MITI and the Japanese Miracle*; Bardhan, *The Political Economy of Development in India*.

[51] Evans, "The State as a Problem and Solution," 154.

[52] Evans identifies industrial capital as the key category of civil society that has the potential to transform the national economic landscape (*Embedded Autonomy*, 17). Bob Jessop's strategic-relational approach has many of the elements Evans attributes to embedded autonomy.

[53] For an extension and criticism of Evans's discussion see Linda Weiss, *The Myth of the Powerless State* (Ithaca: Cornell University Press, 1998).

[54] The recent article on social capital goes some way in dealing with this issue. See Peter Evans, "Government Action, Social Capital and Development: Reviewing the Evidence on Synergy," *World Development* 24, 6 (1996): 1119-1132.

[55] J. Parson, *Botswana: Liberal Democracy and the Labor Reserve in Southern Africa* (Boulder, CO: Westview, 1984).

[56] P. Molutsi and J. Holm, "Developing Democracy When Civil Society Is Weak: The Case of Botswana," *African Affairs* 89, 356 (1990): 323-340. This may be changing given the result of the national election in October 1994, in which the opposition secured nearly a third of the total seats in parliament. Recent strife within the main opposition party may undermine this trend.

[57] Evans, *Embedded Autonomy*, 77-81.

[58] Many individuals will note that Somalia and Botswana are not comparable because of Botswana's huge diamond reserves and its proximity to the relatively developed industrial economy of South Africa. The revenue and location variables are important features that distinguish Botswana from Somalia. I will argue, however, that if the Botswana leaders did not establish relatively effective and streamlined state apparatus in the early years of the country's independence, the revenues would have been wasted. It is interesting to take note, insofar as the location factor is concerned, of the calculated way the leadership managed the risk of either being destroyed or taken over by the apartheid regime (more on this in chapters 2 and 3). Moreover, it is useful to register the difference between the way Botswana managed its relations with South Africa and how Somalia dealt with the oil states of the Middle East. The detrimental and powerful economic, cultural, and political influence the oil states exerted, directly or indirectly, on Somalia is a long and complicated chapter of its history that is yet to be analyzed. For a discussion of the leadership question in Somalia and Botswana, see Abdi Samatar, "Leadership and Ethnicity in the Making of African State Models: Botswana versus Somalia," *Third World Quarterly* 18, 4 (1997): 687-707.

[59] N. Raphaeli, J. Roumanu, and A. C. MacKellar, *Public Sector Management in Botswana: Lessons in Pragmatism* (Washington, DC: World Bank, 1985); K. Good, "At the Ends of the Ladder: Radical Inequalities in Botswana," *Journal of Modern African Studies* 31, 2 (1993): 203-230; J. Isaksen, *Macro-economic Management and Bureaucracy: The Case of Botswana, Research Report No. 59* (Uppsala: Scandinavian Institute of African Studies, 1981).

2

CAPITALISM, COLONIALISM, AND THE BOTSWANA CHIEFS: FRAGMENTATION OR CENTRALIZED POWER?

INTRODUCTION

One recent argument explaining the weakness of the African state claims that spread of the world market and colonialism dovetailed with African social structures to produce multilayered social and political orders.[1] Joel Migdal argues that local power such as tribal chiefs characterize this order. These local and provincial power centers prevent central state authorities from mobilizing resources for development and social transformation. The ubiquitous miniature giants undermine the development of strong state institutions capable of overcoming underdevelopment. Although the world market and colonialism originated outside Africa, Migdal nevertheless identifies the reconfigured local social system as the source of current malaise. Migdal's thesis underestimates a critical force that played a fundamental role in the development of state institutions and their capacity to effect change. His message downplays the centrality of class interest and the social composition of dominant classes in shaping public institutions.[2] How the nature of dominant class(es) affect the capacity of such public institutions and their influences receives short shrift. Most African societies' historical experiences do not match such a claim. The bone of contention is not whether the colonial project played havoc with African societies and weakened the emerging states. Rather, it is why are these states ineffective and more particularly what role do traditional African authorities play in undermining postcolonial states.

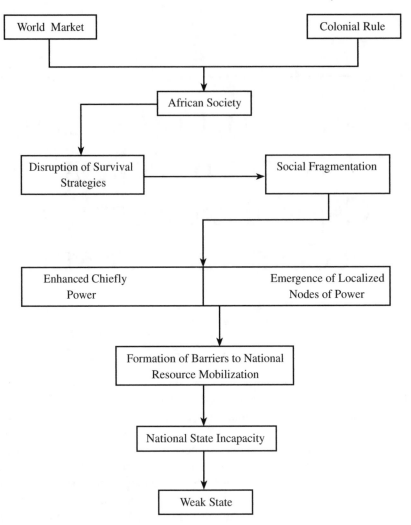

Figure 2.1 Forces Producing Weak African States

Figure 2.1 shows Migdal's straightforward argument. The figure, extracted from Migdal, is slightly modified to illustrate the issues more clearly. According to him, the spread of the world economy into peripheral societies of Africa, Asia, and Latin America subverted the established and predominantly subsistence-based economies. It also played havoc with these societies' survival strategies.[3] The collapse of old survival strategies generated struggles among the population regarding the control of the emerging means of livelihood. It also created conflicts over who was going to dominate the new social order. Colonial European powers emerged as these new forms of social life struggled to unfold. Consequently, colonial rule dovetailed with market forces to shape who had access to and control over resources and ultimately who exercised social control. The indigenous pillars of the new economic and political order were the reformed traditional authorities or chiefs:

> while the old foundations of social control withered and old strategies of survival crumbled, colonialism provided the basis for new bonds of dependency. Often, the new social control of a chief far outstripped what he had maintained before. [Colonial] rulers further strengthened the new bonds by regarding the population as members of social organizations led by chiefs rather than as people with *individual* rights and needs. Any concern with economic development in such a context demanded using the chiefs, inefficient as they were, as conduits to the population. In these circumstances, the strategies of survival, adopted by most of the population necessarily started with the chief's organizational base, the tribe. The tribe was a key organizational ally of the colonial state, and it is impossible to understand the changing nature of the tribe in the twentieth century without noting its relation to the state. Using the tribal organization, the chief controlled key resources, including material goods, jobs, violence, and defense; some of these resources, chiefs received from the state. In addition, the symbolic importance of the tribe was stressed by chiefs as they sought to build the basis of enduring social control. The tribe was catapulted forward as a key structure in the modern world.[4]

Migdal also claims that the distribution of social control among the chiefs in a colony created powerful but localized strong men. These chiefdoms spawned tension between competing rivals within the colony. Furthermore, despite the chiefs' dependency on the colonial administration, the chiefs still exercised significant degree of control over the natives and even what the administration could do on their turfs. Such a social and political structure produced "a weblike society for the twentieth century."[5] In spite of the colonial administration's national scope, the village big men significantly influenced what transpired in their local domains. The emergence of colonial nation states and the fragmentation of authority, particularly when viewed from the indigenous power structure's vantage point, had an enduring and powerful effect on colonial societies.[6] Fragmented social structures and the entrenched power of the chiefs produced weak national states after independence and frustrated national leaders' aspirations:

> the fragmentation of social control—the heterogeneity of rule making in society—greatly restricted the growth of state capabilities after independence. Even with all the resources at their disposal, even with the ability to eliminate any single strongman, state leaders found themselves severely

limited. Any serious campaign to increase their capabilities—to penetrate, regulate social relations, appropriate resources, extract more from their societies—would necessarily undercut the prerogatives and bases of social control of the strongmen. Many state leaders realized that their tenure depended on the social stability the strongmen could offer through their social control; the strongmen had direct access to most of the population, and they could *mobilize people* for specific purposes.[7]

The fragmentation of political and economic life and the tenacity of strong tribal leaders are the heart of Migdal's weak state theory. Postindependence Botswana's experience does not support Migdal's theory. Bechuanaland's British colonial administration depended on traditional "chiefs" to govern the territory between 1885 and 1966. These chiefs jealously and effectively guarded their autonomy and their domains despite their becoming the administration's vassals.[8] This chapter demonstrates that the Bechuanaland chiefs were positioned to realize the benefits of local power, prescribed by Migdal's theory. They commanded the following of their respective communities and frustrated the colonial administration, when necessary, to safeguard their sovereignty over "tribal territories." Contrary to Migdal's claims, the chiefs lost most of their political power during independence negotiations and have not recovered from this loss.

The first part of this chapter presents a brief overview of social structure and power relations in precapitalist Botswana society, particularly emphasizing the traditional leaders' role. The second part evaluates the nature of conflict and cooperation between traditional leaders and the colonial state, especially the way precolonial order was restructured. Finally, the chapter concludes by showing the emerging postcolonial authority structure and the chiefs' location in such edifice.

PRECOLONIAL BOTSWANA: A TRIBUTARY SYSTEM

Precolonial Botswana was one of the most hierarchical social structures in the region.[9] This was a highly organized and centralized society. The center of authority in traditional Botswana nations (*morafe*) was the king (*kgosi*), whose power was unchallenged as long as he ruled well. Given the relatively small size of the Botswana nations and the concentrations of their populations in few large villages, it was possible to keep the centralized political order intact and effective. The link between royalty, particularly the king, and the population was cemented materially and ideologically through the circulation of cattle. The king used force to dispossess those who were disloyal to authority and the traditional belief systems. This centralized political order, headed by an autonomous king, lasted until colonial rule was imposed in 1885.

The morafe organization had several tiers: the household, family group, the ward, and the village. The most basic unit of a morafe was the household.[10] The husband headed this patriarchal unit. It contained a wife (several wives for wealthy men), her offspring, and other dependent relatives.[11] These units owned cattle and fields. They shared grazing and water resources with other larger groups. Several related households formed the next level of social organization, the family group. The eldest man led the family group, united by blood. Even when family group members did not live in close proximity, they still maintained kinship ties. The family group, united by agnatic ancestor, also interacted and maintained relations with other social units through marriage. An elder council, headed by a leader, resolved and mediated disputes between family group members. They also shared major tasks such as large fines which a household was incapable of paying.

The ward was the third level of morafe social organization. A ward (*kgotla*) consisted of several family groups living together in the same section of a village (*motse*). The ward was an important political unit led by a hereditary head man, *kgosana*.[12] Kgosana had clear administrative and judicial power and functions. The kgotla was his headquarters and the main and lowest territorial unit in the morafe administration. Each ward had a kgotla: a meeting place where the group conducted its business. The kgosana represented the king, kgosi, and administered the ward on the kgosi's behalf.

The three types of wards were royal, commoner, and immigrant. Kgosi descendants governed royal wards. Unlike royal wards, commoner wards were governed by commoners (*basemane*) who served at the kgosi's pleasure. The kgosi appointed these men as a reward for supporting him during conflicts with royal kinsmen. Unlike the basemane, royal headmen inherited the title, and kgosi could not "arbitrarily deprive [them] of his property and title."[13] As a result of the security of their tenure, these men occasionally challenged kings. Immigrant wards were created for those groups who sought the protection of the kgosi. The kgosi appointed their headmen from their ranks.

The headmen of all wards acted as an advisory council to the king. New wards came into being as family groups grew and separated into independent wards. Thus, Botswana's social structure had a tendency towards fragmentation because of population growth and conflicts among royal houses.

Another major element of Botswana's social structure was the age regiment (*mephato*). Adults belonged to an age grouping which was formed when boys and girls came of age. The male mephato was called *bogwera*; the female was called *bogale*. The kgosi presided over the mephato initiation. The process instilled a sense of group unity and trained the young about Botswana tradition, dedicating particularly their loyalty to the morafe and its king.[14] The king alone had the power to summon mephato and instruct them to carry out his orders, such as cultivating his fields, subduing his opponents, and hunting for him. They were the king's main force against challengers. "So long as the king enjoyed the support of the mephato, he commanded enough force to coerce compliance."

The king, a hereditary title, stood on the top of this social and genealogical pyramid. Theoretically, the first son of the principal wife automatically ascended to the throne when his father died or became incapable of administering the morafe's affairs. As the Botswana saying indicates, "*Kgosi Ke Ka a tsetswe,*" which means that one is born into kingship.[15] The king was the religious and spiritual leader and the primary law maker and judge. His kgotla was the administrative and the ideological center of his morafe. After the king, his relatives had the greatest influence and prestige.

As the morafe's law maker, the king consulted with his royal and non-royal advisers (head men of the wards). Theoretically, the king had the authority to make laws unilaterally. However, since he depended on his ward men to enforce the law, he discussed proposed laws with them prior to bringing them up for popular discussion in his kgotla.[16] "Popular" discussions of new laws in the kgotla were not "open" to the general public because ward headmen dominated deliberations. Only rarely did commoners who were not the king's confidants challenge proposed laws.

Kinship, religion, material ties, and relations held this social system together. The king, the wealthiest man in the morafe, was the custodian of land and other society resources. He gained his wealth by collecting tributes:

> Apart from being entitled to personal services from his subjects, the chief used to receive from them various forms of tribute in kind. These included Sehuba (specified hunting spoils), Dikgafela (basket of corn after each harvest), and the produce of large fields (Masotla) cultivated for him annually by the inhabitants of his capital and sometimes also by other local groups. He got an ox from the father of every child attending initiation ceremonies, and another as "death token" (Taltlo, Tatodi) whenever an important man died. In addition, he kept all unclaimed stray cattle (Matimela), and most of those paid as fines in his court or looted in war. . . . [H]e also received special tribute from other subject communities.[17]

Cattle was the principal form of wealth, and the kgosi controlled or owned large herds. This wealth was used to entertain guests, provide for religious and other ceremonies, and feed orphans and other needy morafe members.[18] In addition, the king used his herd for patronage to bind to him clients whom he depended on for support. He loaned cattle to these clients who were supposed to care for it and use their products. In fact, the king was referred to as "the milk bail." The kgosi could recall loaned cattle anytime he desired. The loaned cattle, which held together this client system, were called *kgamelo* or *mafisa*. The basemane, appointed headmen, who performed administrative tasks kept kgamelo while that which was loaned to other commoners were called mafisa. The basemane also collected the king's tribute and managed his land. These tasks were beyond the preview of the king's relatives.[19] In nutshell, cattle were a fundamental pillar of the traditional authority structure. Political and economic power rested with royals and appointed clients. Although many constraints limited the king's authority, he nevertheless commanded unfailing loyalty from his people and was the morafe's supreme authority.

COLONIALISM AND THE
TRANSFORMATION OF THE MORAFE

The growing global capitalist economy engulfed Botswana societies long before the Protectorate was declared in 1885.[20] The new order induced five major changes in these societies before colonization. First, it brought industrial commodities to the "shores" of these communities. Second, missionaries spanned the territories, starting with David Livingstone, and led to the Christianization of all major chiefs by the 1870s. In fact, missionaries often became among the chief's trusted advisors. Third, European settlers moved inland from the Cape, dispossessed most Africans and pressured others to concentrate in small areas of land. Fourth, hunters and traders, eager to make fortunes, exploited wildlife in large numbers, leading to the decimation of many species. Fifth, the combined effects of these forces led to changes and innovations in the morafe's administration.[21] For instance, Khama III, the Ngwato king, changed his relationship with many of his subjects by "disowning" the cattle kept by his clients or by "freeing" the serf communities.[22] In spite of such liberalization of the morafe economy, the king remained the largest cattle owner because he invested revenues generated from regulating European trade in cattle. Stray cattle and court fines continued to add to his wealth.

The cumulative effect of these forces produced a vibrant and growing commercial economy in the early decades before matters turned for the worst:

> The economy had been stimulated by mercantile contact with the world economy into a phase of productive growth, which reached its climax when Khama's Country serviced the Cape-to-Rhodesia wagon transit trade. But the railway removed this pole of growth, and the terms of trade turned against the local economy [by the end of the century].[23]

Long before the establishment of a colony the southern African political economy began to strangle the morafe economies. The pressures of European settlers and the ambitions of mining concerns led some of the Botswana kings to seek, with the advice of missionaries, British Imperial Protection for their territories as early as 1866.[24] Not until the British felt (with Cecil Rhodes's help and advice) that the Northern Road, linking the British interest in South and Central Africa, was in danger of being closed by the Boers and Germans in 1885 did they declare and establish the Bechuanaland Protectorate.

Given the parsimonious nature of British colonialism and the absence of immediately visible resources to exploit in the "new" territory, the British did establish a "regular system of administration."[25] Bechuanaland's new British overlord was an administrator stationed in Vryburg who was aided by an assistant commissioner in Gaborones. The scope of his powers was very limited:

> He was to assist the chiefs to resist the invasion of their territories by outsiders, but to abstain from interfering with Native Administration. The Chiefs, it was said, 'are understood not to be desirous to part with their rights of sovereignty nor is Her Majesty's Government by any means anxious to assume responsibility for it.'[26]

The chiefs resisted the Protectorate Administrator's attempt to raise revenues by imposing a Hut Tax in 1889. In fact five years after the declaration of the protectorate, its revenues were a meager 443 sterling pounds in 1890.

The mining interests, like Rhodes, were partially responsible for the extension of British rule to the Botswana territories. They had not forgotten their agenda. Rhodes and Associates formed the British South Africa Company in 1889. This company was willing to "help" the Colonial Administration with its difficult financial circumstances, for about 4,000 sterling pounds a year.[27] Such "generosity" was induced by the knowledge that it was the "intention of the Colonial Office that the company should eventually take over the control of the Protectorate and thus relieve the British Government of the responsibility and expenditure."[28]

The chiefs resolutely objected to the transfer. Their missionaries, aware of the sympathies of the Aborigines Protection Society in England, assisted and advised the chiefs.[29] Three chiefs, Khama, Sebele, and Bathoen, accompanied and advised by Reverend W. C. Willoughby, sailed to England to petition the colonial secretary and to make the depth of their objections known to Her Majesty's government. The negotiations were fruitful as the colonial secretary agreed to their demands: "The Colonial Secretary agreed that each of the Chiefs should have 'a country in which to live, as before, under the protection of the Queen.' In these areas they were 'to rule their own people much as at present,' under an officer who has 'to receive his orders from the Queen through the Secretary of

State.'"[30] Despite this agreement, the issue of the Protectorate being turned over to South Africa was left for the future. In return for this concession from the colonial secretary, the chiefs accepted the imposition of a Hut Tax, which they were to collect. Their reward for collecting the tax was 10 percent of the proceeds.

The May 9, 1891, order of the council set the Protectorate's administrative frame.[31] The order invested all lawmaking powers in the high commissioner. His proclamation became the law of the land. The commissioner's power was wide-ranging. The major constraint on his ability to proclaim new laws was that he had to "respect any Native laws or customs by which the civil relations of any native chiefs, tribes or populations under Her Majesty's power and jurisdiction are now regulated, except so far as some may be incompatible with the due exercise of Her Majesty's power and jurisdictions."[32]

THE PROTECTORATE ADMINISTRATION AND THE CHIEFS

This section presents a brief overview of colonial rule in Bechuanaland. It reviews the dialectical impact of colonial rule on the chiefs. It describes the chiefs' strength and their defense of their privilege. The section assesses the transformation of traditional economic relations and to some degree political hegemony over their people.

For societies such as [Botswana], colonial rulers used their advantage in power to direct resources and authority and enforce sanctions in ways that deeply affected how indigenous forces reconstituted social control. They gave scattered strongmen the wherewithal to build their social control in fragments of the society. . . . Those who shared control with the British, however, were carefully selected: Chiefs, yes; the new educated elites, no. The preference for chiefs by no means eliminated the more educated elites as contenders of social control forever after. It did, nonetheless, affect the long-term balance of power.[33]

The chieftainship was the "center" holding Tswana society together. The chief allocated scarce resources, conducted assemblies and rituals, and represented his polity in encounters with outsiders. Until the middle of the twentieth century, the chieftainship remained the organizing center of northern Tswana life. . . . During Tshekedi Khama's regency as chief of the Ngwato, the chieftainship was surviving its final phase of relative autonomy from state control. In the 1960s, the departing imperialists would erect the apparatus of nation-state . . . over the Bechuanaland Protectorate. As a result, the chieftainship . . . while retaining its form, would lose its claim to exert primary political authority over its subjects and to serve as greatest patron of all.[34]

Migdal's thesis suggests that where indigenous community was fractured into chiefdoms and where the colonial state closely collaborated and used these native authorities, a fragmented social and political structure emerged in the postcolonial societies. Provincial strong men frustrated the independent national leadership's progressive agenda. At a superficial level, the British Protectorate of Bechuanaland with its strong chieftainship seems to fit Migdal's model. But Diana Wylie's work shows this is not the case. This is largely because the weblike society thesis fails to examine the fundamental contradictions of colonialism. While chiefly rule was becoming centralized at the political and administrative levels, the traditional economic and tributary processes that bound the local population to their ruler were coming apart at the seams.

The Protectorate Administration followed Lord Lugard's Dual Mandate framework. The agreement between the Imperial Government and the chiefs, noted earlier, laid the basis for a dual administrative system. The high commissioner and his representatives became the new lords of the Botswana morafes. On May 9, 1891, an Order in Council placed all lawmaking authority in the High Commission's hands.[35] His proclamation became the law of the land. His first proclamation, issued in June 10, 1891, set up the Protectorate administrative machinery. A resident commission and his assistants headed the new administration. They also acted as judiciary authorities. The skeleton European administration supervised, rather than administered African affairs. African affairs were left to the chiefs as long as they did not fundamentally contradict imperial rule. Little changed in this arrangement for the first forty years. In fact, the high commissioner issued only two proclamations during this time.

The colonial administration, in spite of its shallowness in the earlier years, stripped the chiefs of their autonomy. It turned them into the administration's junior partners. Yet, given the nature of indirect rule in Bechuanaland, they retained the power to run their people's affairs within the British colonial administration's confines. The British administration could intervene in the morafe's affairs and overrule the chief. The administration did not exercise this power frequently since this action would have undermined the chiefs' capacity to maintain order. Moreover, constant British intervention in morafe affairs would have required more British administrators, reduced the level of chiefly cooperation, and immediately increased financial costs. The British and the chiefs had to forge a balance. Maintaining such a balance did not rest only with the British as the chiefs were able to protect their interests against the administration.

While colonial rule brought all Botswana morafes under one authority, it also maintained and petrified the divisions between them. Transforming the chiefs into the basic building blocks of indirect rule required dividing the Protectorate into administrative units. These units' defining feature was the "tribe." The invention of fixed tribal reserves fundamentally altered the morafe's geographic basis by turning the chiefs into territorial monarchs. This colonial invention turned the flexible, boundless and expanding morafe into a rigid territorially based order. The tribal reserves' demarcation (initially Ngwato, Kwena, Ngwaketse, Tawana, and Kgatla) in 1895, based on the Boundary Commission recommendation's inscribed into the soul of the Protectorate local identity based on territory and tribal affiliation. The chief had the pride of place in such an edifice (Map 2.1). The chief was the principal native administrator and judge of the Reserves. The morafe traditional administration was adapted to the colonial one. In the apt words of Pauline Peters, the morafe was transformed from state to tribal reserve and then to district.[36] The headmen of the wards or the chiefs' representatives acted as junior judges. Their decisions could be appealed to the chief's court. If the latter court's judgment was not satisfactory, the litigants could appeal to the European magistrate. In spite of the Magistrate Court's supervisory role, the colonial administration rarely overturned decisions of the chief's court.[37]

The Protectorate's administrative infrastructure resembled Migdal's web-like society theory. The Native Reserves, administered by the chiefs, under the "watchful eyes" of British administrators strengthened the chiefs. First, delimiting tribal territories closed off the frontier to morafe members who wanted to break away from the chief's tyranny. The colonial administration supported the chief when his authority was challenged, given Britain's need to maintain traditional authority as a basis of its Protectorate policy. Second, the chief's new authority as the principal native judge and the administration's tendency to side with the chief when conflicts arose meant the chief gained "absolute" authority, something he never had before. This further centralized authority within the morafe.[38] Third, using public and personal resources, the chief created a small tribal administration of secretaries, clerks, and teachers who were dependent on and accountable to him. Fourth, transforming tribute into taxes freed the chief from his dependency on his headmen. While he was freed from these traditional constraints, the residents of the reserves were firmly bound to the new tribal structures that the chief dominated. Fifth, the chiefs' prestige was further enhanced by their tactful, persistent, and successful defense against incorporating the Protectorate into South Africa.

When the colonial administration introduced the Native Advisory Council in 1920, the reformation of traditional authority structure was enhanced further. Before the Native Advisory Council, the administration dealt with each chief separately.[39] The council allowed the administration to deal collectively with all the chiefs despite the fact that the council met only one or two days a year. Initially, the council consisted of the chiefs of Tlokwa, Kwena, Kgatla, Ngwaketse, Rolong, and Malete. Khama of the Ngwato declined to join the council. Included also in the council were other Protector-

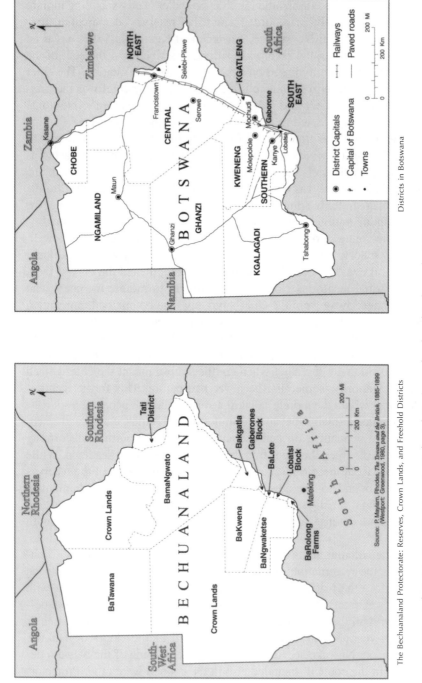

The Bechuanaland Protectorate: Reserves, Crown Lands, and Freehold Districts

Districts in Botswana

Map 2.1: Administrative Divisions in Colonial Bechuanaland and Independent Botswana

Source: P. Maylam, *Rhodes, The Tswana and the British, 1885–1899* (Westport, CT: Greenwood Press, 1980), p. 3. Copyright © by P. Maylam. Reproduced with permission of Greenwood Publishing Group, Inc., Westport, CT.

ate notables. These included highly educated men although the chiefs selected most nonchief members. The council first met at Gaborones but later convened at Mafeking, the Protectorate capital located in South Africa. The council also allowed the chiefs to coordinate their approach toward the administration. The council's main function was advising the administration about proposed policies affecting the territory. Despite conflicts between the administration and council members over a new proclamation on civil marriage and witchcraft (1927), the chiefs' general role in the Protectorate Administration did not change.

Not until 1930-32 did the administration make its first major attempt to reform tribal government. The pretext for reforming tribal administration was that:

> the older order of Chiefs was passing away. A new order was arriving, much better educated and better acquainted with European ways, though for this reason perhaps less closely associated with the people and apt in some cases to use for their personal advantage the authority which their predecessors had utilized in the interest of the tribe.[40]

The High Commission issued two proclamations in 1934. The first (No.74 of 1934) had two objectives: to define the "procedure for the designation and recognition of chiefs, and for dealing with those who did not, or could not perform their duties adequately."[41] This was meant to bring the chief more under the administration's control than has been heretofore. This proclamation also called for the creation of a council of native advisers with whom the chief must consult in carrying out his duties. In essence, this proclamation intended to limit chiefly authority. The second proclamation of 1934 (Native Tribunal Proclamation No. 75) required the chiefs to keep written records of the court and to submit these records to the European magistrate courts.[42] This proclamation was intended to systematize tribal justice.

Before the proclamation could be put into effect, Tshekedi Khama, the paramount chief of the Bamangwato, challenged its legality. Tshekedi, by more or less speaking as the representative of the other chiefs, in the Native Advisory meeting of 1932, argued that the proclamations, if implemented, would fundamentally alter Tswana laws and custom and therefore abrogate the treaty between the chiefs and Her Majesty, the very foundation of the Protectorate.[43] Tshekedi's caustic response underscored the far-reaching implications the proclamations had for Tswana social order:

> I perceive that these laws are intended to define the powers of the chiefs, the function of the Chiefs and their Tribes, and to reduce the existing rights of the Tribes and for this reason I find that the time in which the

matter is being discussed is inappropriate. Looking at the men in front of me, who are called the Protectorate Chiefs today, I find mere boys, and if the subject matter will be found of any benefit to the Tribes, to my mind it should have been discussed with the original seekers of the Protectorate. I do not suggest that the Government deliberately delayed action until the death of our fathers in order that they may discuss the matter with their sons, but I feel that if the matter had been discussed in the time of our fathers, they probably would have understood it better than we do[44].

The debate over the proclamations continued in and outside the Native Advisory Council. The resident commissioner was clear in 1933 that the chiefs were dead set against them.[45] Tshekedi and Batheon, with the help and advice of their lawyer, appealed directly to the high commissioner— over the resident commissioner's head. They hoped to make the proclamation compatible with the 1891 ones. Despite the chiefs' resistance the proclamations went into effect in 1935. Chiefs Tshekedi and Bathoen challenged the proclamation in a special court in Lobatse in 1936, but the judge ruled against their plea. The proclamations became the law of the Protectorate, and the chiefs were required to implement them. However, the administration realized that the chiefs were clearly unhappy with the changes and that they might try to subvert its intent. The Bamangwato chief unevenly carried out the dictates of the Proclamations and in selecting the council that was to advise him. He picked people the administration thought did not include any of the major tribal figures. The chiefs' resistance made the proclamations unworkable. As a result, the administration reformed them in 1943. The new resident commissioner (Charles Arden-Clarke), who arrived in the Protectorate in 1936, involved the chiefs in the process and closely consulted with them to avoid his predecessors' errors.[46] The reforms removed many of the issues to which the chiefs objected:

> As a result, the two Proclamations which issued later in 1943, . . . represented a much greater agreement between Government and members of the Advisory Council, and have secured a far greater measure of co-operation in their working . . . the Tribal Council for which provision was made in 1934 had practically dropped out of the picture. The law of 1934 no longer insisted that the chief shall notify to the Administration the names of his Councillors, or that the Councillors shall constitute a Tribal Council which must be consulted by him in the discharge of his duties.[47]

Although a few more proclamations since 1943 dealt with native administration, none attempted to replicate those of 1934. The Tswana chiefs' authority remained supreme in their reserves. The chiefs' ability to resist political reform from above and the revised 1943 proclamation support Migdal's thesis that local strongmen had the power to derail the agendas of national/colonial leaders.

Although the chiefs successfully resisted political reform from above, they were not immune to the qualitative changes taking place in the social relations of Tswana society. In contrast to Migdal's weblike society thesis, Diana Wylie's research clearly shows that the transformation of social relations dealt a death blow to the chieftainship:

> In Ngwato, the political consequences of southern Africa's industrial revolution burst into public display in 1949 when four thousand men leapt to their feet in the Kgotla and voted their regent out of power. Their act reflected the twilight of the patriarchal era. As the work of survival had been changing in southern Africa over the past century, so had local patterns of political support. After the Second World War, fewer and fewer people believed that patriarchal institutions and values served their interests. The chieftainship and rank had once signified a continuous process of hierarchical exchanges; they were becoming more and more the means by which inherited privilege was justified. In the postwar era not even the elite would need this defense. Their privilege was becoming protected more by law and less by the imperatives of patronage and the rhetorical shield of rank. On the periphery of South Africa's industrial revolution, a patriarchal political system was being transformed from above and below. At the same moment, apartheid policy to the south was seeking to withdraw that system from the flux of history.[48]

The chiefs' "inability" to channel the tide of social change in a way that allowed them to retain their traditional authority was the result of the transformation of the established patronage network. Such networks melded together those in authority and their subjects.

These networks began to dissolve when Khama and other chiefs abolished their ownership rights over the cattle traditionally kept by their clients. Such acts did not impoverish the chiefs. They still claimed all stray cattle, invested their income in cattle and other personal property, collected fines, and used their office and authority to extract resources from traders and others who wanted to settle or do business in their reserves. They remained the wealthiest men in the Protectorate. In fact, Tshekedi Khama was the largest cattle owner in the Protectorate.[49]

Transforming traditional social ties required the commoditization of three crucial resources: cattle, labor, and land. The degree of commodization varied regionally and was uneven among resources. For instance, cattle were the first and most commoditized indigenous product (see chapter 4) until the Second World War. Then labor migrations to South Africa began to absorb nearly 60 percent of all taxpayers in the territory.[50] Communal land was the least commoditized resource in spite of the development of private boreholes.[51]

The British colonial state and the chiefs were the leading forces that transformed these resources. The chiefs were at odds with the British when it came to political reform of their "traditional" authority. The chiefs did not disagree with the administration on economic changes that benefited the former. The privatization of such resources, according to Wylie, gradually corroded the loyalty of the masses to the chief. The elite "were now investing in things more than in people" and social relations.[52]

The decline in patronage, the growth of private property, and the commoditization of what was heretofore collective property melted away, according to Wylie, traditional bonds. The dynastic conflict between Tshekedi Khama and his nephew, Seretse Khama, in the Ngwato reserve in the late 1940s and early 1950s brought into sharp focus the decline of that tradition. The public vote in the Kgotla, which overwhelmingly supported Seretse and led to the defeat of Tshekedi, marked a historic turning point in the social order of Tswana society. To rebuke the reigning chief in a public vote showed the disintegration of the old hierarchy and the demise of the ward's authority. The old order in which patronage provided the social basis of chiefly and patriarchal rule was giving way to a new system. The propertied class no longer required clientele to maintain their social status and economic location.

Despite this event, the patronage-based social order had not yet exhausted its hegemonic power. Although the public vote in the Ngwato Kgotla signaled the decline of the old order, it also meant the defeat of one faction of the royal house rather than the rejection of the chieftainship by the people, as Wylie implies.[53] After all, the weakened but sufficiently powerful traditional order carried the Bechuanaland Democratic Party headed by Seretse Khama to power in 1965. After independence in 1966 the Bechuanaland Democratic Party became the Botswana Democratic Party (BDP). The Ngwato reserve, renamed the Central District after independence, has been the electoral anchor of the BDP. Moreover, other analysts have noted that the party's rural electoral base is in large part due to the traditional patronage system's longevity. This was reinforced by the Party's use of state resources.[54]

Tswana chiefs' authority remained supreme in the reserves, despite the increasing changes in the patronage system until the end of the 1940s. The chieftainship's first major crisis was precipitated not by a new proclamation from the British colonial state, but by the marriage of Seretse Khama, the Bamangwato heir apparent, to an English woman while he was studying law in London in 1948. Tshekedi, the Bamangwato regent, was Seretse's uncle. Tshekedi was against his nephew's marriage, particularly because the tribe was not consulted. The regent was equally fearful that the racist South

African regime might use the marriage as a pretext to incorporate the Protectorate. The Protectorate's incorporation was something he fought since he become a regent in 1925. This did not dissuade the young chief from marrying. Tshekedi continued to fight the marriage and Seretse even after the tribe voted to accept the marriage and Seretse as their chief. The British, eager not to offend the racist regime in the south, joined in the conflict between the chiefs. The British tricked Seretse into visiting London and then banned him from returning to Bechuanaland. Despite his conflict with his nephew, Tshekedi started working for Seretse's return in 1952. However, the conflict lasted until 1956, when Tshekedi journeyed to London and the chiefs were reconciled. The chiefs renounced any claims to the chieftainship for themselves and for their children. During Seretse's exile, the Bamangwato refused to cooperate with the colonial authorities. Bamangwato's support for Seretse clearly demonstrated the legitimacy of the chieftainship in the eyes of the population. The chieftainship still had tremendous appeal in spite of its transformation.

The succession crisis in Ngwato froze colonial attempts to effect political reform. To resolve the crisis the administration and the Bamangwato agreed to create a tribal council. This council would run the affairs of the tribe in lieu of the chief. Such a council had eluded the colonial administration since the early 1930s. The administration proceeded to implement the council program; Seretse and Tshekedi were council members. The two proclamations enacted on November 19, 1957, and November 1, 1957, provided the legal basis of Protectorate administrative reform.[55]

The new Ngwato Council included elected officials from the wards, although the chief retained a significant degree of its autonomy by nominating as many as a quarter of the council members. The council was to assist and advise the chief in his capacity as tribal authority. Seretse and Tshekedi became leading council officials. The council initiative was launched as an experiment in Ngwato territory as other tribes watched the outcome. Similar councils were established in five other territories in 1959.

The colonial administration's plan to reform tribal administration via the tribal council did not go very far. The movement for self-government and independence overtook the administration's agenda. The independence movement began in the late 1940s, even before the Ngwato crisis. Its principal leaders were the two premier chiefs in the Protectorate, Bathoen and Tshekedi. These chiefs used the Joint Advisory Council to press for the formation of a legislative council with law making powers. As Bathoen argued in that Council: "There is a strong feeling among members of the African Advisory Council that whilst admitting that this Council has played its part . . . they have lost confidence in the African Advisory Council. We submit that it is now time that consideration is given to the formation of a legislative Council for the Bechuanaland Protectorate."[56] The administration resisted these demands and continued to advocate the formation of a local council rather than a national legislative council. The chiefs continued their relentless attacks on the administration in the Protectorate and in Britain.[57] Seretse Khama joined the two chiefs once he became a member of the African and Joint Advisory councils.

Finally, the Protectorate Administration signaled that it was willing to entertain the idea of a Protectorate Legislative Council in April 1959.[58] A constitutional committee, formed from the Joint Advisory Council members, drafted proposals. The Protectorate administration and the British government accepted the committee's proposals. The constitution came into effect in December 1960. The new council consisted of 35 members. Ten were elected Europeans. Another 10 were Africans selected from the African Advisory Council. The rest were an Indian and administration members. As a result of the Legislative Council, the Joint Advisory Council disbanded. The African Advisory Council was renamed as the African Council.[59] The African Council's 47 members included seven administration members. The eight chiefs of the principal tribes were ex-officio members. The rest were either elected/appointed by Kgotla or tribal councils.[60] While the committee formulated proposals for the Legislative Council, Bechuanaland in 1959 lost Tshekedi Khama, the most able and articulate traditional authority in the Protectorate. His death foreshadowed the passing of an era.

The Legislative Council, which Tshekedi and Bathoen had worked so hard to establish, ironically closed the final chapter of the age of strong territorial chieftainship. Although the chiefs still had a significant say in selecting Legislative Council members and affairs affecting their people, their role in the territory's general administration slipped significantly.[61]

A novel feature of the Legislative Council was the Executive Council, of which Seretse and Bathoen were members. Including the two most articulate and important chiefs in the Executive Council relegated other, less capable chiefs to the administration's margins. This meant that the latter were concerned about maintaining their chiefly status in the emerging political dispensation. Protecting their individual interests versus the group's meant gingerly negotiating with the new leadership headed by Seretse. Oftentimes they had to accept whatever the new leadership offered. In mid-1962 each nonofficial Executive Council member was paired, as a trainee, to work closely with one of the Protectorate's administrative secretaries.[62] Seretse Khama was assigned to work on constitutional and racial matters, while Bathoen worked with the administrative secretary. This step signaled a closer collaboration between the administration and the emergent African politicians, once they overcame the prolonged legislative council debate.

The legislative council also ushered in a new era in which political parties emerged. This development was partly a product of the massacre at Sharpeville in South Africa, but it was also a response to local conditions.[63]

Bechuanaland People's Party (BPP), the leading political party in the Protectorate, criticized the administration and the traditional elite. In response to this party's agitation and the possible ramification of its rhetoric, the administration and the elite's leading members began to ponder over the formation of a "responsible" party:

> Some informed local opinion considered that a BPP government would be dangerously antagonistic to South Africa, and would stir up racial tensions within the country itself. In consequence Seretse Khama formed the more moderate Botswana Democratic Party in 1962. He was encouraged to do so by the British administration, which was anxious that a suitable national leader should emerge on whom the mantle of power could eventually descend, and was unhappy with the leadership of the BPP. Seretse Khama was the obvious choice for this role. As the traditional heir to the chieftainship of the largest tribe he commanded wide popular support. He had shown his ability and his preference for modern democratic ideas in his participation in . . . the workings of the Joint Advisory Council. . . . His marriage, not many years earlier a considerable embarrassment to the administration, could now be taken as proof of his commitment to non-racialism.[64]

A prominent nontraditionalists group, most of whom were also Legislative Council members, led by Seretse held several meetings in Lobatsi, Mahalaypye, and Mochudi. These meetings led to the formation of the BDP in 1962.[65]

This more moderate BDP convinced the British to speed up the movement towards full independence. Within two years of establishing the Legislative Council, the British Government initiated an exercise that led to the creation of an elected territorial Legislative Assembly. The colonial administration asked political parties, the chiefs, "and other interested persons" to send representatives to a conference aimed at reforming the 1961 constitution. The conference's purpose: to advance self-government. The negotiations began in mid-1963 and concluded at year's end. A principal issue resolved in the conference was the chiefs' role in the future elected government. The administration provided the conferees with position papers on the topics to be covered.[66] Five alternative scenarios outlined the chiefs' future role in the political system: "(a) no special arrangement; (b) an advisory council of chiefs; (c) reserved seats in a unicameral legislature; (d) an upper chamber of a bicameral legislature composed of the chiefs similar to the British House of Lords; (e) a federal system in which the tribal administration would function as regional governments and be represented equally in an upper house of legislature."[67] The chiefs' preference was an upper house with lawmaking powers, but the politicians, led by Seretse Khama, rejected this idea. The chiefs reluctantly agreed to the advisory role in the form of the House of Chiefs. The reformed constitution went into effect in January 1964, and the government began to organize the institutions called for by the new dispensation. In March elections the BDP won an overwhelming majority—28 out 31 seats—and Seretse Khama was appointed prime minister.

Although the new constitution removed the chiefs from the decision-making process at the national level, the government was fully aware of the chiefs' power if they were not handled prudently. They were reminded of their power during the House of Chiefs' first session. The former nationalist-activist Chief Bathoen convinced his colleagues to reject their role in the new order:

> That the House of Chiefs . . . do hereby pass a vote of no confidence in the existence and functions of the House and therefore requests: (a) the dissolution of the House of Chiefs in its present form; (b) that the House be reconstituted to have some six elected members of standing outside the chieftainship; (c) that a parliament of Bechuanaland be constituted with two houses, namely a house of Chiefs and a House of Assembly.[68]

Some of the House recommendations, such as an increase in the number of House members, the government accepted. The rest were pushed aside.

The new government intended to marginalize the chiefs without alienating them. The Chieftainship Bill and the Local Government Bill of 1965, which was enacted in the same year, completed the reform program.[69] The Chieftainship Act regulated the appointments and removal of all traditional authorities. It provided salaries to the chiefs. And it defined their authority, such as allocating tribal land. The Local Government Act promulgated a popularly elected local government at the district level. The district councils took over all the chiefs' legislative authority.[70] The chiefs tried to soften the bite of these laws, but with little success.

The chiefs demanded changes even during the final Bechuanaland independence conference with the British Government in London in early 1966. Chief Bathoen, who represented the chiefs in the conference, raised the issue of a bicameral parliament. Again this was dismissed. When the Protectorate became the independent country of Botswana, the chieftainship's fate was sealed. The final epitaph to the passing of the era of chiefs was Bathoen's resignation from the chieftainship and the House of Chiefs to run for parliament in 1969. He defeated the then Vice President of the Botswana, Quett Masire. His victory underscored the strength of chieftainship and its weakness. Only the most educated experienced and activist of them all had the courage and conviction to completely reject the symbolic role of the chief in

Botswana. The other chiefs were unwilling, and perhaps unable, to challenge the government and risk losing their remaining authority and the benefits of their new position.

The government also recognized the chiefs' potential power and continued to involve them in the public bodies that replaced them:

> the BDP's tactics have been . . . subtle. Each modern democratic institution which was brought into existence to replace a chiefly function incorporates the chief as an ex-officio member or even chairman. Chiefs were paid a stipend for the exercise of the traditional functions which they still retained. Thus, the chiefs were individually faced with a dilemma. Either they could join the new bodies, which enabled them to continue to act as chief and for which they were paid, but which also constitutionally debarred them from party politics. Or they could resign the chieftainship and go into political wilderness.[71]

The chiefs, with the exception of Bathoen, begrudgingly opted to stay out of politics and cooperate with the government.[72] Thus, although the district boundaries largely reflect "tribal" lines drawn by the colonial state (Map 2.1), the chiefs' enormous political authority declined precipitously with independence. Consequently, the constitutional recognition of the chieftainship in Botswana has not induced political instability. Nor has it allowed the chiefs to immobilize the central government's capacity to mobilize resources. Nevertheless, the chiefs continue to command respect and authority at the village level: "where district Councillors, let alone MP's, have yet to impinge on the consciousness of the ordinary people."[73]

CONCLUDING REMARKS

The Botswana government, led by the BDP, has enjoyed nearly three decades of uninterrupted political stability, economic growth, and liberal democratic governance. Contrary to the importance attached to the power of the chiefs and parochial predisposition of this group by the theory of strong societies and weak states, the Botswana government has not fallen victim to the mystical powers of the village. How do we then explain why the powerful chiefs of Botswana, who so successfully resisted British attempts to politically subjugate them, simply gave way to the leadership? First, Migdal's theory overestimates the class distance between the "modernist" elements of this class and those who occupy various levels of the chieftainship. Migdal's book does not address the social and economic distinctions between the old and new leadership. Moreover, it does not consider the possibility of the two groups merging as a result of the social transformation colonial capitalism caused. Wylie's argument posits that while the chiefs were resisting the colonial state's political reforms, they could not induce the British to advance capitalist development in the Protectorate. This argument more accurately represents Bechuanaland's social history.[74] Thus, the conflict between the old and the new factions of the dominant class was not a struggle about capitalist development. Rather, the struggle was about which group was going to put its mark on the further transformation of this society.[75]

The political struggle between the traditional and modern factions of the dominant class in the late 1950s and early 1960s was about the distribution of leadership posts in the state apparatus. The BDP leaders were conscious of the risks involved in denying the traditional group a meaningful role. The latter commanded a significant following among the population that provided government an electoral base. This base helped the leadership to hold the elite together. Chapters 3 and 4 will show how the government used the remnants of the old traditional order and loyalties (e.g., chiefs, kgotla) for state and nation building.

Finally, Migdal's weblike society theory fails to account for the likelihood of the chiefs being affected by and affecting the larger social transformation. For example, Seretse, the Ngwato heir apparent, led the modernist group without forfeiting his royal pedigree. This ambiguous social location allowed him and his party to systematically marginalize the role of traditional authority in the management of national affairs. Moreover, Chief Tshekedi Khama, who led the resistance to the British and South African agenda for the Protectorate, foresaw the decline of the role of the chiefs and the need for nonchiefly national institutions.[76] This demonstrates that parochial traditional authority is not necessarily the basis of weak African states.

NOTES

[1] Joel Migdal, *Strong Societies and Weak States: State-Society Relations and State Capabilities in the Third World* (Princeton, NJ: Princeton University Press, 1988).

[2] Ibid., xv. For a recent discussion of postcolonial states, see Jean-François Bayart, *The State in Africa: The Politics of the Belly* (London: Longman, 1993).

[3] I do agree with him on this matter. Where I part company with his thesis is in its focus on the significance of the provincial power of the chiefs, particularly when that group's changing economic interests are factored out of the analysis.

[4] Migdal, *Strong Societies and Weak States*, 115-116.

[5] Ibid., 123.

[6] Ibid., 130.

[7] Ibid., p. 141. Here Migdal assumes homogeneity among the population because of their tribal tradition.

[8] Michael Crowder, *The Flogging of Phinehas McIntosh: A Tale of Colonial Folly and Injustice, Bechuanaland, 1933* (New Haven, CT: Yale University Press, 1988); Diana Wylie, *A Little God: The Twilight of Patriarchy in a Southern African Chiefdom* (Johannesburg: Witwatersrand University Press, 1990).

[9] Thomas Tlou, "A Political History of Northwest Botswana to 1906," Ph.D. diss., University of Wisconsin, 1972. See also Pauline Peters, "Cattlemen, Borehole Syndicates, and Privatization in Kgatleng District of Botswana: An Anthropological History of a Commons," Ph.D. diss., Boston University, 1983; and also her *Dividing the Commons: Politics, Policy, and Culture in Botswana* (Charlottesville: University Press of Virginia, 1994); Neil Parsons, "The Economic History of Khama's Country in Botswana, 1844-1930," in Robin Palmer and Neil Parsons, eds., *The Roots of Rural Poverty in Central and Southern Africa* (Berkeley: University of California Press, 1977), 113-143; and Isaac Schapera, *Tribal Innovators: Tswana Chiefs and Social Change, 1795-1940* (London: Athlone Press, 1970).

[10] This description of the morafe is based on the work of Thomas Tlou, "The Nature of Batswana States: Towards a Theory of Batswana Traditional Government—The Batswana Case," *Botswana Notes and Records* 6 (1974): 57-75.

[11] Ibid., 58.

[12] Ibid., 58-59.

[13] Ibid.

[14] Ibid., 65.

[15] Conflict over succession did occur within royal families, and this led to civil wars and further fragmentation of the morafe. Jack Parson, *Succession to High Office in Botswana: Three Case Studies* (Athens: Ohio University Center for International Studies, 1990). See also Tlou, "A Political History"; Isaac Schapera, *A Handbook of Tswana Law and Custom* (London: Oxford University Press, 1938).

[16] Schapera, *Handbook of Tswana Law and Custom.*

[17] Schapera, *Tribal Innovators*, 70, 74. See also J. Parson, "Cattle, Class and the State in Rural Botswana," *Journal of Southern African Studies* 7, 2 (1981): 236-255.

[18] Tlou, "The Nature of Batswana States," 70.

[19] Ibid., 72.

[20] Parsons, "The Economic History of Khama's Country in Botswana."

[21] This brief description of the changes brought about by the expanding world economy is gleaned from Parsons, "The Economic History of Khama's Country in Botswana." The changes discussed were not uniformly felt by all communities. See also Schapera, *Tribal Innovators.*

[22] Parsons, "The Economic History of Khama's Country in Botswana," 119.

[23] Ibid., 137.

[24] Lord Hailey, *Native Administration in the British African Territories. Part V. The High Commission Territories* (London: HMSO, 1953), 188.

[25] Ibid., 195.

[26] Ibid.

[27] Ibid., 197. See also P. Maylan, *Rhodes, the Tswana and the British, 1885-1899* (Westport, CT: Greenwood, 1980), chapter 5.

[28] Hailey, *Native Administration*, 197.

[29] Ibid.

[30] Ibid., 199.

[31] Ibid., 202.

[32] Ibid.

[33] Migdal, *Strong Societies*, 141 and 109.

[34] Wylie, *A Little God*, 15 and 18.

[35] Schapera, *Tribal Innovators*, 50.

[36] Peter, *Dividing the Commons*, chapter 2.

[37] Wylie, *A Little God*, 111.

[38] The increasing centralization of morafe administration began in the late part of the nineteenth century and continued with the imposition of colonial rule. See Wylie, *A Little God*, chapter 1; and Simon Gillett, "The Survival of the Chieftainship in Botswana," *Botswana Notes and Records* 7 (1975): 103-108.

[39] Schapera, *Tribal Innovators*, 55.

[40] Hailey, *Native Administration*, 212.

[41] Schapera, *Tribal Innovatorss*, 62.

[42] Hailey, *Native Administration*, 219-221.

[43] Michael Crowder, "Tshekedi Khama and Opposition to the British Administration of the Bechuanaland Protectorate, 1926-1936," *Journal of African History* 26 (1985): 193-214; Crowder, *The Flogging of Phinehas McIntosh*.

[44] Quoted in Crowder, *The Flogging of Phinehas McIntosh*, 26.

[45] Tshekedi Khama also participated in the scholarly debate regarding the nature of the African chieftainship under indirect rule, "Chieftainship Under Indirect Rule," *Journal of the Royal African Society* 34, 136 (1935): 251-261.

[46] Crowder, *The Flogging of Phinehas McIntosh*; Wylie, *A Little God*.

[47] Hailey, *Native Administration*, 224-225. See also Mary Benson, *Tshekedi Khama* (London: Faber and Faber, 1960), chapter 11.

[48] Wylie, *A Little God*, 216.

[49] Ibid., 148.

[50] Ibid., 176.

[51] Ibid. For an excellent discussion of the transformation and struggles over water resources, see Peters, *Dividing the Commons*. R. H. Hitchcock, "Tradition, Social Justice and Land Reform in Central Botswana," *Journal of African Law* 24, 1 (1980): 1-34.

[52] Wylie, *A Little God*, 208.

[53] Ibid., 216. This argument is contrary to some of the recent literature on African development that claims that the trouble with capitalism in Africa is that people invest in social ties rather than engaging in productive investment. See Sara Berry, "Social Institutions and Access to Resources in African Agriculture," *Africa* 59, 1 (1989): 41-55.

[54] Patrick Molutsi and John Holm, "Developing Democracy When Civil Society Is Weak: The Case of Botswana" *African Affairs* 89, 356 (1990): 323-340.

[55] Bechuanaland Protectorate, *Proclamation and Subsidiary Legislations* 39, no. 61 of 1954, 20-62; and *Proclamation and Subsidiary Legislation*, 42, no 57 of 1957, 111-114.

[56] Quoted in Harold Robertson, "From Protectorate to Republic: The Political History of Botswana, 1926-1966," Ph.D. diss., Dalhousie University, 1979, 338-389.

[57] Tshekedi Khama, "The Principles of African Tribal Administration," address at the Chatham House, April 11, 1951. See also his "Developing Representative Government in a Changing Africa: Problems of Political Advance in Backward Territories," *Africa World*, September 1956.

[58] Great Britain, *Bechuanaland Annual Report, 1959* (London: HMSO, 1959.

[59] Robertson, "From Protectorate to Republic," 437.

[60] Ibid.

[61] Ibid., 454.

[62] Ibid.

[63] Neil Parsons, "The Evolution of Modern Botswana: Historical Revision," in Louis Picard, ed., *The Evolution of Modern Botswana* (Lincoln: University of Nebraska Press, 1985), 26-29.

[64] C. Colclough and S. McCarthy, *The Political Economy of Botswana: A Study of Growth and Distribution* (Oxford: Oxford University Press, 1980), 35.

[65] Robertson, "From Protectorate to Republic," 461.

[66] J. H. Proctor, "The House of Chiefs and the Political Development of Botswana," *Journal of Modern African Studies* 6, 1 (1968): 59-79.

[67] Ibid., 61.

[68] Ibid., 66.

[69] Bechuanaland Protectorate, *The Chieftainship Law, Law No. 29 of 1965. Supplement to the Bechuanaland Government Gazette* (Gabarone, December 31, 1965); and *The Local Government (District Council) Law, Law No. 35 of 1965.* Supplement to the Bechuanaland Government Gazette (Gaborone, December 31, 1965).

[70] Proctor, "The House of Chiefs," 66.

[71] Colclough and McCarthy, *The Political Economy of Botswana*, 39.

[72] The relationship between the chieftainship and the government saw a tumultuous year in 1994. The chairman of the House of Chiefs, Seepiptiso (Bathoen's son) was temporarily removed from the chieftainship for allegedly dabbling in politics. He sued the government for illegally dismissing him, and the case was heard by the High Court of Botswana. The moral authority of the chief was rudely brought home to the ruling party in the 1994 National Assembly election in which it lost all the chief's constituency to the opposition Botswana National Front. Furthermore, the High Court ruled against the government, and Chief Seepiptiso was reinstated. See also various issues of *Mmegi*, January-September 1994.

[73] Colclough and McCarthy, *The Political Economy of Botswana*, 38.

[74] Wylie's transformation thesis is supported also by P.J.J. Grotpeter, "Political Leadership and Political Development in the High Commission Territories," Ph.D. diss., Washington University, 1965. Peter, *Dividing the Commons*, chapter 3.

[75] Some of the chiefs have in recent years publicly criticized the government's development strategy, which emphasizes the employment of skilled expatriates. A recent case is the employment of Chinese construction workers at the cost of citizens. The criticism of the chiefs is along nationalist lines.

[76] Tshekedi Khama, "Developing Representative Government in a Changing Africa."

3

Overcoming the Grid of Colonial Inheritance: Building Public Institutions

INTRODUCTION

When Botswana achieved full independence in 1966, informed opinion was unanimous in assessing the country's economic prospects as dismal. . . . the economy had no infrastructure worthy of the name; it had [20] kilometers of tarred roads, no real communications or power network, and an unreliable water supply. . . . by 1976 . . . the country had more than 1,000 kilometers of tarred road, a country-wide telephone network, and was completing an integrated power system in the populous eastern section. . . . This miracle of growth was wrought by an aggressive development plan based on private enterprise and foreign investment, aided by generous allocations from foreign aid donors, and directed by skilled and devoted leaders working within an environment of political stability.[1]

The Republic of Botswana emerged from 80 years of colonial rule in 1966. Foreign domination left behind an impoverished society that many observers of the time described as a "basket case."[2] It lacked two main ingredients necessary to transform its economy: educated and skilled labor and immediately exploitable natural resources. Furthermore, hostile and racist neighbors surrounded it geographically and economically. One of those neighbors, South Africa, had designs to absorb its territory.

Botswana's weaknesses were many in 1966. It had a shallow financial base from which to launch a development program. Its gross national product was 36 million rand with a per capita income estimated between R45 to

Table 3.1 Government Revenues and Expenditures, 1954/5–1964/5 (Rs. 000)

	Ordinary Expend	Total. Expend	CD&W*	Domestic Revenue	U.K. Grants	Total Revenue
1954/5	1,890	2,157	267	1,817	292	2,109
1955/6	2,187	2,556	369	1,940	367	2,307
1956/7	2,462	3,296	834	1,986	1,123	3,109
1957/8	3,267	4,172	935	1,935	1,839	3,774
1958/9	3,226	3,880	654	2,250	1,780	4,030
1959/60	3,826	4,375	549	2,474	1,869	4,343
1960/1	4,541	4,916	375	2,567	2,301	4,868
1961/2	5,763	6,657	895	3,284	3,146	6,430
1962/3	5,852	7,094	960	3,305	3,928	7,233
1963/4	6,590	7,684	972	3,398	4,197	7,595
1964/5	8,185	10,756	1,756	4,413	5,436	9,849

Note: If not for CD & W and U.K. grants, the Bechuanaland Protectorate would have incurred large deficits every year between 1954 and 1965. This trend continued after independence.

*Colonial Development & Welfare.

Source: Republic of Botswana, *The Development of Bechuanaland Economy: Report of the Ministry of Overseas Development: Economic Survey Mission* (Gaberones, 1966: 8).

R60. Botswana in 1966 was one of the poorest societies in the world. Furthermore, the Botswana government depended on its former colonial power's financial support to balance its annual budget. Budgetary grants accounted for about 50 percent of public expenditures during the decade before independence (Table 3.1). The new government of Botswana was indebted to Britain. Moreover, the country's only major resource, cattle, was ravaged by the worst drought in living memory. The drought killed between 30 and 50 percent of the national herd and impoverished the population. In fact, one out of three people depended on public rations for survival on the eve of independence.[3]

The legacy of colonial rule was not only annual budgetary support from the former colonial powers, but an economic order subservient to and thoroughly integrated into a more powerful and racist regime. Botswana, like other colonies in the region, such as Mozambique, Lesotho, Namibia, and Swaziland, served as a cheap labor reserve for the white industrial and agricultural regimes. Neglecting the Botswana economy insured that formal

Table 3.2 Local and Expatriate Labor Power in Botswana, 1966–1991

Year	A	B	C
1966	417	45	372
1971	300	100	200
1976	300	255	45
1981	290	270	20
1991	300	300	—

A. Total requirements of categories I & II manpower.

B. Planned output of local matriculants.

C. Shortfall to be met by recruitment of expatriates.

Category I is persons with a degree or a diploma.

Category II is persons with a minimum educational standard of school certificate.

Source: Republic of Botswana, Transitional Plan for Social and Economic Development
(Gaborone, 1966), 33.

employment opportunities within the country were minimal. In fact, more than half of those employed in the cash economy were migrant laborers in South African mines and farms.[4] This migrant labor force deprived the Botswana economy of the contributions of nearly half of the most able-bodied people. In addition to being a South African labor reserve, Botswana also depended on South Africa for all transport and communication links with the outside world. Furthermore, the South African rand, was also the official currency in Botswana until 1976, when the pula came into circulation. Botswana's monetary, fiscal, employment, and communication/transport dependency on South Africa and Britain posed a formidable obstacle to development.

The dearth of skilled and educated labor and the absence of educational institutions within the country seemed to make the aforementioned barriers insurmountable.[5] The Protectorate Administration's 1960-1964 Development Plan identified 170 primary schools, 3 junior secondary schools, 2 senior secondary schools and a government teacher training college.[6] The Tribal Schools Committee controlled funding for 150 of the primary schools. Some of these were single-room schools, poorly financed and equipped. More than 50 percent of the teachers were unqualified. The net result: the "secondary school system produced only sixteen students in 1965 capable of undertaking higher education." Moreover, only 40 Batswana had university degrees.[7]

This educational system severely handicapped the new regime, forcing it to depend on more expensive expatriates for higher levels of policy-making and professional services (Table 3.2).

As if the dearth of natural and human resources were not enough to impede development, the sociopolitical structure inherited by the new regime could have scuttled its agenda of state and nation building if it were not carefully and appropriately redesigned.[8] Powerful chiefs ran Bechuanaland's eight tribal reserves. These chiefs fought against the Protectorate administration's attempts to undermine their authority and the reserves' incorporation into South Africa. The chiefs were the main native political authorities, and the more progressive of them had national political ambitions.[9] Unifying the nation and creating new national, cultural, and political institutions were also formidable tasks.

The Ministry of Overseas Development Report of 1965 was also pessimistic about an independent Botswana's economic prospects. It suggested that the new government would be dependent on annual budgetary subsidies for the foreseeable future. Apart from Botswana's new leadership, most observers concurred with the report's conclusions.

The new government's leadership was not disheartened by such pessimism. Instead, it boldly and frontally attacked the political, institutional, and economic problems. Its immediate and primary objective was to secure enough financial resources to balance its budget without external support and to establish effective public administration. Renegotiating the Southern African Customs Union, which was concluded in 1969, resulted in extra revenues. These revenues made this objective attainable shortly thereafter. In the meantime, the administration systematically laid the foundation for effective and accountable public institutions that would enable it to carefully plan and pursue its economic objectives. The discovery and the exploitation of copper/nickel, and later diamonds generated the revenues necessary to finance social and physical infrastructural development.

By the tenth anniversary of independence, however, it was clear to the pessimists that the Republic of Botswana had performed a "miracle," turning a South African labor reserve into the world's fastest-growing economy. Botswana's annual growth rate averaged 10.7 percent between 1974 and 1992.[10] Many critics note that such growth would not have been possible without the huge diamond revenues. The diamonds did generate an enormous windfall for the state, but many other states with similar fortunes, such as Nigeria, Gabon, and Venezuela, were ill managed and came to naught. This chapter shows what made Botswana different from these other states. Botswana had a small and united dominant class and a leadership conscious of the importance of building effective public institutions to develop a capitalist economy. Nurturing and protecting these institutions from the dominant class and others was critical to the new nation's success.

CONCEPTUALIZING THE BOTSWANA STATE

Recent studies of African politics have focused on democracy and the transformation of authoritarian regimes in the continent.[11] This literature rarely asks why postcolonial African states failed to develop the capacity to plan and implement a development program. Focus on democracy and plural politics avoids the important issue of institution building. This avoidance is due to the power of the hegemonic ideology of neoliberalism. According to this ideology, the public sector is the primary cause of all that is wrong with any economy.[12] By contrast, Botswana's economic transformation relied on the existence of effective state institutions insulated from major elements of society.[13]

In his pioneering study of the Botswana state, G. Gunderson characterized it as an "administrative state."[14] He noted that its foundation was laid during the colonial era. The British Protectorate administrators made most of the decisions without much input from the native population. The administration's links to the people were the chiefs who transmitted the colonial state's proclamations to their subjects. This arrangement insulated the Protectorate government from public pressure. The bureaucrats rather than the politicians ruled. In the administrative state "resources are allocated by commands issued by administrative elites, and there are no controls by any other social group over the decision-making. Authority in the administrative state flows downward from the rulers to the ruled; administrative elites have complete control over decision-making process."[15] Gunderson blamed the continuation of this administrative tradition and decision making on the marginalized elected political leaders who set the economic priorities for the country: "The new men in the BDP are at the mercy of outside interests, for they have few material resources, little expertise, and few organizational talents. . . . The dominant party 'rule' Botswana, but it is the expatriate-controlled bureaucracy which directs policy."[16] Other scholars shared this characterization of the Botswana policy-making process.[17]

Gunderson's discussion of the state's administrative autonomy[18] was conceptually weak because he was unable to see the likelihood that the administrative elite and elected politicians might share a common agenda. The insulation of the policy-formulating process from society was a deliberate strategy by the political leadership designed to enhance the capacity of the state. Gunderson's work, like some of the scholarship of the time, lacked any clear conception of capitalist development in the periphery and the role of the state in such a process.

The autonomy issue was not reexamined for nearly a decade until Jack Parson's doctoral thesis in 1979.[19] Then, Jan Isaksen more directly and systematically took it up.[20] Isaksen restated Gunderson's thesis, with a twist "... the model proposed is one in which the political elite, with little or no real influence from the grass roots, defines its policy in a very broad way thereby leaving wide policy areas open to the bureaucrats."[21] Isaksen saw the autonomous bureaucrats making policy within the framework set by the political elite. This contribution corrected a principal weakness of the administrative state thesis. The political leadership was no longer considered to be dominated by the bureaucrats.[22] Isaksen went beyond describing the structure of the political bureaucratic relations. He noted that the bureaucrats were fully aware of the latitude within which their economic development formulations must fall. The first development plan made clear that capitalism was the chosen economic order.[23] Furthermore, the dominant class's latitude was significantly circumscribed by the economy's dependency on South Africa.[24] Isaksen suggests the political leaders' awareness of the danger of seriously antagonizing South Africa was married to a public management "style" left behind by the British at independence. The independent government with the help of senior expatriate, predominantly British, bureaucrats continued this public management "style." This strategy bred a conservative managerial style that equated development with conservative financial management and risk aversion.[25]

Other scholars concur with Isaksen. They note that the bureaucratic apparatus's insulation did not mean that political leaders were loath to intervene when necessary, as may be inferred from Isaksen's analysis:

Quite simply, the BDP has the power and the ability to intervene decisively and definitively if it wishes to do so, at any or all stages of the policy-making process, to secure and enforce its strategic policy priorities. . . . After two and a half decades of BDP rule the policy-making echelons of the civil service are *well aware* of what is expected of them both in general and, for the most part, in specific policy terms.[26] (italics mine)

This political-bureaucratic relationship produced a relatively strong state system in Botswana "where probity, relative autonomy and competency have been nurtured and sustained."[27]

ELITE UNITY: A BASIS OF STATE AUTONOMY

The political system is dominated by (and policy is set in the interest of) a coalition of wealthy, well educated, cattle-owning political elites who are committed to rapid economic growth in the framework of a largely free enterprise system. This coalition of traditional leaders, teachers, junior state functionaries, and wealthy farmers was joined by more senior administrators beginning in the 1970s. Altogether, the members of this coalition represent educational and economic characteristics quite unlike the majority of the population.[28]

Seretse's Cabinet colleagues were men whose experience of life had been limited to the segregated lifestyles of southern Africa. They were beginning to gain wider experience, through attending international conference and consultations, but looked to Seretse as the cosmopolitan among them to take the lead in relations with the predominantly expatriate civil service and with foreign relations in general.[29]

The state's autonomy has been central to its ability to establish an effective administrative apparatus. In spite of this, the literature does not fully explore how the state's autonomy facilitated the development of a strong and effective administration while in other countries the consequences of autonomy were the opposite. This oversight in the literature is a result of not focusing on Botswana's social geography and the dynamics of its capitalist transformation. More specifically, the literature does not examine Botswana's broad social relations, which shaped the constitution of state civil-society relations.

Jack Parson's work was among the first to consider the effects of social and class structure on development policy. He felt that the type of social structure was key to understanding the paradox of liberal democracy in a southern African labor reserve.[30] Parson shows that Botswana's liberal democratic politics is based on the partially transformed tributary social relation. The peasantry, which constituted the majority of the precolonial population, remains subservient to the cattle-owning class despite its becoming migrant laborers in South African mines. The peasants' continued loyalty to the dominant class was largely due to two reasons. First, wages earned in the South African mines were not sufficient to cover the reproductive needs of their household. Second, the "flexible" nature of their employment required them to retain their bonds in the Botswana countryside. As such, they were both peasants *and* laborers, hence Parson's apt term, peasantariat.

Botswana's traditional dominant class, the chiefs and other propertied groups, survived and flourished during the colonial period.[31] The colonial state ruled Botswana through the chiefs who remained very strong until the last years of British rule. The primary purpose of the British colonial administration was to insure law and order but not to undertake economic development work. Consequently, it was thinly staffed and strapped for resources.[32] Without a development-oriented interventionist state and a dynamic, private capitalist economy, the cattle-owning class, particularly the royal houses, disproportionately benefited from commercializing the economy and the introduction of schools either in Botswana and in South Africa.

Unlike other regions in African, the Protectorate administration did not employ many natives. Consequently, a large and growing "middle class" did not exist. Even the state's clerical employees were predominantly whites recruited from South Africa.[33] Thus, when Botswana became independent in 1966, neither a native commercial establishment nor an educated bureaucratic class existed. The emerging dominant elite who claimed the state's mantle were mainly large cattle owners who still nurtured patron-client relations with the peasantariat. Moreover, the overwhelming majority of the population was still rural. The BDP under Seretse Khama's leadership capitalized on this relationship and consequently won the overwhelming majority of the seats in the election for the first National Assembly.[34] "The continued electoral success of the BDP demonstrated the unity of a small dominant class in Botswana. The unity of this class was a direct product of the 'gross underdevelopment of the colonial period . . . [and] absolutely modest expectations in the early postcolonial period. The middle class was very small in number, unclear as to its goals.'"[35]

Parson's thesis about the dominant class's unity and its bonds to the peasantariat adds a critical element to our conceptual arsenal. However, Parson did not develop this idea fully. Assessing the unity within a class is a treacherous and difficult business. A simple and straightforward way to measure a class's unity is to examine the homogeneity of its ideological orientation and resource base. For example, does the class consist of only large and medium-sized cattle owners? Or does it have a diverse resource base needing different and contradictory development programs? Do class members share common political and economic strategies? The majority of the leaders who took over the state in 1966 were all large and medium-sized cattle owners. Table 3.3 lists the first three parliaments' members and shows their educational and economic status. The education achievements of these MPs were as following: 13 went to school in Tigerkloof, 2 attended Lovedale, 11 were schoolteachers, 5 had secondary school certificates, 1 had elementary education, 2 had minimal education, 1 was a lawyer, 1 was a clerk, and the background of 6 are not known. In terms of wealth, 27 were large or medium cattle owners, 1 had a small herd, and we know little about the remaining 14 MPs. The small but growing middle class, largely in public service, owned some cattle or hoped to build their own herd.[36]

New middle class members planned to increase their cattle holdings in two ways: insuring the growth of their salary and being promoted to higher posts in the bureaucracy which was dominated by expatriates. The third group was white settlers who owned large ranges or were in commerce. Their main concern was that the government left them free to run their enterprises and protect their private property.

Parson and Molutsi show these groups' agendas were compatible from independence to the mid-1980s as state revenues began to increase with the Southern African Customs Union successful renengotiation in 1969 and with the discovery and exploitation of diamonds in the mid-1970s.[37] The growth in government revenue and the size of the middle class reinforced existing social relations in the cattle industry. Economic growth during the first twenty-five years of independence made the coordination of the interests of civil servants and cattle-owners possible. The Botswana dominant class presented a united front during this time period.[38]

Table 3.3 The Economic and Educational Background of Members of Parliament (First 3 Parliaments)

No.	Party	Education	Cattle Ownership	Other Business
1	BDP	Secondary	Large	NK
2	BDP	Tiger Kloof	Small	NK
3	BDP	NK	Large	Shop
4	BDP	Tiger Kloof	Large	Carpenter
5	BDP	Elementary	Large	Vet. Rep.
6	BDP	Secondary	NK	None
7	BPP	Tiger Kloof	NK	None
8	BDP	little	Large	retail
9	BIP	NK	NK	NK
10	BDP	Teacher	Large	big
11	BDP	Teacher	Medium	Shop
12	BDP	Secondary	Large	vast
13	BDP	Tiger Kloof	Large	Shop
14	BDP	Teacher	Medium	Shop
15	BDP	Teacher	Large	Shop
16	BDP	Clerk	Medium	Shop
17	BDP	Lawyer	Large	NK
18	BDP	Tiger Kloof	Large	NK
19	BDP	Tiger Kloof	Large	NK
20	BDP	Teacher	Large	NK
21	BDP	Lovedale	Medium	NK
22	BDP	NK	Large	Shops
23	BDP	Tiger Kloof	NK	NK
24	BPP	Teacher	NK	NK
25	BPP	BA (Tiger Kloof)	NK	NK
26	BDP	Teacher	Large	NK
27	BDP	Tiger Kloof	NK	NK
28	BDP	Secondary	Medium	NK
29	BDP	Teacher	Medium	Shop
30	BDP	Lovedale	NK	NK
31	BDP	Teacher	Large	Farm
32	BDP	little	Large	Farm
33	BDP	Teacher	Large	Farm
34	BDP	Tiger Kloof	NK	NK
35	BDP	Tiger Kloof	Large	Farm/shop
36	BDP	Teacher	NK	big
37	BNF	Tiger Kloof	Large	NK
38	BDP	Secondary	NK	NK
39	BPP	NK	NK	NK
40	BDP	NK	Large	Farm
41	BPP	NK	NK	NK
42	BDP	Tiger Kloof	NK	NK

NK= Not known.

The small size of the dominant class, its narrow and relatively homogeneous economic base and common ideological views provided a basis for unity. Two factors enabled the state to be autonomous from civil-society organs. The first had to do with the unity of the dominant class and its supremacy at the state level. The second factor had to do with the absence of organized or mobilized social groups whose interests contradict the dominant class. However, these factors were not sufficient to hold the group together.[39] Nor were they enough to insure the expanded reproduction of their collective interest. Guaranteeing continued unity among the dominant class and prosperity required able and conscious leaders. This also required leaders who possessed the determination, foresight, and popular legitimacy to sell the group's agenda as the national interest. This task could not have fallen on more appropriate people than Botswana's first president, Seretse Khama, and his vice president, Quett Masire.

Khama's multiple social locations were pivotal in enhancing the dominant class's unity and the state's autonomy from the civil society. Furthermore, his national eminence and the absence of any challenger to his stature meant that his leadership of the elite was unquestionable. Parson noted that Khama wore many hats:

1. For the peasants, he is a chief.
2. For the small group of educated Africans, he is one of them.
3. For the large cattle-owners, he is one of them.
4. For the chiefs, he is one of them.
5. For the Europeans, by dress, language, behavior and experience, he has much in common with them.[40]

Seretse Khama's leadership cemented a national coalition, dominated by large cattle owners, European interests, and the small but growing African bureaucratic middle class. The unity of the dominant class and the peasantariat's disorganization are two critical concepts in understanding the way in which state–civil society relations evolved in Botswana. Moreover, these two concepts are useful in understanding the problems of the African state.

The coalition's stability, the discovery of copper/nickel and, more importantly, the discovery of diamonds in the late 1960s and early 1970s further enhanced state autonomy from the public. These three factors enabled the state to pursue an economic development program geared toward infrastructural/mining, cattle, and commercial development. The peasantry benefited the least from this growth, and inequality increased.[41] The peasants, however, continued to support the BDP as the mineral-

Photo 3.1.   Founding fathers. The founding fathers of the Republic of Botswana.
Late president Khama (fourth from left, front row) and former president Masire
(third from left, front row).

fueled growth meant the state did not have to extract heavy taxes from
the rural population.[42] Thus, the peasantry did not see the growth of the
economy's other sectors coming at their expense.

Parson's study equates unity with state autonomy and implicitly with
state institutional capacity. This assumption is problematic for two reasons. First, state autonomy from the *dominated* classes does not mean
that the dominant class' collective agenda will be pursued by the state.[43]
Second, such autonomy does not necessarily mean that those directing
state operations are conscious of the nature and importance of the group's
collective project. Nor does it mean that the state will protect it from
members of the political elite. Nor does state autonomy mean that the
state will be able to develop effective state institutions to nurture the
collective project. Parson and earlier authors did not address the relationship between autonomy, capacity, and leaders' consciousness regarding the nature of the national interest. This last point is particularly important to fully appreciate the Botswana experience and recognize its
relevance to other societies.

Photo 3.2. Parliament House. The parliament building, extended in 1995. The older chamber is the small dome on the left of the new clock tower.

Patrick Molutsi, a Batswana sociologist, has revisited inequality, social injustice, and liberal democracy in Botswana. His investigations indicated how the state has pursued the twin but contradictory aims of economic injustice (accumulation by the dominant class) and liberal democratic polity (state's legitimacy with the poor majority).[44] In the absence of a domestic bourgeoisie and a basic infrastructure, the elite decided early on that parastatals, such as the Botswana Housing Corporation and Botswana Power Corporation, would provide the essential infrastructural basis for accumulation. Despite such forays into the economy, the state had no interest in production and openly emphasized the market's critical role.[45] The state enticed international capital, particularly in mining, to join a partnership with it. Thus, these actors dominated Botswana's development program. Moreover, the state has made interventionist decisions without resistance from society-based groups.

This strategy, dominated by the state and international capital has intensified inequality. Despite this, the ruling BDP retained a high degree of legitimacy from the local population, especially in rural areas. The manufacture of such consent in the face of horrific inequality was possibly due to the intelligent use of foreign aid, particularly from Scandinavian social democratic regimes. This foreign aid was effectively used to

Photo 3.3. Debswana House. This is one of the glass towers in the capital's central business district. Debswana House is the headquarters of the Botswana/ De Beers diamond mining company.

provide water, health, and education for the rural masses. Meanwhile, the state's own resources and those from multinational capital were employed to fuel growth.[46]

Molutsi's work builds on Parson's but does not explicitly consider the relationship among the dominant class. Moreover, the importance of leadership and group discipline are assumed away. Despite this blind spot, Molutsi implicitly recognizes that mounting such a strategy, balancing accumulation with legitimacy, entails conscious class agency.

A discussion of why and how BDP leadership translated the state's autonomy into effective action, is missing from Molutsi's and Parson's work. For example, why did the Botswana parastatals and ministries get the job done more efficiently and effectively than their counterparts elsewhere in Africa? After all, many African states were relatively autonomous from domestic social classes at the time of independence.

Translating autonomy into capacity requires the concurrence of three variables. First, a united dominant class must agree on the national interest. Second, those who command state power must be conscious of the

Photo 3.4. Statue of President Seretse Khama. This statue of the first and late President of Botswana stands in front of the parliament house.

nature of the collective project and what it requires from the state to take off. Third, a skilled and loyal technocratic class must exist or be created who can build institutions and plan and implement development programs.

Molutsi and Parson note the dominant class's unity, but they do not address the importance of conscious leadership and the art of creating autonomous and effective state institutions. Few African countries had as undeveloped an administration as Botswana at the time of independence. But unlike Botswana's leaders, other African leaders did not see the need for effective public institutions, capable of maintaining and reproducing state autonomy and implementing the state's development program. Botswana's united and conscious leadership created an effective state machinery for capitalist development.

CONSCIOUS LEADERSHIP AND CLASS UNITY:
THE FOUNDATION OF STATE CAPACITY

The leadership of Botswana has demonstrated a remarkable degree of political responsibility and will in addressing the problems and requirements of the country's public sector management. This, in its turn, is supported by a well-thought out and tried machinery and a set of comprehensive procedures, many of which have a backing in law. The existence of a strong and well-staffed ministry of both Finance and Development Planning ensures good coordination and a satisfactory compromise between the public sector investment program and the need for a balanced annual budget. . . . [T]he various divisions of MFDP [Ministry of Finance & Development Planning] work in close cooperation and this is extended to line ministries in which both the Finance Unit and the Planning Unit are staffed by MFDP personnel.[47]

Recent development literature on East Asia underscores the centrality of a weak dominant class or its absence to the development of an autonomous state and hence the successful execution of capitalist development.[48] This literature is silent about the possibility of a united and conscious dominant class providing a social basis for an autonomous state. Similarly, Marxian literature on the African state in the 1970s and 1980s assumed that the presence of such a class will turn the state into its own instrument. This literature did not examine whether such a force enabled the state to build effective institutions to guide capitalist development. Thus, because of the theory's instrumentalist tendency, it was unable to differentiate between a dominant class turning the state into messy rent havens or creating an effective machine whose objective is capitalist development. Finally, this literature failed to address historical accidents (what realist social scientists call *contingency*). Historical accidents occur when several capable and authoritative individuals rise as leaders from a united class. These leaders articulate and guide the group's agenda and the importance of autonomous state institutions capable of protecting the collective interest of the group and their allies.

In Botswana, the dominant class's leaders created an autonomous and effective state apparatus. A long political tradition produced Botswana leaders conscious of the demands of their class's collective project. This tradition and a set of circumstances enhanced the quality and capability of leadership in independent Botswana. First, the traditional Botswana elite retained a significant degree of autonomy by resisting British colonial rule and Pretoria's attempts to incorporate Bechuanaland into South Africa. Second, the traditional leadership maintained its hegemony over the masses during the period of colonial transformation. Third, the destruction of South African leaders, and the enslavement and dispossession of their people, ingrained in the Botswana leaders a strong sense of themselves and their role as guardians of their society. Fourth, in Botswana the traditional, political, and economic elite were almost one and the same, unlike other African societies. Fifth, the Botswana leaders' long-term independent association with and support from a number of Europeans to fight against South African incorporation[49] meant that the leaders of the regime in power did not suspect those expatriates' intentions. The leaders "freely" choose to associate with these expatriates, and hired them to do specific jobs.[50] Sixth, the dominant class was unchallenged by any other indigenous group. Large numbers of civil servants, major commercial/settler interests, and a mobilized peasantry, inherited from the colonial era, were absent.[51] Mindful of these conditions, their hegemony, and the absence of any meaningful challenge from other social groups, the leadership went about building efficacious institutions to spearhead the transformation of the economy.

The remaining section of this chapter has three primary purposes. First, it discusses the debate over the speed of the civil service's Africanization. In Botswana this process is called localization and includes nonindigenous citizens, such as, other Africans, whites and Indians. I use the debate and the pace of localization as a proxy of how conscious the leaders were of creating an effective state apparatus.[52] Second, this section shows how the policy-making process at strategy setting level is insulated from the influence of groups based in civil society, while giving liberal democratic legitimacy to the process. Finally, this section sketches how MFDP developed into the nerve center of the state apparatus.

Localization Debate

The stimulation of the private sector is an integral part of development policy in Bechuanaland. In this connection it is clear that Government can play a useful role in the shaping attitudes favourable to economic growth.[53]

My Government is deeply conscious of the dangers inherent in localising the public service too quickly. Precipitate or reckless action in this field could have disastrous effects on the whole programme of services and development of the Government . . . potential donor countries might be reluctant to provide aid as they would not wish to see such aid maladministered, and I must again emphasise that we need aid.[54]

The way the leaders of Botswana, particularly President Khama and Vice President Masire, dealt with the development of civil service demonstrates they were conscious of the project's prerequisites. The government decided that private enterprise was the economic system of its choice.[55] They also realized that, given Botswana's underdevelopment, the state's task was to provide infrastructure and public institutional capacity to stimulate economic growth.[56] To fulfill this agenda, the BDP leaders recognized the centrality of an effective and competent civil service. Botswana's first development plan unequivocally stressed the significance of sound planning. Thus, the management of the civil service demonstrated the leaders consciousness and determination.

In most African countries, the Africanization of the civil service was among the first acts of government immediately after independence. Africanizing public service entailed quick and massive promotions of indigenous bureaucrats in the military or civil service to positions previously earmarked for and occupied by white colonialists. Botswana was among the African states who, although eager to indigenize the service, were relatively slow and more deliberate in the speed with which the process unfolded in the senior professional and technical areas.

The government's slowness in this regard may have been due to the fact that the ruling party was not a mass-based national liberation movement. Consequently, an immobilized but previously disfranchised population exerted little pressure to quickly replace the colonialists with Africans. The BDP was in fact part of the colonial administration since its formation in 1962. BDP leading members were "trainee ministers" under the tutelage of Protectorate administrators whom they were expected to replace.[57] The BDP was the colonial state's party of choice. The colonial administration fully supported the BDP to insure a smooth transition to an independent Botswana.[58]

The close relationship between the BDP and the colonial administration is not the sole explanation for the BDP's policies. Such an explanation is myopic and paternalistic, for it presumes that the Botswana leaders were simply towing the colonial line rather than having their own ideas. The leaders' agenda may have dovetailed with the colonial administration's ideological orientation. When such confluence occurred, the BDP government used its contacts to maximum benefit. At other times, when BDP's ideas differed from those of the administration it went its own way.[59]

The BDP government's policy reflected the carefully thought-out agenda of the leaders of the class that dominated the new government. Their plan was to enhance accumulation and sustain their legitimacy with the public. The BDP preferred the term *localization* partly to retain the support of the small, but economically important white population who contributed significantly to the party's coffers.[60] Molutsi's argument that the postcolonial regime attempted to balance these twin, but contradictory, objectives helps us better understand the evolution of civil service policy in Botswana. Although the debate over localization began in 1958 in the African Advisory Council, its full development had to wait for independence. The first real hints of the BDP's localization strategy could be seen in both the 1960–64 and the 1963–68 development plans. These plans affirmed the centrality of a market economy for the Protectorate.

These early plans clearly articulated that the principal development strategy would be based on a market economy, and the government would play a crucial role in this agenda. To fulfill such a role, government institutions would stimulate and assist the market.[61] The BDP recognized that the government must be careful in orchestrating localization. The BDP manifesto for the preindependence election in 1965 clearly showed that the leadership was aware of this dilemma:

> Localization of the Service and In-Service Training: Briefly, while we must guard against the *lowering of standards reached so far* in the Civil Service, by unduly straining after replacing expatriates in the present government, the policy of the Bechuanaland Democratic Party will be to localise the service as fast as *suitably qualified* Bechuanaland citizens become available. We are not sure whether enough has been or is being done to prepare local officers for positions of responsibility in the service, but during the first period of self-government we would see to it that where local men with experience and ability can be found they will be appointed to any post in the Government for which they are qualified. . . . we would see to it that local men are appointed as understudies to serve in almost all positions of responsibility in Government service to prepare them for take over at the independence stage.[62] (italics mine)

The manifesto recognized the need to localize at a "reasonable" speed. Careful "pacing" of localization showed that the BDP was the legitimate party of independence. It also ensured the maintenance and improvement of performance standards in the public service.

The BDP's landslide win in the 1965 election did not change the leadership's mind about their localization strategy. Nor did it change their minds about maintaining and improving the civil service's capacity for resource mobilization and development. The vice president defiantly noted that well-run and efficient public institutions were necessary if resources and budget deficient Botswana was to mobilize overseas resources:

> Even if we could afford to be irresponsible and just appoint people left and right, we must know that we are a poor country. We almost live on donations. Those countries which give us money if they think we put this money into good use, and therefore when we localise we must take account, I mean even if we meant to sacrifice the public good at least we must realize that unless we can use this money which we get externally, unless we can put it to good use, unless we can see that we use it properly we can not hope to continue to get it. It does not matter whether it comes from the United Kingdom . . . , there is no country which would just

throw its good money to another country and not be interested to know how the money is used, and money can only be properly used if it has efficient people to use it.[63]

The small opposition made the civil service question an important political issue. The BDP government was confident although concerned about the consequence of politicized civil service. To make the seriousness of this matter patently clear and put the weight of his presidency behind his government's "go-slow" policy, the president convened a meeting for all public servants at the Gaborone national stadium in late 1967:

> To begin with it is common knowledge that some local civil servants are dissatisfied with the rate at which my government is localising the service, in spite of the fact that we have, in my opinion, carried out localisation faster than we had hoped for. After all we had been quite unequivocal about the fact that we would never sacrifice efficiency on the alter of localisation . . . no one can charge me with going back on promises to localise the service at a faster pace.[64]

President Khama and his party maintained their "go-slow" agenda despite their losses in the 1969 elections and the vice president's defeat by the president's strongest political opponent, former chief Bathoen S. Gasetsiwe. The vice president returned to parliament as one of the "especially elected" members, and he retained his ministerial post.[65] After regaining the electoral momentum in 1974, the president reiterated his old position on localization.[66] To eliminate any doubt about his commitment to the "go-slow" policy, he retained Phil Steenkamp, a former colonial officer of Afrikaner origin who became a naturalized Batswana, as the permanent secretary in the Office of the President. This post was one of the most sensitive in the administration. In addition, he also appointed David Finlay, another naturalized Batswana and former Protectorate officer, as the director of the newly created Directorate of Personnel.[67] These appointments raised the ire of Matante and other leading opposition members of parliament.

Apart from such occasional criticism, the ship of state steamed ahead. The success of the government's team, all expatriates led by the vice president, in renegotiating the Southern African Customs Unions Agreement in 1969 demonstrated the merits of their "go-slow" strategy.[68] If the government had hastily Africanized all civil service positions, the argument goes, it may have been forced to field a team that lacked the training and competency to negotiate successfully. This renegotiated Customs Agreement and the agreement with private firms and donors to finance and develop a copper/nickel complex, commonly known as the Shashe Project, in Selebe Phikwe, enabled Botswana to balance its annual budget for the first time in

1972, without grants from its former colonial master. This was one of the government's major objectives. Its realization fortified the regime's convictions about its approach to development.

The discovery of diamonds and the subsequent negotiations with the De Beers and infrastructural development firms necessitated the employment of a large number of expatriates. The vice president bluntly noted this in his budget speech in 1979/80:

> The rapid expansion of Government activities has resulted in a rapid growth of demand for skilled manpower that exceeds the growth in domestic supply. Thus in spite of the rapid increase in resources allocated to education, the skilled manpower shortage will become worse. In order to bridge the gap, Government will continue to employ expatriates, but in the coming year, the housing shortage in Gaborone will allow only a small increase in the number of expatriates, recruited for service in Gaborone. More importantly, there is evidence that the increase of skilled manpower in Central Government has diverted manpower away from Local Government and the parastatal and private sectors thereby retarding development in these sectors.[69]

The enormous wealth generated by exploiting the country's mineral wealth was final proof that the government's use of skilled expatriate labor, a fundamental tenet of its localization policy, had indeed paid off. The late finance minister and vice president Peter Mmusi succinctly stated government's confidence in its strategy:

> A purposeful government which acquires the expertise to deal with foreign companies on its own terms need not have a fear of domination by foreign companies, however large they may be. The important word is purposeful—and I believe our government has been able to put together strong negotiating teams, has backed them up with well-worked out negotiating mandates, and has then overseen the implementation of our major mining agreements with detailed care as well.[70]

Credit for Botswana's economic success and the minister's subsequent and apparent confidence goes to the republic's founding fathers, Khama and Masire. They saw the merit of institution building and advocated the "go-slow" policy of localizing the civil service. Their "leadership . . . was of unusually high quality."[71] A crucial element of what Harvey and Lewis dub as "high leadership quality" is the leaders' awareness of their goals and what was required to attain them. President Khama and his closest associates were unequivocal about the economy's capitalist nature that they wanted to develop. Other African leaders in the region, some of whom the president (Julius

Nyerere and Kenneth Kaunda) admired and respected, were planning economic strategies supposedly based on African socialism or humanism. Seretse Khama and his government unabashedly pursued capitalist development. He opposed communism and jokingly characterized himself as a capitalist. According to William Henderson, Seretse "often used to joke about being a capitalist among socialists, wryly commenting at one meeting that, although he was a capitalist, he was the only member of the front line team to come to a meeting in a hired rather than private plane."[72]

The choice of a capitalist economy, the leaders' appreciation of the country's underdevelopment, and their decision to use the state as stimulator of the economy, made them realize that efficiently run public institutions were critical to their agenda. Hence, the "go-slow" localization policy. Their awareness of the state's task was married to their political autonomy and legitimacy. This union built the state institutional capacity necessary to plan and implement the capitalist development program. The debate over localizing the senior technical posts in the public service was one of the few areas of government policy the small opposition and some BDP backbenchers criticized. The government, however, stuck to its agenda to build effective institutions and maintain the insulation of the bureaucracy.

MFDP: Institutional Nerve Center

The Bechuanaland Protectorate had neither a dynamic private sector nor a state system capable of inducing economic growth and development. Despite this grid of inheritance, a former member of the Botswana economic bureaucracy noted how quickly this changed after independence:

> The country provided an outstanding example of the successful mobilization of aid resources and their deployment. At a time when the efforts of international agencies and developed country governments were under increasing attack for both the low level of transfers and the way in which these transfers were effected, Botswana provided an example of how aid could be made to work.[73]

Michael Stevens's remarks are at the heart of the problem. How can the dominant class's unity and the leaders' consciousness translate into effective institutional capacity, catering to the collective accumulation project? And how did Botswana become a relatively efficient state model in such a short duration, especially given its history as an impoverished and economically backward British Protectorate? Like their counterparts elsewhere in Africa, the BDP leaders' principal long-term goal was economic development. However, the Botswana leadership also realized that establishing an effective and efficient administrative structure was a prerequisite for economic development. The bureaucracy the British left behind was hopelessly inadequate.[74]

The Protectorate Administration's last two development plans (1960–64 and 1963–68) recognized the importance of planning for the country's development. These plans indicated the government needed to take responsibility for two tasks: developing the country's infrastructure and providing an appropriate social climate for private investment. However, the development plans did not specifically describe the state institutions necessary to carry out this economic development program nor how to build these institutions. The last colonial report on Bechuanaland, however, fully recognized the centrality of such institutions for development. The Porter Report, commissioned by the Ministry of Overseas Development, was published after independence. It stressed the importance of an effective financial and planning mechanism:

> While a certain amount of co-ordination of development activity can be achieved through interdepartmental consultation, . . . *there must be one place in the machinery of government where all departmental plans must be welded into a coherent whole which will enable the general development objectives of government to be achieved.* There will also be the problem of scaling down the finance which is available to the programme which emerges in this fashion. The Economic Planning Unit has therefore two major functions. The first is to make clear to Ministers the economic implications of the general objectives which they would wish to adopt. . . . [T]he second function . . . is to analyze the implications of different allocations of investment programme as a whole, is likely to be more important in the foreseeable future. . . . It is clear that the Economic Planning Unit must, if it is to be *effective, be placed in the centre of the administrative machine and headed by a civil servant of the top rank.* . . . There are, therefore three possible locations for an Economic Planning Unit. . . . There is, however, much to be said in favour of having the Economic Planning Unit report to a single Minister, whether it be the Minister of Finance or a Minister with a general responsibility for long term economic development.[75] (italics mine)

The new government shared the general development strategy prescribed in the previous plans. However, Vice President Masire took exception to the Porter Report regarding Botswana's economic prospects and the country's capacity to effectively absorb more external capital.[76] Botswana's highest priorities were to establish a coordinated institutional capability and to attract sufficient public and overseas private funds. The government acted on the Porter Report's advice by further strengthening the Economic Planning Unit formed in 1965 as part of the Ministry of

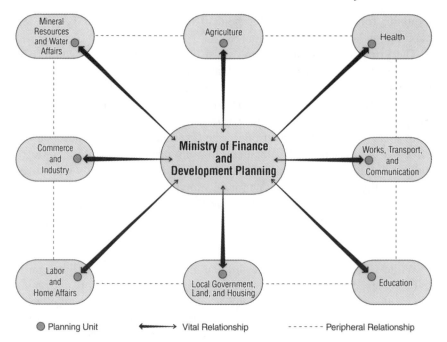

Figure 3.1 Relationship Between Ministry of Finance and Development Planning and Other Ministries

Finance. Botswana also established the Central Statistics Office.[77] Expatriates or former colonial administrators, some of whom became Botswana citizens,[78] staffed all the critical ministry posts. The portfolio of this ministry was given to Vice President Masire, the president's closest political ally and confidant. This signaled that this ministry was the most powerful ministry in the cabinet, outside the presidency. The president did not get involved in a detailed understanding of the economy.[79] Consequently, he relied heavily on his vice president. As such, the vice president was the cabinet's real economic authority.

The government split the Ministry of Finance into the Ministries of Development Planning and Finance a while later. The Ministry's subdivision was the result of internal turf struggles between those left from the colonial administration, who wanted to keep the books, and the vice president and his Young Turks, who were eager to push an aggressive development agenda.[80] Then again the government recombined the two ministries into the Ministry of Finance and Development Planning. This recombination signaled the ascendance of the developmental agenda. Transforming the relationships between the civil service and the government accompanied the ascendance of the developmental agenda.

Botswana inherited and maintained the colonial civil service system with a high degree of autonomy from the government. The latter also established the Directorate of Personnel, which reported to the president's office. The new establishment took over many of the old order's functions, but it also became responsible for developing the human resources skills necessary to develop the economy. This change was essential given the dire need for skilled Batswana to speed up the development process.[81]

Established in 1970, the Ministry of Finance and Development Planning is the institutional brain of the economic policy-making process. Once established, the ministry took off. The activist, Masire, and his technocratic troops, headed by Hermans, consolidated the ministry so that it dominated all other ministries (Figure 3.1). MFDP became responsible for planning, budgeting, and coordinating all development activities. The line ministries were responsible for project implementation. MFDP also liaisoned and negotiated with all aid agencies. The MFDP carefully monitored the implementations of all development projects.[82] The ministry has firm control over the state's financial affairs, as it sets the overall spending ceilings for the annual budgets and the multiyear development plans. Although the ministry has the final say about government finance, its authority is not as firm as it was in the early days.[83]

The MFDP's centrality in agenda setting and management of development planning was the result of the government's experience in the Shashe Project. The Shashe Project was a huge planning and coordination exercise. Its total annual expenditure exceeded Botswana's gross domestic product. As such, the government virtually devoted all of its resources and skilled people to establishing the copper/nickel complex. Given the project's economic dominance, nearly all sectors and ministries depended on the spin-off resources from it. Consequently the government had to coordinate and balance Shashe developments with the rest of the economy. The project's success gave government leaders confidence that they could plan and manage the economy and play a lead role.[84] The government transferred the planning experience from the copper/nickel project to the Ministry of Finance and Development Planning. To insure the MFDP's capacity to spearhead the development agenda, the government set up planning units, staffed by professional planners responsible to the director of Economic Affairs of MFDP, in other ministries. These officers met weekly with the director to discuss and report on progress and possible problems in "their ministries."[85]

The scarcity of skilled professionals necessitated centralizing finance and development-planning authority. However, even when skilled professionals became more available, the centralized structure appeared to be an effective and efficient way to manage the government's business. Institutions which often decried the inefficiencies of centralized public institution praised the Botswana model:

The centralization of the [system] permits a higher quality in estimat-
ing their costs and allows the government to take advantage of bulk
purchasing and economies of standardization. Moreover, this centralization functions as a means of ensuring efficiency and control of operations while leaving line managers with adequate flexibility in carrying out their responsibilities. This efficiency is further encouraged
. . . without influence or political interference. . . . The process of budgetary preparation and control is supported by sets of procedures which
impose the discipline necessary for the production of a good budget
and for its implementation.[86]

The severe underdevelopment of the educational system during the long
colonial period meant that the technical and administrative skills necessary
for development were not available in Botswana. Thus, the BDP government assumed that expatriates would play a crucial role in the near future,[87]
and the government was willing to bend over backwards to attract skilled
young people.[88] Consequently, it retained the few British administrators and
technicians, some of whom became naturalized citizens; among the most
illustrious were Hermans, Steenkamp, and Finlay, who wanted to stay and
serve the new regime.

The government's immediate needs forced employing expatriates in senior positions in a highly centralized system. The new government's first
two major undertakings were renegotiating of the 1910 South African Customs Union and establishing the Shashe Copper/Nickel Project, culminating
with the MFDP consolidation. A small staff from the Economic Planning
Unit, particularly Pierre Landell-Mills and Steven Ettinger, and attorney General Alan Tilbury[89] worked on the negotiations. They had the president's
and vice-president's full backing. Initially, the old colonial guard opposed
the renegotiation. They feared these negotiations might upset South Africa
and create more problems for Botswana. The negotiations were successful,
and the government's financial base improved dramatically.[90] While the renegotiation was in progress, the government was also bargaining with foreign
donors and private investors to invest in the copper/nickel complex. In the
copper/nickel and diamonds case, the government used consultants, given
these projects' complexity.[91] The government knew that it needed first class
technical and negotiating teams to wrestle with giants like De Beers. These
two major efforts' successes demonstrated that employing expatriates was
wise, given the dearth of indigenous skilled labor. Consequently, the government made the employment of expatriates in the civil service and consultants a pillar of its institutions building strategy.[92]

Aid agencies, particularly the British, were a major source of skilled expatriate labor for Botswana. These aid expatriates were often attached to
specific projects and integrated into the civil service during their Botswana

Table 3.4 Professional Officers in Departments of Economic and Financial Affairs, MFDP[ab]

	Mid-1972		Mid-1978		1994		
	Total		Local	Total	Local	Total	Local
Department of Economic Affairs	23		5	25	10	65	59
Department of Financial Affairs	10		6	19	11	24	20

[a] Counting civil servant down to the rank of executive officer.

[b] PS., Secretariat, and consultants include under DEA.

Source: Isaksen, <u>Macro-Economic Management</u>: 51; and Modise D. Modise, Director of Economic Affairs, Ministry of Finance and Development Planning (Gaborone: December 7, 1994).

tenure. This strategy was so successful that the government pressed the United States to send the Peace Corps to Botswana and change the Peace Corps regulations in such a way that these volunteers could be assigned to ministries or wherever Botswana needed them.[93] The United States was reluctant to do this, but Botswana's persistence prevailed.

Given its need, Botswana made unconventional use of the Peace Corps. The Peace Corps administration was reluctant, but again Botswana's tenacity paid off. On one occasion, the government dispatched a young Peace Corps volunteer to London to negotiate with the Britain's Overseas Development Administration (ODA) on Botswana's behalf. The ODA was surprised by the idea, but the process continued.[94] As noted previously, the BDP government made serious efforts to localize the civil service, but it was not in a hurry to do so at the cost of effective and efficient administration. Consequently, expatriates held a large proportion of technical and professional posts in the service.[95] For example, expatriates dominated the most important policy-making organs of the Ministry of Finance and Development Planning until recently as shown in Table 3.4. The relationship between the state's skilled expatriate employees and the political leaders was complementary. The BDP government sketched the broader outlines of its development plan, but the skilled technocrats crafted the details and then implemented the programs. As an insider noted, the bureaucracy had wide leeway as long as its propositions were not

> critically endangering the relationship with South Africa and to refrain from promoting interests which are seen as directly in competition with those of the cattle industry. Within these limits there exists an area of

decision-making for the bureaucracy and bureaucratic politics. The formal political system, and the elite, seldom interferes in this area, but leaves it to the bureaucracy and political elite. Even superficial observation shows contacts and social links bordering on camaraderie. The elite also takes definite interest in and supports plans and implementation. It is, however, the bureaucracy which is usually expected to perceive problems, come out with ideas, take initiative and gain administrative and political support for these initiatives. There is, however, an absence of political sifting of ideas and initiatives which makes the initiator . . . critically important for the direction of policies within the fixed limits.[96]

These expatriates occupied critical bureaucratic positions; therefore they managed the operations of the state apparatus at the behest of the elite. The Batswana who joined their ranks, slowly but steadily, were trained in the same universities and schools of thought as the expatriates. These Batswana also served under these expatriates early on in their careers. Thus, little difference existed between the Batswana and the expatriates about management style and the nature of economic development.[97] The fact that the fundamental administrative procedures governing the ministry's and others' operations were set in the years immediately after independence reinforced this fact. This administrative structure and culture valued effectiveness, orderliness and accountability.[98]

The BDP leaders laid the foundation for stable and relatively effective public institutions by: (a) resisting the pressure to quickly localize technical and professional levels of the public service; (b) insulating the public service from political intervention; and (c) clearly demarcating the political and economic boundaries within which policy making must operate. With the development and establishment of this administrative apparatus and with MFDP as its nerve center, Botswana's economy kept growing.

The Ministry of Finance and Development Planning directs all economic activity and financial management of the state. The ministry is the epicenter of the economic development process. That process has two phases: strategy setting and translating that strategy into plans and projects. The MFDP plays a central role in the latter process, while its part in the former is much less significant.[99] A sketch of these two processes illustrates the state's autonomy in strategy setting as well as MFDP's critical function in translating strategies into substance while guarding the state's purse.

Strategy Setting

This phase of the development process is long-term in orientation and is less frequently tampered with by government. Capitalist economic growth, in which the state plays a leading role, has been Botswana's core strategy since independence. Setting the strategy entails the government producing "white papers," on matters fundamental to the thrust of the economy. They include (a) Financial Assistance Policy (1982); (b) National Policy on Economic Opportunities (1982); (c) Industrial Development Policy (1984); (d) National Policy on Land Tenure (1985); (e) Wildlife Conservation policy (1986); (f) Revised National Policy on Incomes, Employment, Prices and Profits (1990); (g) National Policy on Agricultural Development (1991); and (h) the Revised National Policy on Education (1994).

Andreas Danevad's recent study of the Revised National Policy on Incomes, Employment, Prices and Profits vividly illustrates not only the autonomy of public policy formation from most sectors of civil society, but how the state attempts to legitimize its program.[100] The purpose here is not to address the income policy's substantive issues but to sketch: (a) the general framework of strategy formulation; (b) the relationship between the commission responsible for the production of the paper and nongovernmental organizations affected by the policy; and (c) the role of the Ministry of Finance and Development Planning.

Government follows a standard format in producing a white paper:

> The production of a white paper seems broadly to follow an uniform pattern: a point of departure is often a report by an appointed commission, academic scholars, or private consultants. The report and its recommendations are subsequently considered by the political executive, and a draft policy document is presented to the National Assembly, and finally a white paper is made public.[101]

Botswana's incomes policy since the introduction of the first policy in 1972 has been to restrain wages to attract investment and nurture economic growth.[102] The country has gone through significant economic transformation since independence, and the government thought that the incomes policy, a central tenet of Botswana's development strategy, needed to be updated. A 1989 presidential commission revised and reviewed the incomes policy.[103]

The commission, chaired by the minister for External Affairs, consisted of two members of parliament; five representatives of state employees (one of whom was the governor of the Bank of Botswana and who is a member of the Economic Committee of the Cabinet [ECC]); a member of the civil service association; two representatives of the trade unions; two representatives of private employers; an industrial worker; two from the rural sector, and two scholars, one of whom worked for and advised the Bank of Botswana for many years. The commission's composition led Danevad to conclude that it was not independent from the government.[104] Figure 3.2 depicts the process of reviewing the old incomes policy and producing a new one.

The Revised Income Policy Commission traveled to major population centers to solicit information on incomes and wages. It invited and collected

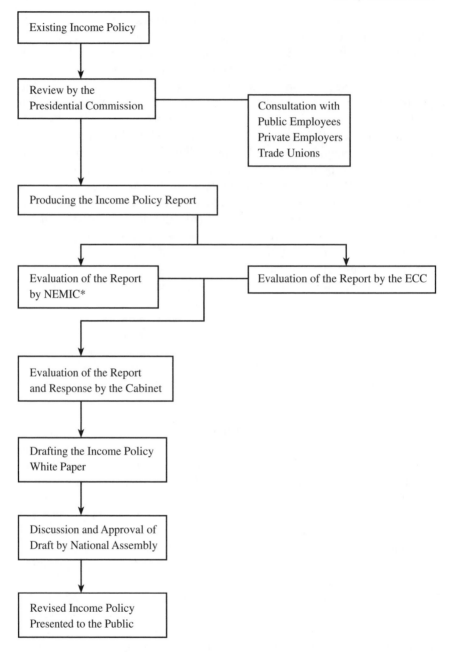

Figure 3.2 White Paper Production Process

Source: Andreas Danevad, *Development Planning and the Importance of Democratic Institutions in Botswana: Report 7* (Bergen, Norway: Chr. Michelsen Institute, 1993), p. 109. Reprinted by permission of Chr. Michelsen Institute.

* NEMIC: National Employment, Manpower, and Income Council

testimonies from anyone concerned about the issue. It received 250 oral testimonies, most of which came from "public and parastatal employees, followed by private employers."[105] After soliciting inputs from the "public," the government- and BDP-dominated commission submitted its report to the government. Trade union and civil society organs representatives did not substantially influence the contents of the report. Senior public employees who followed the commission with advice and who were well represented in the Commission effectively influenced it to recommend a significant increase in the salaries for its cohorts of civil servants. The trade union representative's suggestions, which argued against increased wages for senior bureaucrats and small increases for most public servants, were not included in the report.

Once the commission submitted its report, the government "consulted" with two bodies before drafting its white paper. These were the Economic Committee of the Cabinet (ECC) and the National Employment, Manpower and Income Council (NEMIC). The ECC includes all ministers, permanent secretaries, the governor of the Bank of Botswana, the president, and the commanders of the military and the police. The ECC secretariat is the Employment Policy Unit of MFDP. Thus, the MFDP influences the committee through the presence of its Minister and Permanent Secretary, who are senior to their colleagues and through the use of the Secretariat.[106] NEMIC, which consists of representatives of the government, private employers and workers, is dominated by the first two groups. Given that the ECC is in essence the government itself and that the NEMIC is government- and private-employers dominated and that these council members largely share the government's agenda of keeping wages low and competitive, the discussions of the report was an in-house review, not an examination by outsiders.[107] Once this review was over, the government then produced its draft white paper. The government concurred with nearly half of the commission's recommendations, modified a few, and completely rejected those which would have reduced government involvement in some areas of the economy.[108] The government submitted the draft white paper to the National Assembly for debate. The National Assembly, after two weeks of debate, did not change a single item in the proposed review of the income policy. The white paper became official government policy and was presented to the public. The revised incomes policy partially modifies the old income policy but reifies the dominant class's development agenda.[109] Needless to say, all white paper production exercises follow the same procedure.

The process of producing the white paper clearly shows that government is in the driver's seat and that it does not hesitate to reject those commission recommendations which were contrary to its development strategy. The MFDP influence is not overt, but it is felt through the input of powerful commission members, such as the governor of the Bank of Botswana. Likewise, the cabinet's Economic Committee influenced the commission's report at a later stage. By contrast, the National Assembly, which has the constitutional authority to alter public policy, was "ineffective" for two reasons. First, the BDP controlled 38 of the 40 seats prior to the 1994 election in which the opposition gained 13 seats of the total. Second, the Economic Committee of the Cabinet accounts for nearly half of the BDP members of the National Assembly. Cabinet members from the ECC are also the leaders of the ruling party. Thus, three factors insulate the policy-making process from close public scrutiny: (a) the government's control over the selection of the commission members; (b) members of the government and affiliated groups dominate the commission; and (c) the parliament's weakness. Why does the government appoint such a commission when it has full control over the choice of commission members, sets the commission's mandate, and ultimately decide what becomes of the commission's recommendations? Some critics argue that this exercise is a part of the democratic charade that the BDP regime has been practicing since independence. Others consider this part of the regime's attempts to legitimate liberal capitalist economic strategy.[110] Let us turn to how government strategy is translated into development programs.

Development Planning and Implementation

The broad outlines of development strategy, spelled out in government white papers, have to be translated into plans and concrete projects. The Ministry of Finance and Development Planning spearheads, manages, and controls this process. The MFDP initiates the production of a development plan by introducing a Keynote Policy Paper (KPP). This provides guidelines to all ministries regarding the government's development priorities and fiscal constraints:

> The Keynote Policy Paper has deliberately confined itself to general themes for NDP7. It has not attempted to identify the crucial issues for each sector. This will be done by the sectoral ministries as they prepare Sectoral Keynote Issues Papers. Appropriate emphases will vary from sector to sector, but a number of the themes raised in the present paper should be followed through in each of the sectoral papers. In particular, the sectoral papers should address: manpower and productivity within the sector; pricing and subsidy issues; employment creation and economic opportunities; sustainable development; the appropriate roles of Government, parastatals and private initiative; recurrent costs.[111]

In response to the KPP, ministries develop sectoral keynote issue papers and submit them to MFDP on a specified date. Figure 3.3 shows the process and stages of producing the National Development Plan 7.

Figure 3.3   The Key Stages in the Preparation of the Plan

1. Preparation by MFDP of economic projections for the plan period. These highlight important development issues such as the gap between labour force growth and likely job creations. The projections also provide an estimate of the resources that will be available to Government and the country during the plan period.

2. Preparation by MFDP of a keynote policy paper. This summarizes the economic outlook, identifies the crucial policy issues that will determine the shape of the Plan and proposes the themes to be stressed. The paper is submitted to the Economic Committee of the Cabinet for discussion and endorsement.

3. Preparation by line Ministries of sectoral keynote papers that take up the themes proposed in MFDP's paper. These should be brief (not a "first draft" of NDP chapter) and should concentrate on the new or more crucial issues to be resolved in the course of preparing the sector's plan. Ideally, a keynote policy paper is not more than 6–12 pages long and concentrates on *Issues*, not a shopping list of projects.

4. Preparation by MFDP of initial resource guidelines (ceilings) for the Plan period, allocated among sectors, Ministries and departments in line with the priorities endorsed by ECC. Cabinet approves the ceilings as the basis for drafting of the Plan, and MFDP then issues detailed drafting guidelines to Ministries.

5. The first drafts of the Plan proper are prepared. While sectoral Ministries draft their chapters and prepare projects for part II, MFDP drafts the macroeconomic and review chapters, continuously refining its economic and budgetary forecasts in the process.

6. Drafts are extensively circulated for comment—to all Ministries and all Local Authorities and to various consultative bodies and committees. They form the subject of a National District Development Conference.

7. MFDP reviews and edits drafts, aiming to reconcile proposals with resources available and to ensure consistency. Contentious issues are resolved at ECC or Cabinet level if necessary.

8. The complete draft is submitted to cabinet for approval. It is then tabled in the National Assembly and extensively debated. After any amendments have been agreed and Parliament's approval given the new Plan ceases to be a draft and becomes the blueprint for development policy until superseded by the next NDP.

Source: Republic of Botswana, *Planning Officers' Manual*: 2–5.

The process of producing a development plan as depicted in Figure 3.3 seems participatory. Many actors at different levels of government, from local and district authorities, take part in the deliberations. Danevad's recent study indicated that the process's decentralized appearance does not reflect the actual critical hierarchical relations among the MFDP, the ministries, and the district and local authorities.[112] The public widely shares this assessment. The MFDP dominates and controls the process at every vital stage; from setting the broad priorities in KPP to producing the macroeconomic forecasts through the Microeconomic Model of Botswana (MEMBOT) and establishing the expenditure ceiling with which every sector has to live. Other ministries dispute MFDP's ceiling and broader guidance, but MFDP is the undisputed process leader. The MFDP's central role in producing development plans has somewhat declined. The process has become relatively more participatory since Botswana's diamond-driven economic boom in the early 1980s.[113]

Despite the MFDP's declining role in plan production, it continues to use two methods to dominate economic development.[114] First, before any project can be included into a plan, sectoral ministries must carefully justify the project's economic viability. Those projects which pass the economic viability test and become part of a plan do not get automatic funding unless they are included in the annual development budget.[115] The second way MFDP leads the development process is through its capacity to insure that projects do not exceed expenditure ceilings and may even be reduced when necessary. For the MFDP to release funds a project must satisfy several conditions. First, the project must be in the national development plan and approved by parliament. Second, MFDP must evaluate and approve the project. Third, the funds must be in the development budget.[116] If these conditions are met, a project is included into a ministry's annual budgetary warrant, which the MFDP releases. The MFDP releases these warrants at the beginning of the financial years. If government revenue conditions have changed, however, the MFDP may warrant less than was budgeted for any ministry. This happened in 1982. Under adverse financial circumstances, the vice president and minister of Finance and Development Planning announced to parliament:

> This year we have seen a rapidly changing international situation affecting our budget. If we had known in August what we know now, I would be presenting different figures to this Honourable House. Because of the substantial deterioration in the international and our domestic situation, following approval of the budget, my ministry will only warrant authority to spend 80% of the amounts given in the estimates.[117]

This complex planning and budgetary process, centered in the Ministry of Finance and Development Planning, has enabled Botswana to remain in good fiscal health and insure relatively successful implementation of its development plans. Furthermore, the leadership demands accountable, but autonomous and effective, institutions that can plan and manage the state's affairs. This combination of conscious leadership and insulated bureaucracy has earned Botswana the status of a model state in Africa.

Finally, the Government and MFDP have developed a monitoring and auditing system to insure and enforce proper and legitimate use of public funds. This system has worked exceedingly well, sustaining the republic's reputation as a country free of systemic corruption and excessive rent seeking. When individuals abuse their office, the system holds them accountable. Recent scandals in the Botswana Housing Corporation, a government parastatal, and the periurban land speculation and corruption show that no one can escape the reach of the law. In the latter case, the government removed a minister and the vice president and minister of Finance and Development Planning from their posts for abusing their authority. More recently, many senior members of the ruling party, including the president of the Republic were forced to repay loans they owed to the National Development Bank, whose due date had passed.[118]

CONCLUSION

[Among the developing countries] Botswana stands out in many respects. It has a functioning democratic system, the lines of authority are clearly defined, the civil servants are accountable . . . control over financial management is enforced, plans and planning are taken seriously, technical assistance is utilized effectively, parastatals are managed on sound commercial principles and are not a drain on the national budget and, by and large, there are order, logic, efficiency, probity and rhythm in the conduct of government business.[119]

Independent Botswana inherited a colonial state not worth the name. It did not have an apparatus capable of promoting economic development; nor did it have an agricultural and industrial resource base to marshal for future development. The state's new leadership recognized it needed to establish sound and effective public institutions to carry out its development objectives. Building these institutions required skilled people who were scarce in Botswana. The government used a dual strategy to overcome such scarcity. First, it retained any skilled former Protectorate officers willing to stay. It also solicited donor agencies and countries to assist government by providing trained expatriates. Second, it embarked on training Batswana in significant numbers at home and abroad. The strategy worked well, and the government developed its institutional capacity.

The leadership's unity and legitimacy insured that the policy-making process was managed so that even the National Assembly rarely, if ever, challenged or significantly amended government proposals. Two major factors contributed to Botswana becoming an autonomous state with capacity to effect planned change: insulating the policy-making process from society-centered group and protecting the MFDP technocratic cadre's ability to plan, budget, and monitor program implementation. It also enforced fiscal discipline while remaining free, for the most part, from "political" influence. This chapter's principal thesis is that creating an autonomous state apparatus with significant capacity to affect change did not occur accidentally. Rather, leading members of the dominant class assisted by expatriate technocratic cadre and later on by Batswana bureaucrats carefully and skillfully engineered this autonomous and effective state apparatus. The relationship between conscious and willful political authority and capable bureaucracy was brought together and institutionalized in the MFDP. The ministry has the authority to manage the business of government and the nation. In a nutshell, MFDP played a role similar to that of Japan's pilot agency, MITI, and Taiwan's Economic Bureaucracy. Contrary to the claims of those who advocate decentralization of state authority, the MFDP thus enabled Botswana to forge ahead in spite of the "maladies" of centralization.

To fully understand the nature of the postcolonial African state, its role and ability to transform the economy, requires an appreciation of the motives and the agendas of two groups: those dominant-class members who occupy strategic positions in the state apparatus and those bureaucrats who provided the leadership with technical advice. The MFDP's technical ability to plan, budget, and judicially manage the public purse would not have been possible without a strong and united political leadership. This leadership recognized the importance of disciplined and technically competent public institutions for systemic capitalist development.

Scholars arguing for the centrality of the internal obstacles to capitalist development in Africa and elsewhere in the periphery may think that this chapter lends credibility to their claims. Such an interpretation of the Botswana experience is simplistic and wrong-headed, as it grasps only one imaginary slice of a complex process. Chapters 4 and 5 address the Botswana Meat Commission and Botswana's industrial development strategy. Collectively these make the intertwined importance of internal and external forces apparent. Chapter 4, in addition to this chapter, shows how the Botswana dominant class and state have overcome most of the "internal problems." Chapter 5 shows the enormous difficulties Botswana is having in overcoming the legacy of colonial rule and extracting itself from the regional and international economic and power structure that it inherited.

NOTES

[1] Penelope Hartland-Thunberg, *Botswana: An African Growth Economy* (Boulder, CO: Westview Press, 1978), 5–6.

[2] On the twentieth anniversary of independence, former President Masire recalled the pessimistic attitude that prevailed among the colonial circles at the time of independence: "nothing happens here." Tom Obondo-Okoyo, ed., *Botswana, 1966–1986: Twenty Years of Progress* (Gaborone: Department of Information and Broadcasting, 1986), v.

[3] Jane W. Jacqz, *Report of a Conference on United States Assistance to Botswana & Lesotho* (New York: African-American Institute, June 1967), 1.

[4] Republic of Botswana, *The Development of Bechuanaland Economy: Report of the Ministry of Overseas Development: Economic Survey Mission* (Gaborone, 1966).

[5] T. Luke (Government of Bechuanaland), *Report on Localization and Training* (Gaborone, 1964).

[6] Ibid., xxx, 18.

[7] Republic of Botswana, *Transitional Plan for Social and Economic Development* (Gaborone, 1966), 8.

[8] Lord Hailey noted that Bechuanaland had little potential for political union. This echoed the colonial establishment's pessimistic views. Lord Hailey, *The Republic of South Africa and the High Commission Territories* (Oxford: Oxford University Press, 1961).

[9] The pessimistic view of the colonial establishment reflected the stereotypical view of the nature of African tradition. The establishment failed to understand the fact that chiefs like Bathoen and Tshekedi could lead the nationalist movement while respecting and preserving Tswana tradition. The colonialists confused their assumption with reality. For instance, Bathoen argued for the retention of the integrity of the chieftainship while fully endorsing the national project (see chapter 2).

[10] UNDP, UNICEF, and Republic of Botswana, *Planning for People: A Strategy for Accelerated Human Development in Botswana* (Gaborone: Sygma Publishing, 1993), 11. See also Charles Harvey, *Botswana: Is the Economic Miracle Over?* (Brighton: IDS Discussion Paper 298, 1992).

[11] P. P. Molutsi and John D. Holm, "Developing Democracy When Civil Society Is Weak: The Case of Botswana," *African Affairs* 89, 356 (1990): 323–340; Dickson Eyoh, "From Economic Crisis to Political Liberalization: Pitfalls of the New Political Sociology for Africa," *African Studies Review* 39, 2 (1996): 43–80; William Nunro, "Power, Peasants and Political Development: Reconsidering State Construction in Africa," *Society for Comparative Study of Society and History* 38, 1 (1996): 112–148.

[12] This is despite the moderate changes in the World Bank view.

[13] Jan Isaksen, *Macro-Economic Management and Bureaucracy: The Case of Botswana, Research Report No. 59* (Uppsala: Scandinavian Institute of African Studies, 1981).

[14] G. L. Gunderson, "Nation Building and the Administrative State: The Case of Botswana," Ph.D. diss., University of California–Berkeley, 1970.

[15] Ibid., 7.

[16] Ibid., 434.

[17] Louis Picard, *The Politics of Development in Botswana: A Model of Success?* (Boulder, CO: Lynn Rienner, 1987), 13. P. P. Molutsi, "The Ruling Class and Democracy in Botswana," in J. D. Holm and P. P. Molutsi, eds., *Democracy in Botswana* (Gaborone: Macmillan, 1989).

[18] Gunderson did not use the term *autonomy* in his analysis.

[19] Jack Parson, "The Political Economy of Botswana: A Case in the Study of Politics and Social Change in Post-colonial Botswana," Ph.D. diss., Sussex University, 1979.

[20] There were other important contributions such as C. Colclough and S. McCarthy, *The Political Economy of Botswana: A Study of Growth and Income Distribution* (Oxford: Oxford University Press, 1980); Charles Harvey, ed., *Papers on the Economy of Botswana* (London: Heinemann, 1981). These works did not directly address the inter-

connected issues of state autonomy, capacity, and social structure in the ways that are central to this study.

[21] Isaksen, 18. For a similar but recent expression of this view see R. Gulhati: "The political elite allow the civil servants to play a policy-dominant role because both groups share the same values and similar economic interests, namely cattle rearing." Gulhati, "Who Makes Economic Policy in Africa and How," *World Development* 18, 8 (1990): 1150.

[22] Moreover, as the works of Diana Wylie and Pauline Peters show, there was a great deal of compatibiliity between the agenda of colonial administrators and the chiefs: Wylie, *A Little God: The Twilight of Patriarchy in a Southern African Chiefdom* (Johannesburg: Witwatersrand University Press, 1990); Peters, *Dividing the Commons: Politics, Policy, and Culture in Botswana* (Charlottesville: University Press of Virginia, 1994); see chapter 2.

[23] Republic of Botswana, *Transitional Plan for Social and Economic Development* (Gaborone, 1966).

[24] Isaksen, *Macro-Economic Management and Bureaucracy*, 30.

[25] There was a struggle between the old colonial guard led by Alfred Beebe and the Young Turks who shared the views of the vice president (Quill Hermans, Interview, June 6, 1994). This "conservative" financial management thesis glosses over significant differences between those led by the vice president and old colonial boys. The vice president championed the notion that Botswana had great capacity to effectively absorb resources in order to develop. The position of the vice president and his Young Turks did not mean letting the purse strings loose.

[26] R. Charlton, "Bureaucrats and Politicians in Botswana: A Re-interpretation," *Journal of Commonwealth & Comparative Politics* 29, 3 (1991): 273–74.

[27] Picard, *The Politics of Development in Botswana*, 10. See also N. Raphaeli, J. Roumani, and A. C. Mackellar, *Public Sector Management in Botswana: Lessons in Pragmatism* (Washington, DC: World Bank Staff Working Paper No. 709, 1984).

[28] Picard, *The Politics of Development in Botswana*, 147. See also Dennis L. Cohen, "The Botswana Political Elite: Evidence from the 1974 General Election," *Journal of Southern African Affairs* 4 (1979): 347–372.

[29] Neil Parsons, Willie Henderson, and Thomas Tlou, *Seretse Khama, 1921-1980* (Gaborone: Macmillan, 1995): 239.

[30] Jack Parson, *Botswana: Liberal Democracy and the Labor Reserve in Southern Africa* (Boulder, CO: Westview Press, 1984).

[31] Wylie, *A Little God*.

[32] Until the colonial development and welfare program boosted the revenues base of the colonial state, it barely did much to improve the economy of the Protectorate; see the Pim Commission for indictment of British colonial policy in Bechuanaland: Sir A. Pim, *Financial and Economic Position of the Bechuanaland Protectorate: Command Paper 4368* (London: HMSO, 1933). This is contrary to the claims of Philip Steenkamp, "Cinderella of Empire?" Development Policy in Bechuanaland in the 1930s," *Journal of Southern African Studies* 17, 2 (1991): 293–308.

[33] Charles W. Gossett, "The Civil Service in Botswana: Personnel Policies in Comparative Perspective," Ph.D. diss., Stanford University, 1986.

[34] Parson, *Botswana: Liberal Democracy*.

[35] Ibid., 87.

[36] This elite was a tightly knit group in which everybody knew everyone else: " 'Old Tigers' educated at Tiger Kloof before the mid-1950s constituted the politi-

cal elite in government and opposition. The next generation, now emerging as graduates from the University of Botswana, Lesotho and Swaziland (U. B. L. S.) had mostly been educated at Moeng College—the only large high school in the late 1950s and early 1960s. It was civil servants of the Moeng generation who became permanent secretaries in ministries by the latter 1970s" (Parsons, Henderson, and Tlou, *Seretse Khama*), 15.

[37] Parson, *Botswana: Liberal Democracy.*

[38] Parson discusses the process of social fragmentation of the elite beginning in the early 1980s. The government detected signs of the strain in the coalition. This led to the Presidential Commission on Economic Opportunity (1982). As a result of the commission's recommendations, civil servants were allowed to go into commerce and business. Civil servants argued that the benefits of economic growth were being monopolized by foreigners.

[39] There is a widespread assumption in Botswana that individuals from the Kalange community dominate the civil service and hence the government. It is reported that this notion became a grist for some Tswana politicians and became an urgent political matter. President Khama considered this urgent enough that he had to strongly intervene in order to bring this speculation to an end. The Tswana faction was led by the late Peter Mmusi (Philip Steenkamp, interview, August 15, 1994). Steenkamp was the permanent secretary of the Office of the President. He notes that many senior and very capable civil servants are from the Kalanage community because that commmunity heavily agitated for and invested in schools during the colonial era. This paid off, as many of the students from these schools completed their studies when Botswana became independent and were consequently well placed to take advantage of the professional opportunities. Steenkamp attests to this as he was the district commissioner in the northeast during the time this was taking place.

[40] Parson, "The Political Economy," 335–340.

[41] Government of Botswana, *The Rural Income Distribution Survey in Botswana, 1974–75* (Gaborone, 1975); Bank of Botswana, *Report on the Rural Economic Survey, 1986* (Gaborone, 1987).

[42] The development strategy of the BDP government had three phases (Parson, "The Political Economy, chapter 5, 88–99): a) 1966–74 was the period in which most of the major state institutions were created and the infrastructural boom began. b) During 1975–80, the infrastructural development was consolidated and the initial tensions that began to appear as a result of the previous investment program were managed, i.e., Tribal Grazing Land Policy (TGLP)—partnership with MNCs. This period also saw the growth of state-based middle class who were interested in maintaining existing patterns of growth. c) Parson says that 1980–83 was an era characterized by the appearance of fractures within the dominant coalition and the passing of Seretse. The growth of a working class and its demand for a better wage and working conditions, the aspiration of the middle class to break into the private economy monopolized by Indians and white South Africans, and the tension in the countryside created by the need for further commercialization of the range land via TGLP. Parson thought that during the last phase major cracks were appearing in the unity of the dominant class. Nearly a decade later, the fortress seems sufficiently strong, although one sees cracks. See the *Mmegi Newspaper* (1994–95) for description of factional struggles among the BDP. See also Kenneth Good, "Corruption and Mismanagement in Botswana: A Best-Case Example?" *Journal of Modern African Studies* 32, no. 3 (1994): 499–521.

[43] Note that autonomy is only from the dominated classes, but the distorting effect of the dominant class on state autonomy and the choice of development policy is not fully developed.

[44] P. Molutsi, "Social Stratification and Inequality in Botswana, 1950–1985," Ph.D. diss., Oxford University, 1986. Molutsi and Holm, "Developing Democracy When Civil Society Is Weak."

[45] Molutsi, "Social Stratification and Inequality in Botswana," 101.

[46] Ibid., 374.

[47] Raphaeli, Roumani, and Makellar, *Public Sector Management in Botswana*, 2.

[48] Robert Wade, *Governing the Market: Economic Theory and the Role of Government in East Asian Industrialization* (Princeton: Princeton University Press, 1990); Peter Evans, "The State as Problem and Solution: Predation, Embedded Autonomy and Structural Change," in S. Haggard and R. Kaufman, eds., *The Politics of Economic Adjustment: International Constraints, Distributive Conflicts and the State* (Princeton: Princeton University Press, 1992).

[49] A classic example of this was Tshekedi Khama, who used missionaries, lawyers, and anticolonial, antislavery voices to block the British and South African agenda for the Tswana. See Michael Crowder, "Tshekedi Khama, Smuts, and South West Africa," *Journal of Modern African Studies* 25, 1 (1987): 25–42; and *The Flogging of Phinehas McIntosh: A Tale of Colonial Folly, Bechuanaland, 1933* (New Haven, CT: Yale University Press, 1988).

[50] According to the governor of the Bank of Botswana, the government made brilliant use of qualified and knowledgeable expatriates after independence in the absence of a skilled citizen cadre (Hermans, interview).

[51] Molutsi and Holm, *Developing Democracy When Civil Society Is Weak*.

[52] See Lawrence Frank, "Khama and Jonathan: Leadership Strategies in Contemporary Southern Africa," *Journal of Developing Countries* 15 (1981): 173–198. On matters of consciousness and initiative, see John I. Comaroff, "Class and Culture in a Peasant Economy: The Transformation of Land Tenure in Barolong," in R. P. Werbner, ed., *Land Reform in the Making* (London: Rex Collings, 1982), 85–113.

[53] Bechuanaland Protectorate, *Development Plan* (Gaborones, 1963), 22.

[54] Parsons, Henderson, and Tlou, *Seretse Khama*, 253. This statement was made by President Khama in his first presidential speech in 1966.

[55] There was an agreement between the leaders of the departing colonial regime and Botswana elite regarding the centrality of capitalist economy in the development of independent Botswana. See the continuity between the last development plans of the colonial state and the *Transitional Plan of Independent Botswana*.

[56] Republic of Botswana, *Transitional Plan*.

[57] Bechuanaland Protectorate, *Annual Report* (London: HMSO, 1964).

[58] The leadership of BDP and the administration were very close and shared many ideas. The closeness of the relationship is verified by the words of Seretse Khama on the occasion of the departure of Sir Peter Fawcus, ". . . he will leave many devoted friends behind him and has made a home for himself here that will always be remembered. I, particularly, have had a long and valuable association with Sir Peter, and I wish both Sir Peter and Lady Fawcus a happy retirement." Quoted in W. Henderson, "Seretse Khama: A Person Appreciation," *African Affairs* 89 (1990): 36. This view is also supported by Governor Hermans, interview (Gaborone, June 6, 1994) and David Finlay, interviews (Ramatswa, January 18, 1994). See also Molutsi, "Social Stratifica-

tion and Inequality in Botswana." Colclough and McCarthy, *The Political Economy of Botswana.*

[59] See the history of the relationship between Tshekedi Khama and the British colonial administration. Moreover, the Government of Botswana has had more autonomy from the policy dictates of others, i.e., the neoliberal privatization bandwagon, by keeping its fiscal house in order. See Charles Harvey, "Successful Adjustment in Botswana," *IDS Bulletin* 16, 3 (1985): 47–51.

[60] Charles W. Gossett, "The Civil Service in Botswana," 257.

[61] H.C.L. Hermans, the former governor of the Bank of Botswana was the first permanent secretary of the Ministry of Finance and Development Planning. He notes, in hindsight, that his cadre of Young Turks acted and behaved like central planners to facilitate capitalist economic growth (Hermans, interview, Gaborone, July 6, 1994).

[62] Gossett, "The Civil Service in Botswana," 260.

[63] Republic of Botswana, *National Assembly Official Report (Hansard 22): Part 2* (Gaborone, 1987), 189.

[64] *Botswana Daily News*, November 28, 1967, 2. Also quoted in Gossett, "The Civil Service in Botswana," 273. Many members and expatriates fondly remember this lecture as "when the president gave them hell."

[65] "Specially elected" is a euphemism for appointed members of the National Assembly by the ruling party.

[66] Gossett, "The Civil Service in Botswana," 281.

[67] The Directorate of Personnel is part of the Office of the President. It is an extremely important institution that is fully responsible for development and management of public employment.

[68] Hermans, interview.

[69] Gossett, "The Civil Service in Botswana," 285.

[70] Charles Harvey and Steven Lewis, Jr., *Policy Choice and Development Performance in Botswana* (London: Macmillan, 1990), 119.

[71] Ibid., 9.

[72] Henderson, *Seretse Khama*, 47. At one point in the mid-1970s Vice President Masire turned down President Khama's request for a presidential plane. The vice president insisted that the country could not afford such an expenditure. President Khama accepted the decision of his vice president. Several years later the situation changed, and Khama got his plane (Hermans, interview). Another source suggested that one of the reasons that a presidential plane was not an option for a while was security risks. Shortly after independence, the United States government gave a twin engine plane to Botswana. The plane became a white elephant, for Botswana could not afford to maintain it (David Finlay, interview, Romotswa, July 18, 1995).

[73] Michael Stevens, "Aid Management in Botswana: From One to Many Donors," in Charles Harvey, ed., *Papers on the Economy of Botswana* (Gaborone: Macmillan, 1981), 159. See also David Jones, *Aid and Development in Southern Africa: British Aid to Botswana, Lesotho and Swaziland* (London: Croom Helm, 1977).

[74] Stevens, *Aid Management*, 160; Hermans, interview.

[75] Republic of Botswana, *Report of the Ministry of Overseas Development*, 110–11.

[76] Ibid.; see the preface.

[77] Hermans, interview.

[78] The Economic Planning Unit was staffed by two young expatriates, Peter Landell-Mills and Steve Ettinger. P. Landell-Mills, interview, Gaborone, October 1993.

[79] Hermans notes that Vice President Masire was a keen listener. "One of the most valuable institutions he had in those early days was an informal discussion group held fortnightly in the home of the Hermans. All young planning officers from the ministry, who were initially all expatriate (later joined by a few Batswana), will meet in an evening. The vice president will come and sit on the floor. . . . One of these youngsters will lead the discussion (10–15 minutes) on a planning matter and an intensive discussion will then ensue. The vice president participated and there was a great deal of camaraderie. The seriousness of the vice president impressed and enormously encouraged the young planning officers."

[80] The struggle between the old guard in the Ministry of Finance led by Alfred Bebe and the Developmentalists under the wing of the vice president came to a showdown when Landell-Mills was dismissed by the Civil Service Commission for insubordination. This incident became what is known as the Landell-Mills Affair. The president sided with the Civil Service Commission as that was the legal procedure. The president's action created a rift between him and his vice president, as Landell-Mills was the latter's economic adviser. "Masire felt that Seretse had been got at by colonial rearguard and that Seretse had listened to their point of view before considering his" (Henderson, *Seretse Khama*, 41-42).

I am also grateful to Governor Hermans for some of this information.

[81] David Finlay, interview, Romatswa, January 6, 1994.

[82] Stevens, *Aid Management*, 167. See also Republic of Botswana, *Planning Officers Manual* (Gaborone, June 1986).

[83] Isaksen, *Macroeconomic Management*, 35; Ministry of Finance and Development Planning, *Keynote Policy Paper*, 1989; Baledzi Gaolathe, interview, Gaborone, December 14, 1994.

[84] Hermans interview. See also James H. Cobbe, "Minerals in Botswana," in his *Government and Mining in Developing Countries* (Boulder, CO: Westview Press, 1979), chapter 7.

[85] Isaksen, *Macroeconomic Management*, 34. Republic of Botswana, *Planning Officers Manual*. The weekly meeting had its origin in the fortnightly meeting the vice president used to have in the Hermans home. To insure effective compliance with the government's plans, President Khama received regular economic briefing from the vice president and senior officers of the MFDP and then would quiz his ministers regarding the operations in their ministries. He often embarrassed them by seeming to know more about their jobs than they did. Hermans, interview.

[86] Raphaeli, Roumani, and Makellar, *Public Sector Management in Botswana*, 3.

[87] M.P.K. Nwako, interview, Gaborone, March 22, 1994. Republic of Botswana, *Transitional Plan*. Hermans, interview.

[88] Hermans cites an incident that sums up this attitude. On one occasion, S. Mcarthy, an ODA fellow, was not happy with his government-provided housing. "He kept storming into my office throwing tantrums. He kept saying housing was not acceptable, and that he was not willing to live in type 4 housing anymore. My instinct was to say here is your ticket, good-bye. If that is your attitude, you cannot really make a contribution here. Somehow Vice President Masire, who was my minister, heard about it and then called me in, and said, 'Wait a minute! You got to look at this problem in two ways. One is the short-term view, which is these guys come to Botswana and go away, and they have skills which we lack and they may not be perfect, but they are the best we have. The second is the long-term view. If these youngsters all have good experience here, they are going to fan out and stay in the development business and ultimately we

are going to benefit, maybe not as a country but the development business.' My God, he was right! There are 37 of these guys in the World Bank, and they are some of the best. These World Bank employees are now referred to as the 'Botswana mafia.'"

[89] Hermans, interview.

[90] The lesson of the Customs renegotiations was the value of careful prior analysis and contingency planning if the worst scenario became the only option. Hermans notes that both in the case of the Customs Union renegotiation and the negotiation with De Beers over the diamonds the Botswana team was prepared to walk away knowing that their fall-back scenario was not too bad an option.

[91] The team that negotiated with De Beers on behalf of Botswana included Charles Lipton, a Canadian resource economist from UNDP, Martin Maryal, a former management trainee with De Beers who had fallen out with the diamond giant. The latter provided extremely valuable information to Botswana, such as what would happen if Botswana decided not to sell its diamonds through the Central Selling Organization. As a result of the work of this group, led by Hermans as permanent secretary of MFDP, Botswana was ready to withdraw from the negotiation if terms of the final agreement were not favorable. In fact, Oppenheimer was so furious about the role of Maryal that he threatened to break off the negotiations if Maryal remained a member of the Botswana team. Hermans, interview.

[92] Beledzi Gaolathe, the former president of MFDP for 17 years, noted that the government of Botswana controlled the terms of reference and controlled the process and therefore was not worried that those it hired to do a job would not deliver. If there was a problem with an employee not meeting the terms of the contract, then it simply terminated the agreement. The contracting and consulting system worked very well, and the government of Botswana took ownership of the products. Interview, December 15, 1994.

[93] Botswana was not a Peace Corps recipient country, but it persisted in its request for such status. A U.S. senator's administrative assistant, who was Hermans's brother-in-law, helped Botswana achieve this status. The assistant urged his senator to speak in support of Botswana's request. The senator agreed, and the U.S. administration was persuaded to offer Peace Corps assistance to Botswana. Hermans, interview.

[94] Ibid.

[95] Stevens, *Aid Management*, 172; Isaksen, *Macro-Economic Management*, 37 and 51; Raphaeli, Roumani, and Makellar, *Public Sector Management*.

[96] Isaksen, *Macroeconomic Management*.

[97] Isaksen notes that one of the few differences between expatriates and Batswana bureaucrats is that the latter wanted to spend more on development while the former was financially more conservative.

[98] Hermans reported one of the first administrative manuals was produced by Michael Stevens. Such manuals, which govern the routine operations of ministries and employees became the Bible of the Botswana bureaucracy.

[99] Gaolathe, interview. He notes that the strength of the MFDP has declined relatively as more revenues became available.

[100] Andreas Danevad, *Development Planning and the Importance of Democratic Institutions in Botswana: Report 7* (Bergen, Norway: Chr. Michelsen Institute, November 1993). The discussion of the Revised Incomes policy draws heavily from Danevad.

[101] Ibid., 106.

[102] Republic of Botswana, *National Policy on Incomes, Employment, Prices and Profits: Government Paper No. 2* (Gaborone: Government Printer, 1972), 5.

[103] Danevad, *Development and Planning*, 108.

[104] Ibid.

[105] Ibid., 108.

[106] Danevad, *Development and Planning*, 111–113.

[107] Ibid., 113.

[108] Ibid., 110.

[109] Kenneth Good, "At the Ends of the Ladder: Radical Inequalities in Botswana," *Journal of Modern African Studies* 31, 2 (1993): 203–230.

[110] Molutsi, "Social Stratification and Inequality in Botswana."

[111] Ministry of Finance and Development Planning, *Keynote Policy Paper* (Gaborone, 1989).

[112] Danevad, *Development and Planning*, chapter 7.

[113] Gaolathe, interview.

[114] Ibid.

[115] One of the hallmarks of Botswana's success is the integration of development plans with annual budgets.

[116] Baledzi, interview.

[117] Quoted in Raphaeli, Roumani, and Makellar, *Public Sector Management*, 16.

[118] This does not mean that more systematic ways of eluding the bite of the last are not available. For instance, the National Development Bank was made to write off loans to all farmers after a long and devastating drought. Many have argued that this benefited the rich, mostly civil servants and politicians who had most of the loans. The write-off of these loans was done in this guise of helping poor and small farmers. See Government of Botswana, *Report of the Presidential Commission of Inquiry into the Operation of the Botswana Housing Corporation* (Gaborone, 1992); Government of Botswana, *Report of the Presidential Commission on the Inquiry into the Land Problems in Mogodishane and Other Peri-Urban Villages* (Gaborone, 1991). See *Mmegi*, various issues.

[119] Raphaeli, Roumani, and Makellar, *Public Sector Management*, 10.

4

Translating Class Unity and Autonomy into an Effective Institution: The Botswana Meat Commission

INTRODUCTION

African state institutions, and particularly agricultural parastatals, are said to represent all that is wrong with African societies. These institutions' monopolistic power and financial unaccountability have led to constant and tremendous financial losses that the public must shoulder. In addition, these institutions excessively exploit producers and consumers alike. Africa's fortunes have declined as a result of these institutions' inefficient economic operations and their alienation of producers. They have also politically illegitimized those who command state power.

The dominant literature claims that the privatization of public enterprises and the introduction of multiparty elections will provide a sounder economic and political foundation for the future. Whether the neoliberal doctrine will alter the continent's fortunes is questionable,[1] particularly considering the reasons that multipartism became unsustainable and that public support shifted away from this system in the 1960s. Furthermore, most Africans have had enough of unaccountable political, bureaucratic, and military leaders and unproductive and inefficiently run economies. Despite their dissatisfaction with the old leaders and system, most Africans have quickly realized that the "democratic" regimes that have replaced the old guard in the last decade lack autonomous policy-making capacity.[2] The "democratic" regimes' lack of autonomy is due to their subservience to the dictates of international capital and Western states.

Equating public enterprises with economic and political decay fails to account for the successful experience of such institutions in Botswana since independence.[3] Botswana's example shows that public enterprises can play a critical role in partially overcoming underdevelopment in former colonial societies. Botswana did not have a dynamic private or public sector to stimulate its economy after independence. The new government had but two "choices": either inviting racist South Africa capital to march across the border and reinforce Botswana's status as a Bantustan or establish public enterprises to develop basic infrastructure and provide essential services. The leaders' choice was obvious. They created public enterprises that still dominate the economy. Such enterprises are responsible for water, communications, housing, development, meat, and so forth.

Nearly 30 years of operations have proven the merit of the leaders' choice. However, two critical questions remain. Why have Botswana's parastatals remained relatively effective without burdening the government and the public? And why have they not induced political degeneration? The answer is embedded in Botswana's real politic. Chapter 3 demonstrated that Botswana's dominant political/economic elite were largely the same. Nearly all members of the parliament were large or medium-sized cattle owners who shared a common social and educational background. Furthermore, they have had a patron-client relationship with the majority of rural Batswana. The material basis of this relation is/was in the ownership and use of cattle and water resources. The peasantariat's disorganization and illiteracy reinforced their material dependency. Consequently, the rural population has had little voice in determining economic development, including livestock policy. The BDP's hegemony and the lack of a credible national opposition political party, until 1994, sealed the livestock industry's economic fate. The livestock owning dominant class, via the BDP government, have had relatively free reign in fashioning livestock development policy.[4]

The dominant class was united in its view about further commoditization of cattle and land resources. The unity of this class and its organic but relative autonomy from the peasantariat provided a "sound" political basis for the establishment of the Botswana Meat Commission. The BDP leadership were conscious of the need to develop a competent bureaucracy that could translate policy into substance, without endangering the elite-peasantariat relationship. Consequently, the BMC's mandate was intended to ensure the livestock project's commercial sustainability:

> It shall be the duty of the Commission so to exercise its functions and conduct its business as to ensure, taking one year with another, that its

revenues are sufficient to enable the Commission to meet the outgoings of the Commission properly chargeable to revenue account in terms of section 14 and to make the provision which the Commission is required to make in terms of sections 15 and 16.[5]

The leadership knew it needed effective and accountable management. It also recognized the need to guard its collective interest from the particularistic interventions of the group's individual members.[6] Finally, the BDP leaders were also cognizant of the political importance of BMC and the livestock industry. A well-managed industry, which minimized crude and visible transfer of surplus from poor livestock owners, meant that accumulation did not immediately lead to massive alienation of the rural population. Thus, the BDP retained the loyalty of the peasantariat.[7]

Under relatively autonomous management, accountable to the commission and ultimately the president, the BMC fulfilled its mandate. The BMC expanded its production facilities. Since then it has upheld stringent quality controls over beef processing to meet the unusually high standards demanded of nonmember exporters by European Economic Community, now the European Union (EU).[8] Three factors that prove BMC's superior performance are (a) it has not lost a single shipment of beef exports in the last thirty-one years; (b) it offers producers relatively good prices; and (c) it is willing to guarantee all producers a market during times of distress, such as drought. Moreover, the Ministry of Agriculture's Animal Health and Production Department, a close affiliate of BMC, has kept the country disease-free (particularly from foot and mouth disease) since 1980. Finally, BMC has managed its operations without incurring constant losses within the bounds of its enabling legislation.

The principal argument of this chapter is that BMC has delivered the services necessary to maintain patterns of accumulation in the livestock industry without wrecking the public purse, at least in the short run, or alienating the majority of small producers. In the process, the ruling class has demonstrated its ability to create a nurturing political climate, facilitating BMC'c development as an effective and legitimate national institution.[9] Finally, BMC has remained reasonably free from corruption and unsystematic accumulation. This means that many of the supposedly "internal" factors that writers cite as the main causes of economic stagnation and underdevelopment in Africa were either unimportant in Botswana or have been brought under control. Moreover, BMC's success reveals that the problem is not public enterprises per se, but the political economic context in which they are grounded.

This chapter consists of three topics: (1) the commoditization of cattle, land, and water resources; (2) the BMC's development and its role in the livestock industry; and (3) a summary of research findings and examination of their implication for the debate about the role of public institutions in African development.

THE COMMODITIZATION OF CATTLE

The British Protectorate's declaration of Bechuanaland in 1885 formally connected the autonomous Tswana societies to the emerging commodity-based southern African regional political economy. Cattle from Tswana societies were not a major trade item prior to colonization. King Khama, influenced by Christian teachings, "disowned" all of his cattle that were on loan. Other Tswana chiefs followed his lead. The chiefs, however, continued to claim all unclaimed stray cattle (matimela) and other forms of tribute. Moreover, they used their offices to build the largest herds in their respective areas. As a result of these acts, cattle became private property. The dominant class used serf labor to attend their herds. Two factors contributed to the steady and uneven commoditization of cattle, labor, water, and land resources. These were the imposition of colonial taxes and the population's need for cash to access new imported commodities.[10] The absence of domestic markets for cattle, until the mid-1950s, led to its exportation to regional markets in South and Central Africa (Table 4.1). Botswana exported cattle on the hoof until the permanent establishment of an abattoir in the southeastern town of Lobatse in 1954.[11]

A slower process of commercialization of both water and land, albeit in different and complex ways accompanied the commercialization and privatization of cattle ownership.[12] Tswana societies used water and land communally. Thus, the movement towards privatizing water sources and, consequently, grazing land resulted in conflicts over individual and group rights to these essential resources.[13]

Botswana has an arid, and semiarid climate. Surface water sources are scarce, particularly during the long winter. Consequently, Batswana and their livestock traditionally migrated seasonally to tap different water sources and range land. Communities also moved in search of fodder and safety during times of distress. These communal grazing and water resources were open to all members of the community. These patterns of ownership and use of resources changed with the development of more permanent water sources for livestock and human use in the 1930s. Various Tswana chiefs voiced the need for such developments to ameliorate the effects of drought, a permanent feature of the Tswana environment. They encouraged Protectorate authorities to fund borehole development using colonial resources. The colonial authorities began drilling schemes in the early 1930 to exploit ground water. Borehole development in many parts of the protectorate partially reduced the effect of drought on livestock. Furthermore, the introduction and

Table 4.1 Livestock and Beef Sold in and Outside Botswana, 1911–1980

Year	Export/Lobatse	Local Consumption	Total Cattle Population (%)
1911–12	14,132		
1912–13	15,673		
1915–16	17,664		
1916–17	18,876		
1981–19	26,571		
1919–20	23,569		
1920–21	32,450		
1921–22	25,884		
1922–23	26,046		
1923–24	32,706		
1924–25	25,162		
1925–26	34,434		
1926–27	31,889		
1927	19,870		
1928	30,060		
1929	30,673		
1930	28,177		
1931	26,209		
1932	25,103		
1933	715		
1934	2,871		
1935	24,577		
1936	19,022		
1937	8,515		
1938	21,570		
1939	24,461		
1940	33,928		
1941	33,009		
1942	44,933		
1943	42,931		
1944	35,159		
1945	42,024		
1946	46,994		
1947	53,983		
1948	42,403		

Table 4.1 Livestock and Beef Sold in and Outside Botswana, 1911–1980, *cont.*

Year	Export/Lobatse	Local Consumption	Total Cattle Population (%)
1949	70,403		
1950	70,169		
1951	77,995		
1952	73,168		
1953	71,116	7,546	6.8
1954	74,603	3,803	7.1
1955	71,895	6,503	6.3
1956	70,534	8,051	6.1
1957	64,425	6,908	5.4
1958	69,026	9,707	6.0
1959	97,115	13,297	8.4
1960	85,150	13,100	7.7
1961	89,208	12,312	7.7
1962	109,029	NA	—
1963	127,467	12,755	10.3
1964	123,051	12,721	10.1
1965	155,982	23,000	16.3
1966	148,654	17,000	13.4
1967	95,902	18,000	7.6
1968	103,776	20,000	7.3
1969	93,074	23,000	6.0
1970	128,199	26,000	7.6
1971	167,430	31,000	9.5
1972	156,510	40,000	9.0
1973	209,443	34,000	11.4
1974	186,041	38,000	10.0
1975	188,440	42,000	9.7
1976	211,987	50,000	10.4
1977	196,850	50,000	9.3
1978	149,346	70,000	7.6
1979	229,000	61,000	10.2
1980	140,783	86,000	7.8

Source: M. Hubbard, "Botswana and the International Beef Trade, 1900–1981," Ph.D. thesis, Sussex University, 1983, Table A1. See also M. Hubbard, *Agricultural Exports and Economic Growth: A Study of the Botswana Beef Industry* (London, 1986).

permanent use of the boreholes induced social and environmental problems that are yet to be resolved.[14]

The borehole water schemes, unlike traditional communal resources, were not accessible to all members of the community.[15] The Protectorate authorities, collaborating with the chiefs, funded boreholes through groups of livestock owners called syndicates. The authorities paid for developing the boreholes, while these syndicates were expected to cover the operating costs of these facilitates. The syndicates developed into a hierarchical social order. Its members occupied the pinnacle of a clientist order. These syndicates' clients consisted of two groups. The first group consisted of dependents and related families of original syndicate members. The herds of these client families were considered part of the original member's stock. The second group, called *bihari*, of livestock owners were nondependents, who paid rent to secure borehole access. This rent subsidized many of the borehole operating costs.

The syndicate organizations' borehole development changed access to and use of water and range land resources while maintaining an aura of traditional Tswana communal relations. The British colonial administration believed syndicates were a modern organization through which traditional and "reactionary" beliefs and behaviors could be overcome. The original members of the syndicates were akin to the infamous "progressive" farmers who became vehicles for modernization. By contrast, the chiefs and other Tswana leaders propagated the notion that the syndicates were simply an extended version of traditional communal order. However, the dominant class realized the syndicate framework provided an opportunity for privatizing access to what had been communal property. The size of syndicate membership has fluctuated since their introduction, leading to changes in who gained or lost access to the boreholes. As operating and maintenance costs that is, fuel, increased significantly in recent years, so did belief in and acceptance of private ownership of resources. This led to more clients and bihari losing their privileges. The increasing marginalization of such former syndicate members and private appropriation of communal resources generated intense conflicts in the countryside.

The creation of permanent water sources controlled by syndicates meant that members did not have to migrate each season. Seasonal migration was a central feature of traditional land use and resource management system. However, today many continue to move their livestock away from the borehole during the rainy season to relieve the pressure on borehole vicinity. A new state law that bars against drilling new wells within five miles of existing boreholes further enhances the borehole areas' exclusivity. This edict virtually gave the syndicate direct control of this five-mile area around the borehole. The prevailing practice of free range herding slowed down the push towards privatization of communal resources until the introduction of

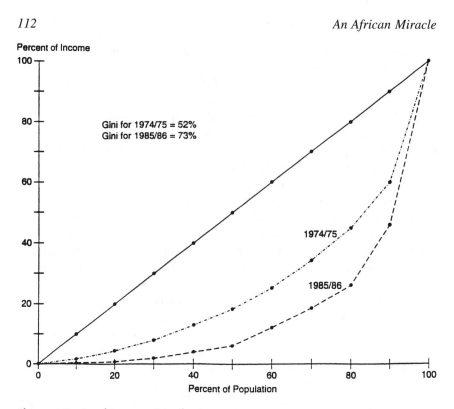

Figure 4.1   Rural Income Distribution in Botswana, 1974–1975 and 1985–1986
Source: Government of Botswana, *The Rural Income Distribution Survey*, 1974–75; Bank of
Botswana, *Report on the Rural Economic Survey, 1986*, Gaborone.

the Tribal Grazing Land Policy (TGLP) in 1975.[16] The community's resistance has partially frustrated the state's and the elite's privatization and commercialization agenda (via TGLP). Despite rural communities' opposition to this agenda, the wealthy continue to monopolize range and water resources through controlling boreholes. Small and medium-sized traditional livestock owners and the large proportion of poor rural inhabitants vigorously object to further concentration of resources in the hands of the elite.

The increasing commoditization of livestock and water resources further exacerbated inequality in Botswana. White settlers took some prime range land in Ghanzi (western Botswana) and the Tuli block in the east of the country. Tswana elite members purchased Crownlands.[17] Access to rural resources is important for the well-being of the population since most live in the countryside. Nearly 45 percent of the rural households do not own cattle, resulting in a highly skewed rural income distribution (Figure 4.1).[18] Furthermore, cattle distribution among owners indicates that inequality has increased. For example, 71.1, 74.4, and 76.2 percent of the poorest (traditional) owners accounted for only 37.3, 27.9, and 29.6 percent of the traditional herd respectively in 1979, 1984 and 1990, while the wealthiest 14 percent of traditional herd owners held 58.1 percent of the herd.[19] In 1993, 91.7 percent of the poorest owners accounted for 37 percent of the traditional herd while the wealthiest 2.4 percent held 39.4 percent.[20]

THE FORMATION AND THE DEVELOPMENT OF BMC

Bechuanaland Protectorate exported livestock to regional markets in South and Central Africa until the late 1950s, when beef exports fully replaced livestock exports. The colonial government attempted to establish an abattoir in the territory as early as 1920. The project, however, had to wait for a major imperial initiative to become a reality. The Colonial Development Corporation's (CDC) inauguration in 1947 served as that imperial initiative. The CDC's function was:

> to initiate, finance and operate projects for agricultural or other development in the colonial empire. [The] need for such expansion of colonial production is of course very much in public mind at this moment owing to the prospect of continuing shortages of certain commodities and increasing difficulty in obtaining adequate supplies of dollars for the purchase of food and raw materials from America. . . . The colonies are almost uniformly in need of further capital investment just as much as the UK and the world at large is in need of increased production of main colonial commodities.[21]

The CDC was a godsend opportunity for the financially starved Protectorate administration. The administration immediately began to plan projects that could tap the CDC's capital and the territory's agricultural resources. Their first choice was a meat-maize complex. This complex, as envisaged by the administration, was to consist of an abattoir capable of processing 70,000 head of cattle annually. It would also include ranching and farming schemes. The town of Lobatse in southeast Botswana was selected as the site of the abattoir. As soon as the project was announced, the old livestock trading establishment and northern livestock farmers began to resist because of the abattoir's location. The project went through difficult birth pains and suffered from CDC's managerial blunders. The abattoir opened in 1954, two years behind schedule. The CDC dropped the "maize" farming and ranching schemes after an unsuccessful start. Two years after the abattoir opened, demand for Protectorate beef in the regional market declined.[22]

The fortuitous and timely opening of the British market for beef produced in the colonies saved the abattoir. Despite the British export market's opening, CDC project's managerial and marketing problems were far from over. By 1958, the administration considered "nationalizing" the industry. The CDC and the colonial government took the first step toward nationalization when they agreed to a new arrangement. The CDC retained the abattoirs' management. Both were vested in the ownership of the project. The CDC's management contract was to expire in ten years. After this the government would take over the entire operation. This agreement led to the creation of Bechuanaland Abattoirs Ltd.

The managerial issue was not the only problem facing the Lobatse-based operation. The northern producers were not happy with the increased cost of sending their cattle to the far southeastern end of the Protectorate. They demanded a second abattoir in Francistown. The Northerner (Ngwato) producers were a powerful force since they held nearly two-thirds of the territorial cattle. The Protectorate Administration formed an alliance with Seretse Khama. After the death of his uncle, Tshekedi Khama, Seretse was the most prominent African politician in the Protectorate. He was also the Ngwato community's "head" and an influential member of the Livestock Industry Advisory Board. Together, the Protectorate administration and Seretse Khama put the resistance of the north to an end. This signaled the emergence of a coalition between the administration and large African cattle producers.[23] As the territory moved toward independence, Seretse Khama and his newly formed BDP, which the administration supported, used the abattoir's nationalization and fair cattle prices as their main political slogan.[24] It is important to note that all the leading members of the BDP were large cattle owners. The industry was nationalized, and the BMC was established in 1966, the year of the country's independence.

The BMC is a non–profit making enterprise. Its purpose is to serve the industry's interest. It had been the sole exporter of meat and its by-products from Botswana. The commission is affiliated with, but autonomous from, the Ministry of Agriculture and reports directly to the president of the Republic. The president appoints the chairman and all commissioners and can affect policy change and veto any Commission decision.[25] Furthermore, the commission's autonomy meant that resources will not be extracted from the industry to benefit other sectors. In fact, the converse of this relationship has been the case. The commission manages the industry primarily for its stake holders' benefit.[26]

Large cattle owners, senior civil servants many of whom have their own herds, cattle owning businessmen and politicians dominate the commission (Table 4.2). Of the 52 commissioners who served as the policy-making body of BMC since its formation until 1994, 24 members were/are large and medium cattle producers, 21 were senior civil servants, 11 were businessmen, 4 were politicians, and only 1 member represented small traditional producers. Moreover, the first chairman of the commission, who was appointed in 1968, was the retired chairman of Barclays Bank, South Africa.

Table 4.2 Members of the Botswana Meat Commission

Commissioner	Profession	Cattle owner/herd size
1	Politician	Large
2	Colonial officer	NA
3	CDC	NA
4	Businessman	Large
5	Businessman	Large
6	NK	Small/Medium
7	NK	Medium
8	Businessman	Medium
9	Civil servant	Medium
10	Civil servant	NA
11	Banker	Large
12	NK	Large
13	NK	Small
14	NK	Medium
15	Politician	Small
16	Civil servant	NA
18	CDC	NA
19	Civil servant	NA
20	NK	Large
21	NK	Medium
22	Civil servant	Medium
23	Civil servant	NA
24	CDC	NA
25	Civil servant	NA
26	Civil servant	NA
27	Businessman	Very Large
28	Politician	Large
29	Businessman	NA
30	NK	Large
31	Businessman	Small
32	Civil servant	NA
33	Civil servant	NA
34	Civil servant	Medium
35	Civil servant	NA
36	Civil servant	Small
37	Civil servant	NA
38	Businessman	Large
39	Nurse/co-op	Small
40	Businessman	Medium

Table 4.2   Members of the Botswana Meat Commission, *cont.*

Commissioner	Profession	Cattle owner/herd size
41	Businessman	Large
42	Civil servant	NA
43	Businessman	Large
44	Civil servant	Small
45	Businessman	Medium
46	Politician	Medium
48	Civil servant	Medium
49	Civil servant	NA
50	Civil servant	NA
51	Civil servant	Medium
52	Businessman	Small

Source: David Finlay, Gaborone, interview, November 22, 1993. Defining large, medium and small cattle owners is rather problematic. However, anyone with less than 40 head of cattle is considered to be a poor or small farmer. See J. Solway, "Commercialization and Social Differentiation." Note these numbers add to more than 52 as some commissioners dabbled in more than one professional field. Our sources suggested that small producers as identified in this table are not traditional small producers, who usually own less than 40 head of cattle. The exception to this is the nurse who represented small traditional producers. Mrs. Eva Moagi, interview, Gaborone, December 15, 1993. Mrs. Moagi was a nurse by profession who also represented small traditional farmers in the commission. She was one of the commissioners for three terms of three years each. NA = Not available; NK = Not known.

He owned one of Botswana's largest ranches.[27] The vice chairman was also a freeholder with a large cattle interest. Most important of all, the president of the republic, reputed to control around 18,000 head herd, was the largest cattle owner in the country.[28] The commission's clear mandate and its autonomy from "politics" was coupled with management competence. Many senior technicians and managers were expatriates long after independence, although many young and well trained Batswana slowly but steadily joined the professional cadre's ranks.

Although large producers and other members of the dominant class dominated the BMC, policy makers recognized that a well-managed BMC could also benefit small producers. This is obviously important to the BDP government, which depends on the support of the majority of Batswana voters who are rural dwellers.[29] Most of these voters are small and indigent cattle producers. The upshot has been that a well-managed BMC has nurtured the collective interest of the dominant strata and provided services to many small producers. Including indigent cattle owners in the fold did not reduce existing patterns of inequality. It simply modernized inequality.[30] This strategy helped keep the numerically superior small producers "loyal" to the BDP, allowing the BDP regime to remain in power without resorting to naked coercion.

ECONOMIC OPERATION OF BMC

Despite difficulties, notably drought, the BMC has maintained, expanded, and defended the export markets for its products. It had to bring the full weight of the government's diplomatic skills to bear to obtain and retain its access to the precious EEC market. This task required President Khama to intervene and lobby by visiting Brussels. The BMC's success in sustaining the industry's health in increasingly tough markets to access depended on its ability to properly manage its domestic production operation.

The BMC expanded its facilities' capacity to take advantage of its growing market. Balefi Tsie notes that "by the middle 1970s BMC's throughput had exceeded its slaughter capacity by nearly 50%, i.e. 120,000 to 209,000."[31] The Lobatse abattoir remained the only one of its kind in the country until 1983, when a small regional facility was built in Maun. Nine years later, the third, and larger, abattoir was established in Francistown (Map 4.1). BMC completely paid for the Francistown abattoir. The cost of this abattoir was 54 million pula, half of which came from BMC's development reserve. The other half was a loan from local commercial banks. These two abattoirs were important additions. Their establishment immediately reduced producers' transport costs in those regions who had to transport their livestock to the distant abattoir in Lobatse. In addition to these physical improvements, the BMC invested in other profitable enterprises, notably the ownership of a Cayman Islands insurance company. This insurance company saves the BMC £150,000 annually through self-insurance.

BMC increased the number of animals processed, the cattle throughput, from about 150,000 head in 1966 to the peak of 239,293 head in 1984. Net sales grew to over 222 million pula in 1994. Table 4.3 shows BMC's net sales. The advantages of having such high-grade abattoirs in a livestock-based economy include the facts that producers are assured of a safe and reliable market and that animal prices are stable since the BMC is mandated to buy whatever becomes available. This approach means that producers do not suffer as badly as their counterparts in other semiarid African countries.

The BMC, unlike other similar parastatal institutions in Africa, remains sensitive to the producers' needs. Their cattle prices kept pace with international market price trends, particularly the EEC's very high prices. The BMC producer prices increased from a base price of 100 in 1960 to 645 in 1980, reflecting the lucrative EEC market. The upward trend in producer prices continued into the 1990s although at a slower pace.[32] Despite such income growth, small producers constantly complain about BMC's prices.[33] How-

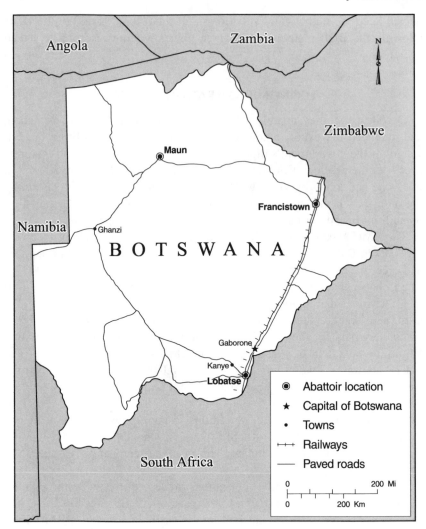

Map 4.1   Botswana Map Showing Sites of the Three Abattoirs

ever, when questioned further, the small producers' concern appeared to be that their stock rarely get a super grade in BMC standards. This grade is assigned to high-quality, heavy stock.

In addition to consistently adjusting the prices it pays its cattle suppliers, the BMC has also established a stabilization fund. This helps the commission during deficit years. Botswana law prohibits the BMC from being in a deficit for more than one year or from depending on the state for annual subsidies in order to balance its books. Likewise, it is also legally forbidden

Table 4.3   BMC Cattle Throughput and Net Sales, 1966–1994 (P 000)

Year	Throughput	Net Sales*
1966	132,232	6,805
1967	88,535	11,120
1968	103,776	10,593
1969	93,074	9,334
1970	127,317	11,915
1971	167,180	14,962
1972	156,510	19,547
1973	209,443	31,297
1974	186,041	34,711
1975	188,440	33,889
1976	212,000	44,814
1977	197,000	42,042
1978	149,000	31,327
1979	228,961	75,893
1980	140,783	39,847
1981	202,001	71,186
1982	237,135	87,549
1983	233,900	96,286
1984 **	239,283	96,745
1985	193,843	73,220
1986	160,000	128,535
1987	112,498	120,288
1988	140,000	95,380
1989	134,558	146,789
1990	146,729 @	159,791
1991	158,457	161,302
1992	213,635	212,858
1993	181,000 @	172,987
1994	158,000	222,279

* Net sales amounts were recorded in RSA rands from 1966 to 1975. From 1976 to the present, all sales have been negotiated and recorded in Botswana pula.

** 1984 recorded the highest kill but a low cold dressed weight because of the severity of the drought, which reduced the average cattle weight.

@ Approximate figures drawn from graphs.

Source: Botswana Meat Commission, *Annual Reports* (Gaborone, 1966–1994).

Table 4.4 BMC Financial Operations, 1966–1994 (P 000)

Year	Surplus*	Bonus	Tax Remission	
1966	491	491	0	
1967	614	614	0	
1968	1,132	1,120	0	
1969	781	781	0	
1970	1,012	1,000	0	
1971	1,909	1,899	0	
1972	3,694	3,656	0	
1973	6,546	6,492	0	
1974	2,433	2,304	0	
1975	922	0	0	
1976	1,533	1,502	0	
1977	- 1,022	0	0	
1978	—**	0	0	
1979	6,388	6,388	0	
1980	- 38	0	0	
1981	3,748	3,540	0	
1982	8,969	8,350	0	
1983	5,740	5,740	0	
1984	1,866	0	0	
1985	10,388	8,489	0	
1986	9,130	8,797	0	
1987	9,725	9,725	0	
1988	10,374	9,519	0	
1989	13,289	10,121	239	
1990	9,328	4,725	191	
1991	6,660	0	10,361	(50%)
1992	17,039	17,039	6,796	(50%)
1993	5,479	5,479	9,400	(50%)
1994	23,790	23,790	11,440	(50%)

* Net surplus is calculated after all production and contingency program costs are deducted from total revenues. No net surplus means no bonus as shown in 1978.

** There was a net surplus of 688, of which 349 was put into capital reserves, and 339 was transferred to stabilization fund.

Source: Botswana Meat Commission, *Annual Reports* (Gaborone, 1966-1994).

from making and keeping a profit. The commission must return all excess surplus funds to farmers after it has deducted all its operating cost and necessary reserves from its income. Producers received bonuses 22 out of the last 27 years, a remarkable record (Table 4.4). In addition to increasing producer prices, the commission has also defended the industry's interest by convincing the government to hold down taxes to allow producer prices to increase at a healthy rate.

> Taxation of income from cattle was set on a lenient basis by the Income Tax Act of 1973 and made even more so by the amending Act of 1979. . . . The leniency of farming taxation lies not in the rates charged on taxable income (those being the same for all other individual or companies) but in the generosity of deductions allowed.[34]

The commission's efforts paid off in the form of a 50 percent tax remission in 1991, 1992, 1993, and 1994. In addition to this tax remission, the government spends substantially more money on the industry than it receives from it. The government spends nearly 60 million pula ($1 = 2 pula in 1992) a year on the industry (i.e., animal health) while it extracts, through taxes, only 20 to 30 million pula.[35] Tsie notes the other ways the state invests in cattle which the BMC does not pay for, but that benefits the cattle elite:

> The post-colonial state has also put the cattle industry on a sound footing by securing a loan (11 million Pula) from the EC for the erection of a vaccine factory (BVI). The provision of free vaccines, subsidized cattle-feed, a bull subsidy scheme and the erection of 5,000 kilometres of cordon fence in several parts of the country all reveal how massive state intervention has been in the sphere of cattle production. . . . state intervention occurs under the auspices of a state dominated by cattle owners. The manner in which the cattle industry has become a preserve of accumulation by large cattle owners was reflected in the intensive opposition mounted by MPs in 1987 when the Company Tax rate was raised from 35% to 40%.[36]

The government is able to generously support the industry with the availability of revenues from diamond exports. Whether it will be able to maintain this transfer of resources in the future will depend on the size of the royalties and the electoral pressure on the BDP. Transferring resources from the state to the private sector occurred even before the government decided to remit 50 percent of BMC's tax liabilities in 1990–1991, 1991–92, and 1993–94.

The transfer of resources from the state sector to cattle producers is symbolic of the economic centrality of livestock to the majority of the Botswana

Photo 4.1. Cattle.   The mainstay of rural livelihoods is very inequitably distributed among the population.

population, and this group's political power. The state's rationale for this
generosity may be due to its intention to keep as many people in the rural
areas earning income from their stock in the absence of industrial and services employment in the urban areas.[37] The industry's privileged position in
the economy made it an attractive investment avenue for the local population, particularly those with excess cash, such as senior civil servants.[38] The
latter's increased investment in the industry has further reinforced the
industry's political and economic clout. This investment has strengthened
an elite alliance between well-paid civil servants, commercial farmers, and
large traditional farmers.

The transfer of public wealth to the livestock industry is not shared equitably among livestock producers. Three ways exist in which poor, traditional producers gained less than medium or larger traditional and commercial producers. First, marketing of livestock was/is one mechanism through
which smaller producers receive less for their livestock. For example, BMC
set the price it paid suppliers at the beginning of the season at a level that
was relatively low to insure that it covered all of its costs, and without creating disincentives for farmers. If there was a surplus in its coffers at the
end of the year, then BMC would pay bonuses to suppliers who directly
sold livestock to it. The rub is, until recently, the marketing system was
organized and managed in such a way that a producer needed to get a quota

Photo 4.2. BMC. The well-managed facilities made it the most profitable parastatal of its kind in the continent.

from BMC to deliver a certain number of animals to one of its abattoirs on a particular date. To obtain a quota, a producer needed to own at least 40 head of livestock. Since most producers owned less than this number, they had to sell their stock to traders, other larger farmers or agents.[39] These intermediaries received the BMC bonus at year's end. This system generated such a political heat that the president forced the commission to abandon the system. The commission introduced a new quarterly method of setting producer prices in order to adjust prices more quickly. "Producer prices were increased by 11% at the beginning of the year. In August 1993 seasonal producer prices were introduced, which with upward adjustment of higher grades resulted in another price increase. . . . This change was introduced in order to align producer prices with external markets."[40] Moreover, the BMC abandoned the rigid quota system, giving small producers greater access to BMC. Despite these important changes, the number of traditional farmers selling directly to BMC has declined since 1979 (Table 4.5). Currently, more farmers are selling directly to local abattoirs who pay relatively higher prices compared to BMC's prebonus prices.[41]

N. H. Fidzani found that the quarterly pricing system, intended to reward those who sold their stock when it was not in peak condition, does not help

Table 4.5 Ratio of Cattle Sold to Different Buyers, 1981–1993

	Traditional		Commercial	
	BMC	BMC/Other	BMC	BMC/Other
1981	72.8	7		
1982	68.2	5.1		
1983	70.9	5.3	29.6	46.5
1984	55.0	24.2	60.3	17.3
1985	67.1	9.9	33.5	62.5
1986	69.6	6.0	60.0	15.5
1987	51.7	19.8	30.3	57.9
1988	65.5	10.1	34.6	44.0
1989	58.8	13.0	34.6	44.0
1990	58.5	11.1	28.7	39.0
1993	29.9	21.9	10.8	11.1

Source: Ministry of Agriculture, *Annual Agricultural Statistics* (Gaborone, 1981–1990 and 1993).

small producers. Indigent farmers are unable to take advantage of this price structure as they need the bull for tilling their fields when prices are high, in October through December. During the next high price period, January to February, the animals are recovering from the weight they lost during plowing.[42]

The second way small producers lose is through the regressive livestock tax system. The BMC collects a fixed tax from every head it purchases. A small producer who sells only two beasts per year pays as much per head as those who sell several hundred annually. This money is used to develop the industry, especially animal health. Under this system larger producers gain significantly more than small producers.[43] Third, small producers' stock does not earn high prices from BMC, as they are often lightweight.[44] This is so for three reasons: (a) poor cattle producers cannot afford to get the feed necessary to fatten their stock; (b) indigent producers cannot grow the quantity of fodder needed for such purposes; and (c) this group cannot get loans from banks to invest in improving their stock as they lack collateral. Since poor traditional farmers keep their cattle in communal lands, banks do not accept communal land as collateral. In contrast, commercial farmers and large traditional producers hold title to their land or own other assets that banks accept as collateral. Consequently they have access to the capital necessary for improvements. Finally, the large subsidy to the industry means that large traditional and commercial producers who dominate the livestock market disproportionately capture the benefits of these public investments.

The aforementioned structural conditions reinforce the existing patterns of wealth ownership. Thus, BMC policy strikes a fine balance of reproducing current socioeconomic inequality without unduly alienating and forcibly dispossessing the poor. While not redressing land and cattle ownership inequality inherited from the past, it has included small producers adequately to prevent serious discontent and social upheaval yet. Such policy shows a complicity with structural conditions that severely curtail significant improvements in small producers' economic well-being. Despite such inequality most producers seem to have a stake in the system.

THE LIMITS AND LESSONS OF BMC

This study of the BMC shows how the dominant class manufactured, at least in the livestock industry, the "success model"[45] that has come to symbolize its unique achievements in Africa. The commission has successfully generated capitalist economic development in the livestock industry over the last three decades. Similar bodies in Africa have given way to decay. The commission has maintained the industry's economic health, literally and figuratively, for almost three decades. First, it marshaled the state's diplomatic power and influence to access the lucrative and protected EU market. Once it gained access, it meticulously enforced the community's onerous animal health standards. Secondly, the commission managed its financial affairs without falling into the two main terrible traps of African parastatals: huge losses and heavy extraction of resources from producers. Third, the commission has increased suppliers/producer prices and consistently returned bonuses to producers despite its monopolistic power. Finally, those running the BMC did it in such a way that smaller and more numerous producers, who benefited the least from the industry's development, continued to support the BDP, an organization dominated by large producers and other capitalist interests. The BMC directly contributed to the sustainability of liberal democracy in Botswana while protecting the dominant class's collective interest.

The achievements of BMC in particular and the Botswana state in general contrast sharply with the decay of African public institutions. The crisis of the African state fundamentally represents the incapacity of the African dominant class to create public institutions capable of successfully and systematically imposing a developmental agenda on the African people. The cause of their failure is their inability to recognize that their collective project requires discipline within their own ranks. They need to protect public institutions from themselves and other social groups. The operations of the BMC demonstrate that, unlike their counterparts on the continent, the Botswana dominant class recognized their social position and the necessity of building effective public institutions to insure the reproduction of their common interest. Three elements account for BMC's success. First, conscious, strong, and disciplined leadership led a united dominant class. Second, the political leadership gave BMC a clear mandate. Third, the leadership appointed skilled managers and gave them sufficient autonomy from particularistic and individualist political intervention. At the same time, they held these BMC managers accountable.

BMC's impressive economic accomplishments contributed to the existing political order. However, the BMC "model" has several unique features that limit its usefulness elsewhere. First, the "model's" development presupposes a unified and class-conscious elite whose dominance is unchallenged. Social conditions in most parts of the continent are more complex and fragmented than in Botswana. The dominant class's unity, its small size, and its dominance in the industry facilitated the evolution of uncontroversial and narrowly defined livestock development strategy. Second, a former colonial power's support and the accessibility of the lucrative and heavily protected EU market helped to sustain BMC's strategy. Such favorable circumstances are not necessarily present elsewhere. Some preliminary discussions in BMC and government circles question the industry's future when Lome 4 expires in the year 2,000. The thought of Lome 4 expiring and Botswana losing the EU market are frightening prospects:

> As a result of the new GATT agreement, the Lome Convention, together with the beef protocol, is being challenged. This has very serious implications for our continued access to the European Union markets, which take 70–80% of our beef. Reduced tariffs and the removal of tariff barriers will open up our beef to serious competition from other major world beef producers. Again, I have to re-emphasise the point that unless the Botswana beef industry can remain competitive it is going to have to *face the threat of extinction* in the near future. The removal of tariff barriers and the reduction of tariffs and subsidies mean that only efficient livestock industries will survive.[46] (italics mine).

This prospect is frightening when coupled with the possible liberalization of Botswana's second most important market, South Africa. Third, BMC's livestock development strategy has depended on transferring resources from other state sectors. "Surplus" state revenues generated by diamond exports, made such transfers possible. The recent recession in the industrial capitalist countries has resulted in declining revenues from the diamond exports. This has not yet adversely affected the cattle industry. Moreover, if the EU market becomes liberalized, the state will have to transfer more resources to the industry to keep it competitive. The industry's dependency on resource transfer from other sectors indicates that its strategy is not self-sustaining. As such, states strapped for cash will not be able to pursue this strategy. Fourth, the decline or absence of surplus-generating sectors, whose resources can be shifted to support the cattle industry, will require Botswana to reconfigure its strategy. This change may destabilize the coalition of social classes that kept the BDP regime in power. A breakup of this alliance may undermine the liberal democratic nature of Botswana politics. Whether leaders of the opposition will seize such an opportunity and engage in progressive agrarian reform while building on the BMC's institutional strength is open to speculation.

Despite these limitations, BMC's strategy has at least three major positive lessons for other African dominant classes. First, the dominant class learned through BMC operations that their nurturing of their collective project did not need to completely deprive the subaltern classes of the benefits of good management and economic growth. BMC's second lesson is that the crystallization of dominant-class unity is a double-edged sword. It can enhance discipline within the groups' ranks to nurture the collective project to buttress systematic accumulation. It could also lead to the reproduction of the status quo without major transformation and the creation of new productive sectors. The absence of conscious leadership, keeping the collective project as a development priority in most of Africa led to the failure of parastatals and other public institutions. The BMC shows how parastatals can significantly contribute to economic recovery when set within the appropriate political and managerial conditions.

NOTES

[1] Howard Stein, "Theories of Institutions and Economic Reform in Africa," *World Development* 22, 12 (1994): 1833-1849. See also Stein, ed., *Asian Industrialization and Africa: Studies in Policy Alternatives to Structural Adjustment* (New York: St. Martin's Press, 1995); Abdi Samatar, "Structural Adjustment as Development Strategy: Bananas, Boom and Poverty in Somalia," *Economic Geography* 69, 1 (1993): 25–43.

[2] For an analysis of this see the important contribution by Claude Ake, *Democracy and Development in Africa* (Washington, DC: Brookings Institution, 1996). See also Ato Sekyi-otu, *Fanon's Dialectic of Experience* (Cambridge: Harvard University Press, 1996).

[3] Keith Jefferies, "Public Enterprises and Privatization in Botswana," in Thomas Clarke, ed., *International Privatization Strategies and Practices* (New York: Walter de Gruyter, 1994), 380–396.

[4] The government and the cattle-owning elite it represented attempted to transform communal range and water resources to advance its capitalist project via its Tribal Grazing Land Policy of 1975. This attempt was only partly successful because of the resistance of the poor. See Government of Botswana, *National Policy on Tribal Grazing Land:*

Paper No. 2 of 1975 (Gaborone: Government Printer, 1975); R. H. Hitchcock, "Tradition, Social Justice, and Land Reform in Central Botswana," *Journal of African Law* 24, 1 (1980), 1–34.

[5] Government of Botswana, *The Laws of Botswana*, vol. 10, chapter 74:04 (Gaborone, 1987), rev. ed.

[6] The near absence of corruption and rent seeking during the first twenty years of independence and the discipline of the political leadership is in sharp contrast to more recent years as demonstrated by two recent government commissions. Government of Botswana, *Report of the Presidential Commission of Inquiry into the Operations of the Botswana Housing Corporation* (Gaborone: Government Printer, 1992); and *Report of the Presidential Commission of Inquiry into Land Problems in Mogodishane and Other Peri-Urban Villages* (Gaborone: Government Printer, 1991). See also the critical article by Kenneth Good, "At the End of the Ladder: Radical Inequalities in Botswana," *Journal of Modern African Studies* 31, 2 (1993): 203–230.

[7] This clearly supports Molutsi's thesis, "Social Stratification and Inequality in Botswana, 1950–1985," Ph.D. diss., Oxford University, 1986.

[8] The former executive chairman of BMC, David Finlay, reported that beef exporters to the EEC/EU, such as Botswana, must satisfy stringent standards that member producers are not required to meet (David Finlay, interview, Ramotswa, November 22, 1993).

[9] The viability of this institution depends on the state's ability to maintain its access to the lucrative EEC/EU market. The current agreement, Lome IV, which allows Botswana to export its beef to the EU market at generously subsidized rates, will expire in the year 2000.

[10] Diana Wylie, *A Little God: The Twilight of Patriarchy in a Southern African Chiefdom* (Johannesburg: Witwatersrand University Press, 1990); Pauline Peters, "Cattlemen, Borehole Syndicates and Privatization in the Kgatleng District of Botswana," Ph.D. diss., Boston University, 1983; Jacqueline Solway, "Commercialization and Social Differentiation in a Kalahari Village, Botswana," Ph.D. thesis, University of Toronto, 1986.

[11] A small abattoir was established in Lobatse but did not operate for long.

[12] Soloway, "Commercialization and Social Differentiation."

[13] Peters, "Cattlemen and Borehole Syndicates"; Hitchcock, "Tradition, Social Justice and Land Reform in Central Botswana"; Jack Parson, "Cattle, Class and the State in Rural Botswana," *Journal of Southern African Studies* 7, 2 (1981): 236–255.

[14] This section draws on Pauline Peters's thesis, "Cattlemen, Borehole Syndicates." See also her book, *Dividing the Commons, Politics, Policy, and Culture in Botswana* (Charlottesville: University Press of Virginia, 1994).

[15] I am thankful to Sophie Oldfield for her assistance in the following three paragraphs.

[16] Hitchcock, "Tradition, Social Justice, and Land Reform in Rural Botswana."

[17] John Stephen Morrison, "Botswana's Formative Late Colonial Experience," in S. J. Stedman, ed., *Botswana: The Political Economy of Democratic Development* (Boulder, CO: Lynn Rienner, 1994), 38.

[18] See Government of Botswana, *The Rural Income Distribution Survey in Botswana, 1974–75* (Gaborone, 1975); Bank of Botswana, *Report on the Rural Economic Survey, 1986* (Gaborone, 1986). See also Christopher Colclough and Stephen Macarthy, *The Political Economy of Botswana: A Study of Growth and Distribution* (Oxford: Oxford University Press, 1980); Central Statistical Office, *Population Census Data* (Gaborone, 1991); UNDP, UNICEF, and Republic of Botswana, *Planning for People: A Strategy for Accelerated Human Development in Botswana* (Gaborone: Sygma Publishing 1993);

Isaad Mazonde, *Ranching and Enterprise in Eastern Botswana: A Case Study of Black and White Farmers* (London: Edinburgh University Press, 1994).

[19] The traditional cattleherd accounted for 82 percent of the national herd while the rest is in the hands of commercial farmers. Ministry of Agriculture, *Annual Agricultural Statistics* (Gaborone, 1979, 1984, 1990, 1993).

[20] This trend is also confirmed by a 1993 British study that showed that the proportion of the total and rural populations living under the poverty datum line grew from 45 to 55 percent and from 51 to 64 percent, respectively, betweeen 1974 and 1989. Natural Resources Institute, *National Resources Sector Review, Botswana: A Strategy for ODA Technical Assistance* (Chatham, UK: 1993), 27. See also Robert L. Currey, "Poverty and Mass Unemployment in Mineral-Rich Botswana," *American Journal of Economics and Sociology* 41, 1 (1987): 71–87.

[21] Quoted in Michael Hubbard, "Botswana and International Beef Trade, 1900–1981," Ph.D. diss., Sussex University, 1981, 186. See also Michael Hubbard, *Agricultural Exports and Economic Growth: A Study of the Botswana Beef Industry* (London: Routledge, 1986).

[22] Morrison narrates this crisis and the subsequent political-economic struggles between the colonial administration in the Protectorate and the CDC in his dissertation, "Developmental Optimism and State Failure in Africa: How to Understand Botswana's Relative Success," Ph.D. diss., University of Wisconsin-Madison, 1988.

[23] Hubbard, "Botswana and International Beef Trade," 211. Morrison, "Developmental Optimism and State Failure in Africa."

[24] Hubbard, "Botswana and International Beef Trade," 226.

[25] David Finlay, interview.

[26] Morrison, "Botswana's Formative Late Colonial Experience," 34.

[27] Mr. R. White bought a large ranch in the Ghanzi before being appointed to head BMC. Botswana Meat Commission, *Annual Report, 1968* (Gaborone, 1968): 4–5.

[28] P. Landell-Mills, interview, Gaborone, October 19, 1993.

[29] Parson, *Liberal Democracy and Labor Reserve.* It should be noted that the BDP heavily lost all the major urban areas in the 1994 election and narrowly won some rural areas. The electoral losses of the BDP in urban areas marks the waning of its hegemony on the country's fastest-growing population centers.

[30] See P. Raikes, *Moderning Hunger: Famine, Food Surplus and Farm Policy in the EEC and Africa* (London: James Currey, 1988).

[31] Balefi Tsie, *The Political Economy of Botswana in SADCC* (Harare: SAPES Books, 1995), 246.

[32] Hubbard, "Botswana and the International Beef Trade," 269.

[33] In particular, small producers strongly argue that BMC does not pay them for by-products such as hides, bones, and so on. We interviewed about 25 small communal farmers in the Kanye District in February 1994. The by-products issues was raised in many commission meetings. In response to a question raised by one of the commissioners, Mr. Nielson, who is managing director of the BMC office in London, explained in a memo that farmers' compensation for the so-called "fifth quarter" (hides, etc.) is built into the price they get (O. K. Nielson, Memo [London: Botswana Meat Commission, October 15, 1990]).

[34] Hubbard, "Botswana and the International Beef Trade," 274.

[35] David Finlay, interview. See D. J. Hudson, "The Taxation of Income from Cattle Farming," in Charles Harvey, *Papers on the Economy of Botswana* (London: Macmillan, 1981), 66–81. Although more recent figures are hard to come by, some informed au-

thorities reported to us that the proportion of expenditure revenue has changed a great deal.

[36] Balefi, *The Political Economy of Botswana*, 259–261.

[37] David Finlay, interview; Republic of Botswana, *Government Paper No. 1 of 1973* (Gaborone, 1973).

[38] Hubbard, "Botswana and the International Beef Trade," 264.

[39] Hitchcock notes other problems related to marketing that small producers face: "cattle must be driven long distance to market. During the course of moving the animals, many of them lose condition. A second problem is that many small holders are unable to sell cattle directly to . . . BMC." He also indicates that "there is no question that the majority of rural Botswana have access to relatively few livestock" ("Comment," *Botswana Notes and Records* 19 (1987): 173. See also I. McDonald, *Report on Cattle Marketing in Botswana* (Gaborone, 1982). The development of producer marketing co-ops has helped ameliorate some of the marketing problems. The co-op charges 2.5 to 5 percent of the gross value of the animal.

[40] Botswana Meat Commission, *Annual Report*, 1992–93.

[41] A 1993 study noted that BMC accounted for nearly 71 percent of the national off-take while the remaining portion is split between local abattoirs and domestic slaughter. N. H. Fidzani, "Understanding Cattle Off-take Rates in Botswana," Ph.D. diss., Boston University, 1993, 8–9.

[42] Ibid., 146–47.

[43] Dr. Tsholofelo Diteko, interview, Gaborone, December 12, 1993; Philips Bimbo, interview, December 17, 1993, and August 19, 1994.

[44] Eva Moagi, interview, Gaborone, December 15, 1993. Mrs. Moagi represented small producers in the commission.

[45] Louis Picard, *The Politics of Development in Botswana: A Model of Success?* (Boulder, CO: Lynn Rienner, 1987); N. Raphaeli, J. Roumani, and A. C. MacKellar, *Public Sector Management in Botswana: Lessons in Pragmatism* (Washington, DC: World Bank, 1985).

[46] Botswana Meat Commission, *Annual Report, 1993–94* (Gaborone, 1994), 15. See also Botswana Meat Commission, *Beef Digest*, November 1994. The significance of the EU market subsidy for the Botswana beef was estimated to be 51 million EUC in 1986. Cited in Tsie, *The Political Economy of Botswana*, 267.

5

COLONIAL AND IMPERIAL LEGACY: THE BARRIERS TO INDUSTRIAL DEVELOPMENT IN BOTSWANA

INTRODUCTION

The extraordinary growth of the Newly Industrializing Countries (NICs) in East Asia has been held up in contrast to the stagnation and decline of African economies. This is a flawed comparison as it cites domestic forces (this is known as the *internalist argument*) as the major socioeconomic constraint to development. The World Bank reiterated this argument in its 1989 and 1994 reports on Africa.[1] This chapter shows that these so-called domestic forces were indeed manufactured during the colonial century. A careful reading of Botswana's social and economic history clearly implicates the colonial project in underdeveloping "native" entrepreneurship, education, and other skills. Second, Botswana's integration as a Bantustan into the South African economy has significantly hampered Botswana's industrial development efforts. This developmentalist state's two most important industrial policy instruments—the Botswana Development Corporation and the Financial Assistance Policy—have not been able to overcome the legacy of the past. Consequently, whites, mainly from the South, and Indians who have access to capital still dominate the economy.

The internalist argument claims the free market will induce economic development if African public policy is pragmatic and the state confines its activities to creating an enabling business climate. The hallmark of this literature is to argue that the prospects for economic development would be significantly enhanced had it not been for the state, traditional social, and cultural forces.[2] Advocates of this position often point to the East Asian NICs as a model of what might have been possible in Africa.[3] They suggest that, until the 1960s, African countries like Ghana were as well positioned to industrialize as South Korea, Taiwan, and other NICs. These countries were as underdeveloped as many in the continent.

The underlying objective of this current is to jettison the centrality of the colonial heritage and the postcolonial global context as one of the major defining features of the continent's failure to successfully embark on industrial transformation and capitalist development. Recent writings on East Asian industrialization contradict the internalist thesis's claims, which understate the "The Colonial Origins" of that region's industrialization.[4] As Robert Wade noted:

> Whatever a "typical" underdeveloped country is, Taiwan was clearly not one during the 1950s, contrary to most neoclassical accounts. It had a long experience of fast manufacturing growth, going back to the 1930s, an unusually productive smallholder agriculture, more than average literate population . . . . (108) The development of Taiwan, as well as the two Koreas, has to be understood in the context of Japanese colonialism. . . . A good communication infrastructure was laid down, not for the narrow purpose of extracting some primary raw material, but with the aim of increasing production of smallholder rice and sugar. . . . With respect to industrial development, too the Japanese colonialism differed from others. . . .
>
> During the 1930s, prompted by rising wages in Japan, and the government's plan for war, the administration began to develop in Taiwan such industries as food processing, textiles, plywood, pulp and paper, cement, chemical fertilizers, aluminum and copper refining and ship building. (73–74).[5]

This reference to the legacy of Japanese colonization is not meant to glorify and justify their brutal rule, but to identify the economic structures they put in place and the consequences of that heritage. In addition to building an economic infrastructure, the Japanese colonial state institutionalized an interventionist approach to capitalist development:

> The administration took the role of a strong state in the economy, pushing their development plans forward with legislation and state-backed and-directed financial institutions. If their economic policy was growth-oriented and interventionist, it was also distinctly capitalist, promoting the rights of private property and the growth of private enterprises. . . . A format for business-state relations emerged in which the state played a more prominent role in the economy than was typical even in Meiji Japan.[6]

Although Japanese imperial capital and the state dominated strategic and major sectors of the economy, Japanese colonial law did not systematically bar the colonized from owning and operating commercial and productive assets.[7] When the Japanese withdrew as a result of their defeat, they left behind a productive economic infrastructure and a seasoned, although small, business class. This heritage is qualitatively different from what the European colonial regimes left behind in their African colonies.[8]

Two features distinguish an effective capitalist state from an ineffective one: the state's autonomy from civil society and the creation and existence of a network of relations between key members of the administration and those segments of the capitalist class who have the capacity to create and manage productive enterprises.[9] Peter Evans's embedded autonomy captures this relation. However, it does not explicitly discuss the state's ability to preside over the development agenda and push the business class in the directions it deems beneficial. Alice Amsden more forcefully deals with the state's role in the context of embedded autonomy.[10] Accordingly, the autonomously embedded state simultaneously supports *and* disciplines the capitalist class to advance productive capitalist development.

Dennis McNamara's, Robert Wade's, and Bruce Cumings's work about the colonial origin of new East Asian industrialism clearly marks the critical importance of historical and geographic contexts. The Asian tigers inherited two pivotal elements in economic development: a basic productive economic infrastructure, and state–civil society relations geared to advancing the economic project. Moreover, their inherited social and political context was married to the cold war environment. This environment gave preferential trade arrangements and enormous aid to the noncommunist regimes of Korea and Taiwan. These infrastructural and historical conditions were necessary, but not sufficient, for Asian tigers to emerge as dynamic capitalist economies. The other necessary ingredient was autonomous and conscious leaders committed to capitalist development. Chapter 3 showed that Botswana's leaders were significantly autonomous from civil society. They were also conscious of the economic task ahead of them. This chapter shows Botswana has not been able to develop its industrial capacity. It has not able to do this despite the leaders' consciousness and their commitment to capitalism and pragmatic policies. This is so significantly because of the social and geographic legacy of British colonialism and the regional dominance of apartheid South Africa.

The absence of an indigenous and dynamic business class manifests the legacy of colonialism. This class's absence prevents the postcolonial state from networking with the progressive elements of this class to foster industrialization. This legacy continues to shackle Botswana as foreign and nonindigenous groups dominate the economy. Although Botswana has progressed in indigenizing the economy, its principal industrial policy instruments are still unable to break with the past. The combination of British colonial economic policy of "do nothing," and the domination of the regional economy by South Africa via Botswana's membership in the Southern African Customs Union since 1910 continues to shape the pathways and prospects of industrial development in Botswana.

The present chapter consists of five themes: (1) the entrepreneurial context Botswana inherited from British colonial rule; (2) the slow emergence of Botswana's industrial strategy between independence until 1982; (3) the history and performance of the state's two principal instruments to nurture industrial development: the Financial Assistance Policy (FAP) and the Botswana Development Corporation (BDC); (4) the performance of a sample of manufacturing and industrial firms supported by the government through BDC and or FAP (I evaluate these firms' performance on three criteria: level of indigenous ownership, level of employment generated and articulation between these firms and the rest of the economy, that is, raw material sources and so on. Moreover, I compare these firms' achievements with the lack of changes in indigenous ownership and management of commercial enterprises in the major shopping malls in the country's four largest population centers); and (5) the short distance Botswana has traveled in transforming the economy's commercial and industrial sectors.

COLONIAL CONTEXT AND ENTREPRENEURSHIP IN BOTSWANA

[E]conomic [development] is bound to be slow unless there is an adequate supply of entrepreneurs looking out for new ideas, and willing to take the risk of introducing them. Thus a private enterprise economy will be retarded if it has not enough businessmen, or if its businessmen are reluctant to take risks.[11]

Chapter 3 pointed out that the dearth of physical infrastructure and human resources in Botswana matched Batswanas' poverty in the commercial and entrepreneurial sectors. South African whites and Indians still dominate the commercial and industrial sector.

The absence of a Batswana business-owning class was the result of a deliberate colonial policy. This policy allocated business licenses to Europeans and Indians. The colonial regime prohibited African participation in commerce since the early part of this century. The systematic denial of business opportunities to Batswana began in earnest when the administration forced a commercial company, founded in 1909–10 and owned by the Great Khama, to close.[12] Khama established the firm to reduce the dominance of white traders in his nation. He also wanted to secure his personal and his traditional administration's economic future.

Three factors contributed to Khama's declining fortune and his subsequent concern about the future. His forfeiture of traditional tribute; the decline of the wagon trade resulting from the establishment of the railway; and the collapse of the cattle economy due to drought and disease epidemic. Although Khama was the firm's sole owner, he named it after his firm's two European managers, Garrett and Smith. The colonial administration did not want the company to carry the chief's name although it had no problem with the arrangement as long as Khama was not "an active partner." Garrett, Smith & Co. apparently competed against the principal trading firm in the area, Bechuanaland Trading Association (BTA):

> Garrett, Smith & Co., blessed with Khama's capital, moved in to take over or 'support the accounts' of small trade outlets in the Ngwato and Tawana (Ngamiland) Reserves. It saved a number of traders from bankruptcy, and one supported account alone amounted to £4,000. It not only had more stores than B.T.A. but it rescued stores at places where the B.T.A. might otherwise have had a monopoly, and gave them prestige of being 'the Chief's stores.' There was no need of a royal proclamation for the Ngwato to patronize their local branch of 'Khama & Co.'[13]

Garrett, Smith & Co.'s activities and growth were not lost on BTA. It launched a pernicious campaign to revoke the firm's license and bar the chief from involvement in commerce. BTA's manager used the company's political connections and the racist South African press to compel the colonial administration to act against Khama.[14] The administration forced the chief to "withdraw from all trading interests." The company's folding in 1916 had far-reaching consequences for Botswana and more particularly Batswana. If Khama's attempt in commerce had been successful, other *Batswana* states and individuals with means would have copied it. Such development would have helped the growth of indigenous entrepreneurship that Batswana sorely lacked at independence and even today.[15]

The demise of Khama's enterprise meant that the few indigenous people with resources, mostly chiefly families, were blocked from partaking in Bechuanaland's incipient but developing market. This administration then proceeded to favor Europeans first and Asians second when issuing trade licenses. By 1932, these two foreign interests held all trading licenses. The Europeans had 131 licenses; the Asians controlled 13. This excluded Africans from the "modern" economy until nearly the end of the Second World War.[16]

Then Batswana began to challenge these discriminatory laws and commercial practices. The colonial administration succumbed to the pressure. Africans had 10 licenses in 1949 and 53 licenses ten years later.[17] As the independence movement gained momentum, increasing numbers of Africans

Table 5.1 Number of Trading Licenses in Botswana

Race	1932	1949	1959	1968
African	0	10	53	136
Asian	13	20	NA	95
European	133	155	185	208

NA = Not available.

Source: Calculated from figures provided in Alan Best, "General Trading in Botswana, 1908–1968."

obtained a foothold in retail trade. The number of African store owners increased, so that African-held licenses accounted for nearly one third of all licenses two years after independence (Table 5.1). This pace gained such momentum that the 1973–78 National Development Plan showed that citizens held 70 percent of all trading licenses. This included whites and Indians who had Botswana citizenship. This numerical growth of citizen-owned businesses did little to redistribute commercial capital as the Plan lamented:

> More than 70 per cent of all trading licenses are held by Botswana citizens, but that figure gives no indication of the proportion of total trade that is carried out through establishments owned by Botswana citizens. In fact by far the greater part of internal trade is conducted through non-Batswana-owned establishments. In addition, non-local enterprises carry out the "prime" retail and wholesale business in the urban areas, while it is left to small-scale Batswana-owned enterprises to provide for the needs of the suburban and rural communities. The smaller traders have no wholesaling system which they can rely on, and they have to travel long distances to acquire small stocks from semi-wholesalers or larger retailers in the urban areas.[18]

Because whites and Indians dominated the commercial economy, Africans were denied concomitantly the opportunities to nurture entrepreneurial skills and gain experience in trade. This reinforced the grip of the forces left behind by colonial policy.

FORMULATING INDUSTRIAL STRATEGY

Botswana's activist and development-minded government walked into a tight trap as both the public and the indigenous private sectors were impoverished. Until the late-1970s and early 1980s, the public sector was resource poor. As a result, the government allotted the premier role in the country's development to the private sector.[19] But there were no Batswana with sufficient capital to partake in the activities of the private sector. As such, the private sector–centered development strategy required that the principal actors in the market be white and Asian "paper-citizens"[20] with capital or entrepreneurial skills. The Government was mindful of the dilemma of the benefits of development accruing to foreigners. However, it had little maneuvering room.

The country's industrial strategy in those early days, such as it was, was embedded in the private, foreign investment inducement development program:

> The expansion of the industrial base—presently very small—is a prime objective of Government policy. Botswana has duty-free access to surrounding countries, an advantage to be fully exploited if industrial development is to occur. . . . Private enterprise will only be interested in investing in Botswana if there is a profit to be made, if they are assured of a stable and friendly environment and if they are allowed to export their profits if they wish to do so. These conditions the Government accepts. In order to make this quite clear and to create added incentives, the Government will devise fiscal relief for new investors and is prepared to examine sympathetically any specific proposals investors may choose to make.[21]

Botswana's membership in the Southern African Customs Union (SACU) conditioned its liberal development policy.[22] Botswana has been a member of the South Africa–dominated organization since 1910. Goods move freely in the customs area without duties. All duties are collected at the point of entry in South Africa. These duties are then distributed among member countries on a predetermined formula. Botswana felt that the Customs Union was biased against the smaller nonindustrial SACU members (Lesotho, Swaziland, and Botswana) and in favor of South Africa. As a result, Botswana renegotiated their agreement, which resulted in a more favorable arrangement in 1969. The new agreement led to a significant increase in Botswana's income from the common custom's revenue (Table 5.2). This increase helped the government balance its annual budget for the first time in 1972 without grants from Britain.[23] In addition to increasing the government's income, the new agreement also stipulated that Botswana and other smaller countries could use the "infant industries" clause to protect new industries from South African competition for up to eight years. Only three industrial firms successfully exploited the "infant industry" clause: The Breweries, Bolux Milling, and Sugar Industries.

In addition to being a SACU member, Botswana was also part of the rand currency area until 1976, when it launched its own currency, the pula.

Table 5.2   Customs and Excise Government Revenue (Million Pula After 1976)

Year	Customs/ Excise	Total Gov't Revenue	Custom Excise as (%) of Domestic Revenue
1968/69	1.4	NA	NA
1969/70	5.1	NA	NA
1970/71	4.6	NA	NA
1971/72	8.3	NA	NA
1972/73	12.5	NA	NA
1973/74	20.9	NA	NA
1974/75	30.4	NA	NA
1975/76	24.6	87	NA
1976/77	29.3	87	NA
1977/78	37.8	118	NA
1978/79	49.8	NA	NA
1979/80	73	301	NA
1980/81	102	307	NA
1981/82	104	323	NA
1982/83	114.3	394	NA
1983/84	157	563	NA
1984/85	156	803	NA
1985/86	149.2	1,133.4	NA
1986/87	192.3	1,547.5	NA
1987/88	234.1	1,825.0	13.6
1988/89	292.6	2,556.2	12.0
1989/90	353.1	2,751.0	13.0
1990/91	478.2	3,740.7	13.2
1991/92	761.6	4,069.4	19.0
1992/93	998.4	4,652.2	22.0
1993/94	822.3	5,359.4	15.3
1994/95	711.8	4,397.5	16.2
1995/96	829.4	5,457.7	15.2

NA = Not available. In the years immediately after independence and before revenues from diamonds materialized, customs revenues accounted for a higher proportion of government domestic revenue.

Source: Figures from 1968/9 to 1973/4 are from the World Bank, Botswana: *Development Strategy in a Mineral-led Economy, Basic Economic Report, Volume 1, Report No. 735-BT* (Nairobi: Eastern Africa Regional Office, 1975). Data for 1982/3 to 1995/6 are from the Bank of Botswana, *Annual Report 1994 and 1996* (Gaborone, 1994), S62. For a general analysis of the Botswana economy in the 1970s, see Bertil, Oden, *The Macroeconomic Position of Botswana: Research Report No.60.* Uppsala: Scandinavian Institute of African Studies, 1981.

In other words, Botswana did not have an independent monetary policy to protect its economic interest. Botswana saw membership in the rand currency area as an advantage as it did not have to worry about foreign exchange constraints since the rand was an internationally respected currency. In fact, membership in the rand currency area was a point the government emphasized in its development plans to lure foreign investors to the country. Using its incorporation into the South African economy, the government attempted to entice investors. Investors could locate in Botswana and sell to South Africa without duties. Despite this inducement, not many industrialists moved across the border even at the height of the liberation war in South Africa. Consequently, South Africa remains the source of almost all of Botswana's imports (Table 5.3).

Botswana's industrial development strategy has had two phases since independence. The first phase was by necessity largely confined to creating the economic climate to lure foreign investors. This phase also laid the economy's infrastructural needs. This policy framework formally lasted until 1984, when Botswana produced its first industrial development white paper.[24] The second phase retained most of the elements of the earlier period. However, the state became more active in promoting industrial investment since 1982.

The 1968 Industrial Licensing Act, which called for the registration of all enterprises "employing more than 9 workers and using 25 Horsepower or more"[25] formalized Botswana's liberal industrial strategy. Botswana's membership in SACU and its desperate financial circumstances dictated its liberal industrial program. These conditions dovetailed with the leadership's capitalist commitment. Given this context, the government had limited ways to entice foreign investors and induce industrial growth. First, Botswana signed agreements with the United States. These agreements committed Botswana to respecting the sanctity of private property and guaranteed investors their resources would not be nationalized. The government went further and became a "signatory to the International Convention for Settlement of Investment Disputes under the auspices of the World Bank.[26] Second, Botswana created a regionally competitive, company income tax, 30 percent. This tax rate gave investors generous incentive and depreciation terms. Moreover, the tax rate included no restriction on profit repatriation.[27] Third, in addition to the lack of foreign exchange controls, two other factors contributed to making Botswana an integral part of the South African economy: the free flow of goods in the Customs Union and the use of the rand as the national currency. Fourth, Botswana made developing a physical infrastructure the centerpiece of its development strategy to facilitate industrial operations. Fifth, Botswana encouraged skilled expatriate employment to make up for the dearth of local skills in all enterprise areas.

Table 5.3 Imports by Country/Continent (Thousand Pula)

Year	CC Area	Other Africa	UK	Other Europe	USA	All other	Total imports	CCA* % of total
1980	466,845	360,158	7,319	5,837	16,310	4,339	537,808	87
1981	581,330	42,046	7,515	11,398	14,836	6,796	663,921	87.6
1982	608,838	44,751	1,600	12,273	11,550	10,440	703,852	86.5
1983	669,876	59,305	10,129	42,038	8,547	16,049	805,944	83.1
1984	698,116	78,200	27,637	58,521	16,540	16,246	895,260	78.0
1985	814,280	81,720	53,120	81,958	30,639	33,467	1,095,184	74.4
1986	1,021,532	101,161	32,836	82,147	37,805	55,937	1,331,418	76.7
1987	1,250,954	121,674	36,248	106,182	29,703	27,695	1,572,455	79.6
1988	1,681,991	146,581	124,772	109,922	45,636	56,290	2,172,191	77.8
1989	244,624	194,458	93,581	187,314	36,313	63,321	3,019,612	81.0
1990	2,979,702	206,826	90,123	222,963	41,301	78,553	3,619,467	82.3
1991	3,291,831	218,761	143,196	151,715	48,847	73,315	3,927,665	83.8
1992	3,373,930	208,786	103,733	177,559	38,900	67,154	3,970,062	85.0
1993	3,553,777	213,380	112,022	192,339	140,791	85,363	4,296,972	82.7

* CCA = Common Customs Area.

Source: Republic of Botswana, *Statistical Bulletin*, 18, 3 (1993): 19.

While attempting to lure foreign investors to establish industrial enterprises in Botswana, the government recognized that, given Botswana's tiny domestic market and its reputation as a barren and remote backwater of South Africa, liberal inducements may not be sufficient to attract enough worthy investors. It also was concerned that a progressive and steady process of indigenization of the economy continue to occur if such investments materialized. To counteract these tendencies the government established three organizations: the BDC in 1970; the Botswana Enterprise Development Unit (BEDU); and the National Development Bank (NDB). The BDC, which is discussed later, is a parastatal mandated to operate as a commercial enterprise, its purpose is to identify profitable opportunities in the country and then recruit investors. If investors are not forthcoming, the BDC could use its own funds to establish such enterprises. Furthermore, its function is to insure that Batswana had a stake in these opportunities. If individual citizens are not available, then the BDC retained a share of the enterprise.

Another way the government hoped to stimulate development was to encourage local entrepreneurs. As a result, it formed the Botswana Enterprise Development Programme. This programme was renamed Botswana Enterprise Development Unit (BEDU). The BEDU was part of the Ministry of Commerce and Industry, established in 1973.[28] The BEDU's first task was to "provide advice, guidance, and training to Batswana entrepreneurs and to help them negotiate financial assistance."[29] To facilitate BEDU's functions, the government created its own limited liability company, the Batswana Enterprises Development Company (BEDC). The BEDC was designed to manage all capital funds requirement and develop industrial estates in the country's major urban centers. It was also to provide facilities, procure raw materials for small entrepreneurs, and help them gain credit.

The third organization, NDB, secured all credit for small-scale, local enterprises. The Ministry of Finance and Development Planning oversees the NDB.[30] The BEDU started quickly, spending 1.6 million pula. By the end of the Plan period, BEDU had assisted 78 businesses, which employed over 900 people.[31] The mandate of BEDU was redefined in the early 1980s. Its function shifted from supplying a comprehensive support package to small and medium-sized citizen-owned enterprises to providing "technical and professional leadership and direction for the effective delivery of an integrated commercial and industrial extension service as well as to facilitate the transfer of industrial technology."[32]

The "Local Preference" scheme, which went into effect in 1978, is another policy instrument government used to insure that local producers of industrial products have a chance to compete with foreign enterprises.[33] To qualify for preference under this scheme, a quarter of production costs of a local product must take place in the country. Furthermore, the government

Table 5.4 Industrial Employment in Botswana, 1973–1996

Year	Manufacturing	% Change	Trade/Industry	Mining	Electric/Water	Construction	Transport Communication	National Employment
1973	2850		22525	3525	325	7225	8600	45050
1974	3300	15.8	25400	4100	525	8075	9400	50800
1975	3850	16.7	28525	4525	650	9000	10500	57050
1976	4275	9.9	27100	5450	750	6125	10500	54200
1977	4150	-2.9	27500	5500	950	6900	10000	55000
1978	4500	8.4	31000	4700	1200	9300	11300	62000
1979	5500	22.2	25200	6300	1300	9800	2300	50400
1980	5600	1.8	28100	7200	1500	10400	3400	56200
1981	6400	14.4	34500	7300	1600	15300	3900	69000
1982	7200	12.5	36800	7100	2200	16600	3700	73600
1983	9800	36.1	38100	7200	1900	15300	3900	76200\
1984	9500	3.1	40600	7500	2000	16100	5500	81200
1985	9900	4.2	43100	7300	1900	18300	5700	86200
1986	12200	23.2	47700	7500	2000	20900	5100	95400
1987	14700	20.5	56300	7000	2200	25700	6700	112600
1988	16400	11.6	62900	7500	2300	28800	7900	125800
1989	22200	35.4	73700	7600	2100	43500	7300	147400
1990	24300	9.5	81300	8100	2100	38300	8500	162600
1991	26300	8.2	90291	7700	2500	52000	9800	180582
1992	22000	-16.3	82800	8300	2600	40000	9900	165600
1996	23683	7.7	NA	8100	2671	22555	8781	234116

Source: Central Statistics Office, *Labour Force Statistics* (Gaborone: 1991/92, 1993); and *Employment Survey*, (Gaborone: September 1985) 10. Central Statistical Office, *Statistical Bulletin* 22, 1 (Gaborone, 1997:55). Republic of Botswana, *National Development, 1979–85*.

gave other preferences to local contractors through the tendering process without violating the terms of the Customs Union.

Botswana's postindependent leaders knew that infrastructural development was a prerequisite for attracting foreign investment. Consequently, it invested heavily in building roads and establishing electrical, communication, and transport systems. Moreover, immediately after independence Botswana expanded and upgraded the educational system and developed an appropriate administrative structure to support it. These developments absorbed the bulk of the state's resources and energies during at least the first decade.

Five factors defined the fundamental liberal thrust of Botswana's industrial development strategy for the first 18 years of independence: (a) infrastructural developments and BDC investments; (b) credit and service support for small and medium Batswana entrepreneurs through BEDU; (c) Local Preference schemes; (d) free trade within the Customs Union; and (e) free currency flows (until 1976). Despite the absence of a highly interventionist state in the area of industrial development, employment in the industrial sector grew significantly during the period (Table 5.4). The number of jobs in mining, manufacturing, electricity/water, construction, and transport and communication grew from 22,525 in 1973 to 34,500 in 1981, amounting to a 6.7 percent annual growth rate. Manufacturing jobs, a critical industry subsector, grew from 2,850 in 1973 to 6,400 in 1981, a 15.6 percent annual growth rate. This is a remarkable growth rate despite the absence of intensive government intervention.[34]

Botswana's industrial program was making significant progress in addressing one of the nation's industrial objectives: to generate sufficient *employment* for the population. Furthermore, Botswana made significant inroads in increasing the proportion of the sector owned by citizens (Table 5.5). The proportion of Batswana-owned formal manufacturing operations increased from virtually zero at independence (excluding the state-owned BMC, which was the largest industrial firm in the country) to 9 percent in 1978/79 and then to 15 percent in 1984. In addition to the growth of citizen-owned enterprises in the manufacturing sector, the number of firms jointly owned by citizens and foreigners increased from 26 percent to 32 percent during this same period. Despite these improvements in advancing citizen-held interests in the economy, noncitizens continued to dominate the private industrial sector not only in terms of business numbers, but more significantly the proportions of total value of capital owned.

The slow pace of indigenization of the economy, particularly the commercial and industrial sectors, became a critical issue in public debate in the late 1970s and early 1980s. First, serious concerns existed that noncitizens, who controlled the commercial and industrial sectors, were capturing the benefits of the wealth generated by Botswana's rapidly growing diamond

Table 5.5 Citizen Versus Noncitizen Ownership of Industry

Industry	Batswana-owned			Mixed Ownership			Foreign-owned		
	1978/79	1984	1994	1978/79	1984	1994	1978/79	1984	1994
Building material	1	0	89	2	0	20	5	0	24
Garments/textiles	0	8	47	4	8	43	9	8	70
Wood/product	2	1	21	1	6	18	2	5	24
Tanning/leather	0	0	4	1	4	6	1	3	7
Metal and products	1	9	63	1	7	38	17	21	75
Beverages/food	1	1	—	2	7	8	9	5	4
Print/publishing	0	0	—	0	0	—	1	0	—
Agro-products	0	1	68	4	4	34	5	3	43
Meat/products	1	0	4	0	1	1	0	1	2
Chemical/rubber	1	0	8	3	2	29	1	14	45
Bakery products	0	3	—	0	3	—	0	7	—
Paper products	0	0	16	0	2	9	0	4	23
Plastics/product	0	0	8	0	3	21	0	4	20
Electrical wares	0	1	9	0	3	11	0	6	19
Handicraft	0	0	3	0	1	4	0	2	6
Miscellaneous	1	0	—	5	0	—	7	0	—
Total	8	24	340	23	51	242	57	83	363
% CHANGE	9.1	15.2	36	26.1	32.1	25.6	64.8	52.5	38.3

Source: Republic of Botswana, National Development Plans, 1970–1985. The figures for 1985–94 were supplied by the Ministry of Commerce and Industry, personal communication, September 21, 1994.

exports. The second issue was that, despite the growth of employment, the rate of job creation was not keeping pace with the number of future job seekers.[35] Finally, the government realized that the economy needed to diversify away from cattle and diamonds, particularly since these sectors were not going to generate growing numbers of future jobs. These concerns led to a significant reform in Botswana's commercial and industrial strategy. The Presidential Commission on Economic Opportunity[36] was the first signal in the policy shift. This commission was commonly referred to as the Mmusi Commission, named after the late vice president, Peter Mmusi, who headed the commission. The commission was mandated to come up with recommendations on how more opportunities could be created for citizens in the private sector.[37]

INDUSTRIAL STRATEGY, 1982-1995

Three factors significantly contributed to the government's willingness to reformulate its industrial policy in the early 1980s. First, Botswana's financial situation improved dramatically with further discoveries and exploitation of diamonds. The government begun to accumulate a healthy balance of payments and reserves and, therefore, gained tremendous fiscal flexibility it did not have before (Table 5.6). Second, the public institutions and some of the physical infrastructure that the country lacked when it became independent were now in place. As a result, the government did not have to be so preoccupied with establishing these institutions and infrastructure.

The government anticipated the growth of its revenues and pondered how it could use these resources to induce further and sustained growth in the industrial and particularly in the manufacturing sector. Third, the government was very concerned about stimulating industrial growth in order to provide employment for its rapidly growing population.[38] In anticipation of the new financial climate, the government engaged two consultants to examine the prospects of increasing employment and inducing industrial growth.

The employment question fell to a group headed by Michael Lipton; a German consultant assessed the prospects and problems of Botswana's industrial development.[39] The Lipton report recommended forming an employment unit in the MFDP to coordinate the government's plan to intensify its efforts in increasing job creation.[40] The German study identified four problems the industrial sector was facing: institutions supporting industry were either weak or nonexistent; raw materials and skilled labor were lacking; and there was essential need to build a public agency to promote the sector and the industrial opportunities in the country. The German study recognized that the government of Botswana had been

Table 5.6 Diamond Exports and Total Government Budget Balance, 1968/9–
1995/6 (Million Pula)

Year	Value of diamond exports	Gov't budget balance
1968/9		-8.4
1969/70	3	-7.5
1970/1	20	11.7
1971/2	20	-13.7
1972/3	30	-27
1973/4	32	-16.4
1974/5*	32	-14.3
1975/6	37	-12.5
1976/7	46	-21
1977/8	75	-5
1978/9	186	10.6[#]
1979/80	236	17[#]
1980/1	135	-3
1981/2	243	-18
1982/3	464	-21
1983/4	616	102
1984/5	1049	188.2
1985/6	1226	414.2
1986/7	2253	539.3
1987/8	1979	513
1988/9	2861	768.5
1989/90	2614	536.5
1990/1	2942	798
1991/2	2899	697.2
1992/3	3340.2	881.3
1993/4	3727.4	878.3
1995/6	5271.6	269.9

Note: Currency was in South African rand until 1976.

 * Figures before this date are from the World Bank, 1975, 15.

 # These are estimates, and the author has been unable to get actual figures.

Source: Bank of Botswana, *Annual Reports 1993, 1994* and *1996*.

working on institutional issues and training the labor force while using skilled expatriates in the interim. It suggested continued developments in these areas and new and strong emphasis on the promotional needs of the manufacturing sector.[41] Botswana accepted the Lipton and the German study recommendations. Consequently, the government created an Employment Unit in the Ministry of Finance and Development Planning. It also created a promotional agency: Trade and Investment Promotion Agency (TIPA), in the Ministry of Commerce and Industry.

FINANCIAL ASSISTANCE POLICY AND INDUSTRIALIZATION

The government took the consultants' advice. The Employment Policy Unit, in collaboration with a small group from the other ministries, worked on the substance of the government's future employment creation strategy. Their work became the seeds of the Government White Paper No. 1 of 1982.[42] The parliament approved the Financial Assistance Policy (FAP) on April 13, 1982. This paper articulated the government's intentions to support the industrial sector more vigorously.[43] Although the government had not yet articulated a fully developed industrial strategy, FAP was to be the most important new policy instrument to advance the industrial project. The establishment of FAP was to complement the government's other principal industrial policy instrument, the BDC.

Mindful of the failed attempts by most Third World governments to induce industrial development through planning, subsidization, and/or ownership of plants, Botswana's new attempt to promote industry was in keeping with its philosophy of encouraging the market and letting investors and entrepreneurs choose their own course.[44] FAP gives investors the necessary freedom while insuring the use of public money to maximum advantage. To insure the mutuality of these aims, FAP circumscribed the terms under which public money will be used to assist industrial enterprises:

First, Government funds should only be used to support those new ventures (or expansions of existing ventures) where we can reasonably expect the benefits to Botswana, in terms of new incomes and new jobs created, to outweigh the costs of assistance or grants. Second, the assistance from Government should be temporary, that is, it should only last for at most five years. By adopting this approach, there is a better chance of new developments being viable on their own, and even contributing eventually to tax revenue. If we did not have a system to stop assistance to new ventures after some time, we would quickly come to the point where we did not have enough money to help any more businesses or individuals, and no more new projects could be assisted.[45]

Photo 5.1. Infrastructure. Development of infrastructure has been at the forefront of the government's agenda. One of Gaborone's major thoroughfares.

Under these conditions FAP was to (a) contribute to economic diversification, away from mining and cattle; (b) to facilitate local entrepreneurs' movement into the industrial sector; (c) increase the share of Batswana-owned productive firms; (d) attract foreign investors into the country; (e) produce goods for import substitution or for exports; and (f) increase productive employment and income.

Broadly speaking, FAP's assistance to enterprises came in two types: automatic and case-by-case grants. The FAP awarded automatic grants to new investments in manufacturing. All other new, productive investments and expansion of old establishments could apply for case-by-case grants. A new manufacturing project could also apply for case-by-case assistance. Others could not for both types of assistance.[46] Entrepreneurs could apply for FAP grants only after the authorities had carefully examined the project's viability and contributions.

Enterprises eligible for FAP support are divided into three project sizes: large, medium, and small-scale. The investment size the project intends to make defines its scale. Large-scale projects with investment over 750,000 pula are eligible for four types of grants:[47]

(a)   an initial capital expenditure grant related to the jobs that will be created for Batswana;

Photo 5.2. Industrialization. Botswana was able to beat other countries in the region to attract foreign investment. Hyundai, South Korea's car company, chose Botswana over South Africa. Most of the cars produced by this plant are sold across the border in South Africa.

(b)   grants to reimburse a portion of the wages of unskilled and semi-skilled workers;

(c)   grants to reimburse a portion of off-the-job training costs; and

(d)   grants related to the value of sales from the project.[48]

FAP disbursed second and third grants over the five-year period.

Medium-scale projects are those with investments ranging from 10,000 to 750,000 pula.[49] Projects falling in this category were eligible for the same grants as the large-scale operations. However, the authorities use a simpler method to assess their viability. Authorities favored citizens for these projects without further financial inducement.

Small-scale projects possess investment capital worth up to 10,000 Pula. Only Batswana may be eligible to invest in such industrial enterprises. The criterion for evaluating these projects' viability is: do the investors have the requisite managerial skills? If so, then the project becomes eligible for a portion of its start-up costs. The proportion of these initial costs that may be covered by the grant ranges from 5% to 95%.[50] Four factors improve grant size: rural location of a project, ownership by women, the number of jobs

Photo 5.3. New glass tower in Gaborone.   One of the new towers that now dominate Gaborone's skyline and are symbolic of Botswana's wealth and status as a
middle-income country.

created, and owner-operated projects improved the size of the grant. To encourage rural industrialization, the grant cover a higher proportion of initial
costs in rural areas.[51]

The MFDP in 1995 completed its third assessment of the policy. The
government engaged external consultants for all three evaluations. It also
accepted a significant number of the recommendations of the 1984 and 1988
evaluations. These evaluations provide most of the data in this section. The
resource FAP committed has increased greatly. By the end of 1993, FAP has
supported over 4,000 projects (Table 5.7). The cost of the FAP grants has
been (1982–93) 160,439,000 pula at the 1993 prices.[52] Small-scale projects,
which are reserved for citizens only, showed the fastest growth rate in terms
of the number of grants, despite the temporary decline between 1986–87.[53]
Small-scale projects' share of the total money spent increased from a low of
9 percent in 1986 to 33 percent in 1993. Industrial sector grants accounted
for the majority of the small-scale enterprises in total money distributed and
number of projects funded. The projects supported in the small-scale industrial sector ranged from sewing and knitting to leather work and carpentry
(Table 5.8). The small-scale sector accounted for less than a third of the

Table 5.7 Number of FAP Grants, 1982–1993

Year	Small		Medium/Large
	Agriculture	Industry	
1982	39	199	11
1983	75	103	21
1984	66	109	19
1985	31	110	24
1986	39	149	34
1987	34	133	63
1988	28	142	67
1989	50	220	51
1990	240	324	58
1991	231	338	58
1992	76	415	40
1993	17	432	38
Total	926	2,674	474

Source: Ministry of Finance and Development Planning, *The Third Evaluation of Financial Assistance Policy (FAP)*. Draft Report Submitted by Phaleng Consultancies (Pty) Ltd. March 1995.

Table 5.8 Number of Small-scale Industrial FAP Grants by Sector

Sector	Grants
Sewing/knitting	1393
Brick molding	532
Welding/metal	220
Carpentry/furniture	134
Bakery	225
Leather	71
Other	205
Total	2,807

Source: Ministry of Finance and Development Planning, *The Third Evaluation of Financial Assistance Policy (FAP)*. Draft Report Submitted by Phaleng Consultancies (Pty) Ltd. March 1995, p. 48.

Table 5.9 Distribution of Medium and Large Projects by Sector and Subsector

Subsector	Medium Agri mining		Medium Industrial	Large	Total
Agriculture	109		4	113	
Bakery			24		24
Building material		4	57	3	64
Chemical/ rubber			26	1	27
Electric/paper/plastic			47		47
Leather/ footwear			14	1	15
Metal			43	6	49
Textiles			75	3	78
Wood			23	1	24
Other food			39	2	41
Other industrial			1		1
Gems		1		1	2
Total	109	5	349	21	485

Source: Cameron L. Smith, Raphael Kaplinsky, John Menz, and Babutsi Beauty Selabe, *Evaluation of the Financial Assistance Policy: FAP and Its Role in Botswana Business Development* (Gaborone: Government Printer, May 1988): 71.

Table 5.10 Distribution of Medium and Large Projects by Sector and by Ownership

Citizenship	Medium Agri Mining		Medium Industrial	Large	Total
Citizen	71	3	152	5	231
Noncitizen	10	1	141	7	159
Joint venture	17	1	48	7	73
Other			1	1	2
No record	11		7	2	20
Total	109	5	349	22	485

Source: Cameron L. Smith, Raphael Kaplinsky, John Menz, and Babutsi Beauty Selabe, *Evaluation of the Financial Assistance Policy: FAP and Its Role in Botswana Business Development* (Gaborone: Government Printer, May 1988): 72.

Photo 5.4. Radical inequality. The slums of old Naledi (part of Gaborone), where at least a third of the capital's population live.

grants committed during the program's life, but it generated nearly 5,000 net jobs (1,600 in agriculture and 3,400 in industry) at the average cost of P2,700 and P1,600 for agriculture and industry, respectively.[54] The sector affords Batswana, especially women who accounted for nearly 48 percent of committed grants, entrepreneurial opportunity, and training. These opportunities did not exist before FAP implementation. The small-scale sector fulfilled two program objectives: employment generation and entrepreneurial development. It minimally satisfied the third purpose of economic diversification. However, it failed to increase production to replace some of the country's imports.[55]

The medium- and large-scale program, which accounted for nearly two-thirds of the committed FAP money, funded 485 projects since FAP's inception. Nearly a quarter of these projects were agricultural while five were in mining (Table 5.9). Medium- and large-scale enterprises that became operative and survived the teething problems created nearly 6,000 jobs at the cost of P4,700 per job per year.[56] According to the third evaluation, the medium- and large-scale projects were not as cost-effective as small-scale projects. Unlike the small-scale projects, medium- and large-scale FAP grants were open to citizens and noncitizens alike. Despite the disadvantages Batswana faced in such operations due to lack of capital, and managerial and entrepreneurial experience, citizens accounted for a little under 50% of these grants (Table 5.10). Furthermore, the proportion of projects in this group that is citizen-owned is slightly less than in 1988. Citizens owned barely more than half of the enterprises in 1988.[57] As such, citizen ownership declined marginally since 1988. Agriculture accounted for about a third of the citizen-owned medium and large-scale enterprises. Citizens owned a little more than a third of the large/medium industrial enterprises.[58]

The FAP has had an important impact on the Botswana economy. First, FAP grants created over 10,000 jobs between 1982 and 1993. The employment growth rate in the manufacturing sector, one of FAP's prime targets, grew at the unprecedented rate of 20.6 percent annually since the policy's inception, while the comparative rate for the sector during the preceding period was 10.7 percent.[59] This phenomenal growth rate is not solely attributable to the FAP, as the manufacturing grew faster than even if all FAP-induced jobs were in the sector. The fantastic growth of the sector was partly a product of Botswana's general economic boom, resulting from the tremendous growth of diamond revenues and its competent management by the government. Employment in Botswana did grow. However, we do not know exactly how much of this growth is due to FAP inducements, an upturn in the economy, or other factors.[60]

The three policy evaluations concur that the small-scale program is by far the most successful in achieving policy objectives. The small-scale sector has generated the most cost-effective jobs. Second, FAP-supported projects contributed to the diversification of the economy by creating employment in noncattle and mining sectors. The FAP did not significantly reduce imports or generate exports. For example, the proportion of major food and industrial imports to Botswana did not decline since the introduction of FAP.[61]

Third, FAP created many small-citizen producers who did not exist before. This is a significant development although most of these producers are at the bottom end of the production process. Therefore, they are dependent on other suppliers who are not Batswana. In the medium- and large-scale FAP projects, the ratio of citizen to noncitizen owners has improved compared to the years before FAP. However, the ratio of citizen to noncitizen owners has declined slightly since FAP's early years. Moreover, FAP data do not show the ratio between indigenous and naturalized citizens. However, my own spot check suggests that the latter group figures prominently in medium- and large-scale operations.

Fourth, FAP inducements attracted some foreign investment, demonstrated by the number of noncitizen medium and large-scale projects. Some of these investors, however, were already operating in the country. Grants by FAP paid for expanding existing enterprises, not creating new ones. FAP evaluations of 1984 and 1988 noted that some foreign operators were already planning to invest in Botswana; FAP grants represented a windfall.[62] Furthermore, earlier FAP evaluations and my interviews with a dozen medium and large producers show that many are planning to mechanize most of the jobs created as a result of FAP grants. Others indicated that they will relocate their plants to other countries when the FAP grants are exhausted.[63]

The tremendous growth in industrial employment since the FAP's inception in 1982 was partly due to BDC's wide-ranging investments activities in the 1970. Furthermore, the BDC continued to support many firms created or expanded through FAP inducements. In spite of the overlap between the BDC and FAP, the former is not as sectorally focused as the latter. Nevertheless, the BDC spent significant proportions of its resources in industry.

BDC AND INDUSTRIALIZATION[64]

The dearth of major commercial and industrial sectors and entrepreneurs to jump-start the economy after independence induced the government to initiate that process. Botswana created its own investment corporation. The BDC, established in 1970, was the government's principal commercial, industrial, and agricultural development agent.[65] The BDC is responsible for identifying, through feasibility studies, viable economic opportunities in Botswana and then seeking out prospective investors. Where such investors were forthcoming, BDC was allowed to take a minority interest in such projects. If foreign investors were not available, the BDC has the mandate to invest in such enterprises and own the entire operation. The BDC's mandate extends beyond inducing commercial and industrial development. It is also to insure that citizens receive the benefits of this development. If local citizens are unable to exploit such opportunities, which was almost always the case in the early years, BDC minority shares in these investments insure some "citizen" participation.[66]

BDC was incorporated under the Company Act of 1959, which governs the operations of nearly all of Botswana's parastatals. One of the act's fundamental pillars was to insure that these parastatals did not become a constant financial drain on the public sector:

> The Company shall conduct its business affairs upon a commercial basis, and in prompt, efficient and economic manner. It shall exercise special care and give due regard to the economic and commercial merits of any undertaking it promotes, assists, finances, or manages, so that, taking one year with another, it shall not be allowed to operate at a loss; however, though each such undertaking should be evaluated strictly on its merit, nevertheless, such evaluation should include consideration of the over-all long-term interests of and benefits to Botswana.[67]

The government expects the BDC to fulfill two sometimes contradictory roles, those of a commercial and of a development agency.[68]

While the Company Act mandated that the BDC operate as a development and commercial agency, it gave the board of directors tremendous degree of managerial autonomy.[69] The government (usually by the minister of Finance and Development Planning) nominates the board. The number of directors increased from 8 in 1971 to 13 in 1994. The number of BDC employees grew steadily from a handful to 107 in 1993 as its operations expanded. The chair of the board is the permanent secretary of the Ministry of Finance and Development Planning, whose ministry the BDC comes under. The board's autonomy is limited only by the tenets of the Company Act and the broad guidelines of the *National Development Plan*. The Board guides the BDC investment agenda, but the managing director is responsible for the corporation's daily operations and is accountable to the board.[70]

The government of Botswana was the sole share owner of the BDC until 1979, when it was joined by the Nederlandse Financierings (FMO), the Deutsche Gesellschaft für Wirtschaftliche Zusammenarbeit (DEG), and the International Finance Corporation of the World Bank (IFC). These agencies subscribed for 600,000, 300,00 and 300,000 shares respectively (8.25 percent redeemable, cumulative, nonvoting preference shares) while the government held all ordinary shares. The purpose of this association was that "these new shareholders will provide a depth of international experience and contacts not hitherto available to the Corporation."[71]

Botswana was dependent on Britain to balance its annual budget; and therefore it did not have surplus revenues when the BDC was founded. Initial funds for the BDC also came from United Kingdom development funds.[72] The corporation started its operations with modest capital. After Botswana became financially independent, it set up a loan fund—the Public Debt Service Fund (PDSF)—to support its parastatals. The PDSF financed the BDC and charged 14.6 percent interest on these loans.[73] To further help the BDC consolidation, over the years the government transferred ownership of some of its assets, such as the President Hotel, the Holiday Inn (the Gaborone Sun), and so forth to BDC.

The BDC invests in three kinds of firms. Subsidiary firms are those in which the BDC holds 50 percent or more shares. These include firms that the BDC owns completely. Those firms in which the BDC holds between 20 percent and 50 percent of the shares are associates of the BDC. The third type of businesses are those which receive only loans from the BDC. These firms are called affiliates. The BDC charges commercial rates and higher for loans. It may consider concessional rates if national social benefits are involved. Subsidiary and associate firms can also apply for BDC loans. Nearly two-thirds of BDC-supported firms were subsidiaries until about 1984 (Table

Table 5.11 BDC Firms

Year	Subsidiary	Associate	Affiliate	Total
1972	7	4	1	12
1973	10	8	2	20
1974	19	8	2	29
1975	20	9	3	32
1976	24	6	4	34
1977	21	7	4	32
1978	23	6	5	34
1979	23	6	4	33
1980	23	6	4	33
1981	26	6	3	35
1982	28	7	4	39
1983	29	8	6	43
1984	33	9	10	52
1985	31	13	16	60
1986	35	14	22	71
1987	33	15	40	84
1988	36	17	37	90
1989	37	21	38	96
1990	38	23	43	104
1991	35	26	46	107
1992	36	26	47	109
1993	34	24	59	117
1996	37	24	61	119

Source: Botswana Development Corporation, *Annual Reports* (Gaborone: 1972–1993 and 1996).

5.11). The BDC owned most of these businesses. Fully owned BDC firms are concentrated in agriculture and the estates.

The BDC initially concentrated its investments in the development of commercial and industrial infrastructure; that is, industrial parks and shopping malls. These investments were prerequisite for commercial and in-

Table 5.12 BDC Investment in Various Sectors, 1970-1993 (%)

Year	Estates	Finance	Indus/Comm.	Agric.	Hotel/Tour	Transp.	G	Total (000 pula)
1970-75	62	2	11	10	14	1	-	5026
1975-80	48	3	32	2	10	1	-	8982
1980-85	31	2	14	15	11	11	2	26057
1986	37.6	14.7	20.6	9.7	7.5	10		57317
1987	41.7	11.6	24.5	6.4	5.9	1		72975
1988	44.4	5.1	22.2	5.9	18.7	3.6		90130
1989	31.4	6.2	24.8	4.7	32.7	0.3		131559
1990	27.3	4	31.2	3.5	33.8	0.3		210561
1991	37.1	3.4	36.2	3.3	19.7	0.4		247871
1992	44.7	3.7	34.6	3.3	12.8	0.7		271565
1993	45.7	3.5	34	3.1	13.2	0.6		341632

Source: Botswana Development Corporation, *The First Fifteen Years, 1970–1985* (Gaborone, 1985). This publication is the source of the figures for 1970 to 1985. The rest of the data was provided by the BDC's group internal auditor, Mr. B. D. Phiri (Gaborone, June 17, 1994).

dustrial operations to be successful. They were also immediately profitable and insured that the BDC functioned within its mandate. Commercial and industrial property, hotels and tourism, and residential property accounted for 76 percent of BDC's investments in the first fifteen years of operations.[74] The complete dearth of physical infrastructure inherited from British colonialism, required the BDC to devote such a high proportion of scarce resources into real estate. For instance, given the complete lack of urban housing in Botswana, BDC had to build housing for its staff and plan and build the Malls of Selebi Phikwe, the Broadhurst industrial and commercial estate in Gaborone, and other factory shells. By contrast, industry and agriculture absorbed 21 percent of BDC funds during this period. Financial services and transport each took 1 percent. The absence of infrastructural development in Botswana during the British colonial state contrasts sharply with the accomplishments Japanese colonialism in Taiwan.

The BDC continued to invest a high proportion of funds in estates development, although this gradually declined in relation to commerce, industry, and agriculture (Table 5.12). Investment in industrial property absorbed a little more than half of the estate sector. In 1993 the BDC's gross investment totaled P336.6 million (note the discrepancy between this figure given by BDC's internal auditor and those for 1993 in Table 23). Estates, industry, services, financial institutions and agriculture accounted for P162, 89.6, 62, 11.8 and 11.2 million pula respectively.[75]

The BDC's investments have been wide-ranging and have affected every sector of the economy. In spite of spreading itself too thin, the BDC has been a profitable public enterprise. It returned dividends to its shareholders, primarily the Botswana government, and also paid taxes to the national treasury. Characteristic of most of Botswana's parastatals, the BDC made profits in 24 out of 25 years between 1971–1995. The only year it had a loss was its first year of operation (Table 5.13). Despite its loss in the first year, the BDC paid 220,035 rand in taxes. The BDC has not drained the state's purse even when it made a loss. Since the profit figures in Table 5.13 are after taxes, then the BDC has been solvent from its first year. Profits grew unevenly over the years although the general trend has been upward, peaking in 1992. Profits were relatively modest in the first decade but increased significantly in 1980 and remained nearly stagnant for most of that decade. Then profits grew again at high rates from 1987 to 1992. This is a remarkable record by any standards.[76]

Finance and estates investments have been BDC's most profitable sectors. These sectors and a few firms in industry, trade, and commerce, such as Kgalagadi and Botswana Breweries, and Sefalana Holdings are BDC's cash cows. By contrast, most of the BDC's unprofitable investments are in industry and agriculture.[77]

Table 5.13   BDC Profits and Taxes (000 Pula)

Year	Growth of Profit/Loss	Profit Rate*	Taxes
1971	- 69.564		220.035
1972	384.198		175.0
1973	525.160	36.7	200.0
1974	505.2	- 3.8	157.932
1975	115.474	- 77.1	16.281
1976	0.189	- 99.7	6.833
1977	21.361	11202.1	5.472
1978	169.160	692.0	59.3
1979	406.433	140.3	203.264
1980	1,353	232.9	204
1981	706	- 58.1	279
1982	1,002	42.0	481
1983	1,036	3.4	648
1984	1,258	20.4	537
1985	39	- 97.0	399
1986	1,008	96.1	666
1987	1,679	66.6	873
1988	3,751	123.4	1,166
1989	3,818	1.8	1,957
1990	7,450	99.1	2,480
1991	4,248	- 45.0	234
1992	11,866	179.3	188
1993	961	- 92.0	2,388
1994	20,641		253

* Calculated by the author.

Source: Figures before 1976 are in South African Rand. Botswana Development Corporation,
   Annual Reports 1971-1993.

The steady growth in BDC-assisted businesses meant the establishment of infrastructure, the diversification of the economy, and employment growth in Botswana. Employment by BDC companies grew from 0 in 1970 to 1,629 in 1978 (Table 5.14). The rate of employment generation from 1978 to 1993 increased at a phenomenal average annual rate of 14.5 percent. Thus growth in employment was the product of the increasing number of BDC-supported firms. More specifically, the industrial firms among the BDC group generated most of the jobs during the period. The number of industrial firms increased slowly from 1 in 1972 to 7 in 1982. After this slow growth, BDC-supported industrial firms took off and increased ninefold in the next 11 years. The swift and steady growth of the number of industrial firms after 1982 coincides, not with changes in BDC policy, but with the FAP introduction. Thus, the combination of BDC support and FAP subsidies accelerated the development of productive firms and employment.

The BDC's principal mandate was to foster feasible business enterprises while inducing development. One of its secondary responsibilities was to assist citizen entrepreneurs in participating in the country's commercial and industrial economy. The BDC was required to assist potentially viable local enterprises and also find foreign investors to complement their efforts and jointly establish businesses. Moreover, BDC was to insure that the benefits of the economic growth did not accrue to foreigners only. For this reason, the BDC took shares in foreign investments that had no citizen partners.

The Botswana government and the BDC were aware of the dearth of sufficient number of citizens who had the resources and/or skills to establish their own businesses even with the BDC's. Consequently, the BDC became the citizen participant in most foreign investments in Botswana. If there are no interested foreign investors, the BDC invests its own resources in potentially viable businesses. Under such circumstances, the BDC creates a firm and appoints management that is answerable to it.[78] In some cases, private citizens identify feasible enterprises but do not have either the managerial wherewithal or sufficient resources. Then the BDC locates able and willing foreign partners. The BDC has successfully induced business expansion. More critically, it has also made citizen participation a reality. The majority of citizen participation in BDC-supported businesses took the form of BDC shares, not private citizens. This kind of citizen participation troubled some members of the National Assembly who claimed "That this Honourable House has observed with dismay the way the Botswana Development Corporation has conducted its affairs in a competitive manner to the disadvantage of local entrepreneurs."[79] The Corporation defended its record of supporting private citizens but acknowledged the disabling business-related problems faced by Batswana:

Table 5.14 Employment in BDC-supported Firms, 1971–1996

	Agriculture	Estates	Finance	Industry	Service	Tourism	Transport	Total	# Firms
1971									12 (1)
1972									19 (1)
1973									29 (3)
1974									34 (4)
1975									36 (5)
1976									32 (4)
1977									34 (5)
1978	715	15	39	269	143	448	111	1,629	33 (5)
1979	702	14	40	301	147	509	131	1,844	33 (7)
1980	252	11	49	952	264	789	NA	2,317	35 (6)
1981	206	15	64	1,008	134	647	142	2,216	39 (7)
1982	220	15	61	1,173	112	860	176	2,627	43 (12)
1983	224	15	87	1,974	89	983	195	3,455	52 (22)
1984	238	15	92	2,458	*	990	230	4,023	60 (28)
1985	313	15	91	3,263		801	263	4,746	71 (34)
1986	286	15	121	4,121		953	254	5,750	84 (44)
1987	268	15	134	4,856		1,092	332	6,697	90 (47)
1988	329	32	178	5,638		1,146	162	7,485	96 (54)
1989	334	32	162	6,932		1,137	142	8,739	104(61)
1990	332	29	218	8,171		1,190	171	10,111	107(54)
1991	368	20	190	6,125	3,298	1,516	166	11,683	109(55)
1992	473	15	213	6,392	3,696	1,616	142	12,547	117(61)
1993	531	10	220	7,135	2,429	1,708	125	12,158	119(59)
1996	940	68	126	9,585	NA	1,071	23	11,855	

* Prior to 1984 the Service Department did exist and was called small business. The government abolished the small business department in 1989 and established a new service department. In the last column the number inside the brackets is the number of industrial firms. NA = Not available.

Source: Botswana Development Corporation, *Annual Reports*, 1972–93 and 1996.

In many instances, citizens of Botswana have approached BDC with viable business plans, yet they lacked the experience or expertise to properly implement the project. In such cases, BDC will conduct a careful search for potential partners who have the necessary skills and manpower to ensure the businesses' success. Usually, this will involve going to the international market-place. BDC will identify suitable foreign companies, assess their respective merits, and invite the representative of selected companies to Botswana for briefing and discussion. If all goes well, the result will be a joint partnership between a foreign company and local investors, that will, in turn, benefit further local businesses.[80]

After noting how the corporation assists perspective Batswana entrepreneurs, the BDC memo catalogued the number of citizen-owned or partially citizen-owned establishments in its group. The memo showed citizens have a significant stake in 35 businesses out of its 117 firms. A few of these firms had failed. While most establishments in the memo exemplified the ways the BDC helped citizens gain business competence and then run their own affairs independently, some big ones are either naturalized Indians, white firms, or firms where the citizen is BDC.

Examples of successful private indigenous citizen businesses include Marothodi and Mopipi, which produce silk–screen printed garments, and uniforms and industrial protective gear, respectively, and Wayguard Securities. Naturalized Indians and whites–owned firms are Jamal Trading, Abes Furniture, Algo Industries, and Botswanacraft.[81] The BDC is the citizen participant in the Owens Corning Pipe of Botswana firm. Most firms the BDC memo identified as "citizen"-controlled or owned are small and mainly in nonindustrial sectors.

The limited scope and range of citizen-controlled or owned business is not necessarily a product of the BDC trying to discourage Batswana business formation. It may be more reflective of the poverty of colonial policy that guarded against the indigenous entrepreneurship development in Botswana. The BDC's mandate—mainly to foster profitable business enterprises while operating its affairs without a loss for more than one year at a time—compounds the difficulty involved in overcoming such a colonial heritage. To operate profitably, the BDC has to attract proven enterprises with owners who have the managerial prerequisites. This process favors foreigners and BDC's short-term bottom line. However, it does not help Botswana achieve its long-term goal of vigorously incubating indigenous Batswana entrepreneurship and businesses.

Colonial and imperial legacy and a BDC development strategy driven by short-term profitability has significantly impeded the pace of indiginization of the private sector, except at the low end of the business and employment hierarchy. A retired senior and distinguished civil servant, currently one of a handful of indigenous Batswana trying to break into the upper echelons of the industrial sector, bitterly remarked, "Tragically, the Government reserves bittens for us while whites and Indians dominate all major and profitable sectors of the economy."[82]

POLICY TOOLS AND INDUSTRIALIZATION

Botswana's economy has gone through a revolution since independence. The development of physical and social infrastructure and the creation of thousands of businesses led to significant growth in employment and a moderate level of economic diversification. The FAP and the BDC played a vital role in this transformation. Despite these advances, Botswana has yet to break away from two major constraints inherited from the colonial era. These constraints are entrepreneurial underdevelopment and the integration of this society into the South Africa–dominated regional economy. The economy's weak private commercial and industrial sectors illustrate Botswana's inability to overcome this legacy despite its wealth and relatively effective public institutions.[83]

This section evaluates the progress towards (a) indigenization of the ownership of industrial and commercial enterprises; (b) development of indigenous managerial and other skills; and (c) linkages between BDC- and FAP-induced commercial and industrial development and the local economy; in order to gauge how much Batswana dented the legacy of colonialism in the commercial and industrial sectors. BDC- and FAP-supported enterprises and a survey of businesses located in the main shopping malls in Gaborone, Lobatse, Francistown, and Mochudi provide cases to highlight these problems.[84]

The question raised in the National Assembly was misdirected as it pointed to the BDC competing with local entrepreneurs. The question is: have the BDC and other government instruments been successful in (a) indigenizing the industrial and commercial sectors? (b) inducing managerial and technical skills development of indigenous Batswana? and (c) enhancing and improving linkages between new investments in the industrial sector and the local economy?

Table 5.15 shows the role which indigenous Batswana and local resources played in a sample of BDC- and FAP-supported industries. The sample contains large, medium and small industrial enterprises. The table demonstrates that indigenous, private Batswana owned or controlled less than a third of the enterprises. Furthermore, the Batswana businesses were small in terms of numbers of people employed and size of capital investment. Second, the number of firms managed by native Batswana was even less than those owned and controlled by them. Native Batswana managed only 4 of these 20 firms. Those firms managed by Batswana were, again, very small. Third, although native Batswana were more nu-

Table 5.15 Ownership, Management, Skilled Employment, Source of Input, and Markets of Manufacturing and Industry in Botswana

Firm Type	Ownership	Nationality of Management	Skilled employee	Source of inputs	Market
Soap	Foreign, BDC	White Zimbabwe	Noncitizen	RSA, ROB	Domestic
Furniture	Indian	Indian	Noncitizen	RSA,BR,ROB	Domestic
Furniture	White Motswana	Indian	Noncitizen Batswana	RSA/ZIM/UK/ROB	Domestic
Garment	Motswana Ghanaian	Motswana	Noncitizen Batswana	RSA, Asia, Swiss	Domestic/export
Garment	SA white	White Zim	Batswana	SA	Export
Textile	Indian Motswana	Indian	Noncitizen	SA, ZIM, ZAM, Saudi	Export
Silk screen	Motswana	Motswana	Batswana Noncitizen	RSA	Domestic
Textile	Indian	Indian	Noncitizen	RSA,ZIM,ZAM	Export
Shoes	Italian	Italian	Batswana	Zimbabwe, RSA, Italy	Export/ Domestic
Leather	Swiss	RSA	Noncitizen, Motswana	ZIM, RSA, Malawi	Export
Leather	Motswana	Motswana	Noncitizen, Motswana	ROB, ZIM, RSA	Export/ Domestic
Leather	Motswana	Motswana	Batswana, Noncitizen	RSA,ROB	Domestic
Sugar	White Zimbabwe	White Zimbabwe	Batswana, Noncitizen	RSA	Domestic
Biscuit	Indian	Indian	Batswana, Noncitizen	RSA	Domestic
Roof tiles	Indian	Indian	Batswana, Noncitizen	RSA, ROB	Domestic
Construction	Motswana, Noncitizen, BDC	British	Batswana, Noncitizen	RSA, ROB	Domestic
Concrete	BDC	S. African	Noncitizen, Batswana	RSA, ROB	Domestic
Building material	BDC, American	British	Noncitizen, Batswana	ROB,RSA	Domestic
Tire	BDC, Motswana	S. African	Batswana, Noncitizen	RSA	Domestic
Heating	Iranian Motswana	Iranian Motswana	Noncitizen, Batswana	RSA,ROB	Domestic

ROB = Botswana; RSA = Republic of South Africa; ZIM = Zimbabwe; ZA = Zambia.
Source: Author's field notes, 1994.

Table 5.16 Ownership and Management of Select Commercial and Industrial Enterprises by Nationality in Botswana

Business type	Number	Ownership			Management		
		W	**I**	**B**	**W**	**I**	**B**
Restaurants	30	15	11	4	8	12	10
Groceries	21	5	6	10	4	7	10
Bakery	5	2	3	0	2	3	0
Plants	4	2	1	1	0	1	3
Liquor	3	2	1	0	2	1	0
Bottle	9	0	0	9	0	0	9
Tailoring	7	0	0	7	0	0	7
Book/stationery	7	6	1	0	4	1	2
Silver/china	3	1	2	0	0	2	1
Curios/tourist	3	2	1	0	1	1	1
Pottery	1	1	0	0	1	0	0
Opticians	4	0	4	0	0	4	0
Dry cleaning	2	0	0	2	0	0	2
Travel agency	4	3	1	0	3	1	0
Pharmacy	13	4	9	0	4	9	0
Sports	4	1	3	0	0	3	1
Hair care	5	1	0	4	1	0	4
Hardware/construction	14	2	12	0	2	12	0
Pool care	2	2	0	0	2	0	0
Shoes/clothing	94	52	37	5	12	35	47
Electronic	16	5	9	2	5	6	5
Furniture	11	11	0	0	1	3	7
Auto repair	7	6	1	0	6	1	0
Auto sales	7	3	4	0	3	4	0
Total	276	126	106	44	61	106	109

W =South African (white); I =Indian; B = Indigenous Batswana.

Source: Author's fieldnotes, 1994.

merous among skilled workers on the shop floor than at the managerial levels, they nonetheless constituted a small minority among skilled workers. Moreover, most technical, conceptual, and senior skilled labor on the shop floor were noncitizens. Native Botswana occupied the majority of skilled posts in only three firms. Again, most of these firms were small and the quality of required skills was not high. Fourth, column five shows the sources of input that go into the industrial production process. In nearly every case almost all inputs came from South Africa. In a few instances they came from Zimbabwe, Zambia, and Malawi.

The leather industry's case is revealing. A logical assumption is that leather for manufacturing shoes and other leather products comes from Botswana, given the existence of BMC abattoirs. This is not the case for three out of the four leather products firms. The BMC's tannery processes leather to the wet-blue stage. Most of this is exported to Italy and elsewhere.[85] The lack of significant amounts of local raw materials or processed inputs in the manufacturing sector shows that this sector is not dynamically linked to the local economy. Finally, while nearly 75 percent of the industries produce for the domestic market only the remaining 25 percent have broken into the export market.[86] Thus, the manufacturing sector contributes to import substitution and foreign exchange earnings. However, it lacks the necessary backward and forward linkages to stimulate the growth of other productive sectors in the economy.

The insignificance of indigenous Batswana participation in the ownership and management of industrial enterprises is repeated in the commercial sector. Foreigners, particularly Asians, own or manage most businesses in the major shopping malls in the urban centers of Gaborone, Lobatse,[87] Francistown, and Mochudi. The latter group are predominantly Indian. The majority of the whites are South Africans (Table 5.16). Of the 276 businesses surveyed, indigenous Batswana owned only 44 (16 percent); whites and Indians accounted for 126 (45 percent) and 106 (39 percent), respectively. White ownership is mainly in the form of South African chain enterprises. All indigenous Batswana–owned firms are small. For instance, nearly 40 percent of these enterprises were bottle and tailor shops with little operating capital. These businesses also have little access to credit from commercial banks. By contrast white and Indian operators have a much greater resource base, and they are able to access credit from commercial banks. Furthermore, there is a claim among the few indigenous operators that the growth of their enterprises is not only constrained by the barriers to commercial credit and their own experience, but also the impenetrable network between South African wholesalers and the local white and Indian businesses. Government statements on the subject in the 1973–78 national development plan and my field interviews support this claim.[88]

Indigenous Batswana have greater opportunities in managing businesses than in owning them. Of the businesses surveyed indigenous Batswana managed 39 percent; whites and Indians managed 23 percent, respectively. Indigenous Batswana–owned firms accounted for nearly 40 percent of the businesses Batswana managed. By comparison, Batswana-managed Indian businesses are proportionally negligible. At the macrolevel, Indians owned and managed 106 enterprises. Only two Indian firms are managed by Batswana or anyone else. This means that whites own more than half of the Batswana-managed businesses. With the BDC's and FAP's help, indigenous Batswana gained a foothold in industrial and commercial enterprises. These advances provide some necessary experience in managing and running businesses that may become useful for future enterprise expansion or investments in other areas where Batswana have yet to make their mark. Indigenous Batswana seem to be tethered to the small and often undercapitalized commercial and industrial enterprises, despite the economy's growth and the government's sustained effort.

CONCLUSION

Independent Botswana lacked immediately exploitable resources. In addition, the regional imperial power, apartheid South Africa had Botswana in its grip. As a result of these two factors, the Botswana government had to gingerly find a formula for inducing industrial development within the framework of market economy. Two factors meant that the state and nonindigenous forces had to take the lead in spurring economic activity: the dependency of government on foreign assistance to balance its budget and the dearth of indigenous entrepreneurs. The government saw its role as creating an attractive political economic environment that would lure foreign capitalists to invest in the country. It immediately initiated infrastructural development and signed agreements with the United States and the World Bank to guarantee the sanctity of private enterprise. The government knew these assurances and infrastructural developments were not enough to attract investments in sufficient quantity; consequently, it established the BDC with several objectives in mind. First, it wanted to insure that commercially viable projects did not go to waste due to the dearth of foreign investors. Second, since Batswana did not have surplus capital to partake in their economy, the government wanted to insure that all the benefits of economic development did not accrue to noncitizens. As a result, the BDC became the citizen participant in many investments. Third, the government did not want the BDC to burden the public purse, so it gave the corporation sufficient autonomy yet demanded and enforced that it operate as a commercial enterprise.

Fourth, the government expected the BDC to generate employment through its investments and operations.

Apart from the liberal and business-friendly environment, the corporation was the government's only instrument to induce commercial and industrial development for the first decade and a half after independence. With limited financial resources, the BDC managed to establish essential commercial infrastructure. Simultaneously it invested in many viable projects in most sectors of the economy. As result of the BDC's investments and other related government activities, employment increased significantly while citizen ownership of commercial enterprises also grew, but less noticeably.

The government realized growing surplus revenues from its diamond exports that decreased its financial vulnerability in the 1970s. Just as the government's fiscal health was improving and funds were accumulating, unemployment increased faster than the number of jobs created in the economy. In addition, the public was concerned that the benefits of economic growth were accruing disproportionately to noncitizens. To counteract these tendencies, the government introduced the FAP and legislated its industrial strategy. As a financial support system, FAP encourages productive industrial investment while advancing and enhancing the indigenization and feminization of enterprises. Rather than replacing them, the FAP complemented the activities of the BDC. The FAP induced tremendous growth, particularly of small enterprises and those owned by Batswana women. Employment grew substantially as a result of FAP inducements; ownership of large and medium-scale industrial enterprises significantly remained in the hands of nonindigenous entrepreneurs for the most part.

Botswana's two premier state programs designed to foster economic growth and industrial development received clear mandates and autonomous management free from particularistic political interventions. In addition, the government of Botswana carefully monitors the activities of the two programs to keep them accountable and to insure that they evolve to address the economy's changing needs. The BDC's and FAP's solvency, accountability, and effectiveness support the claim that Botswana's dominant class have built capable public institutions. These institutions guard the integrity of the collective *capitalist* project against the provincial interest of individual members of that group. Furthermore, these efforts show that Botswana has successfully induced capitalist development while attempting to diversify its base and reduce its dependency on South Africa.

Botswana's substantial accomplishments might have been greater had the British colonial state not left behind such deep educational, entrepreneurial, and infrastructural deficits. Botswana's industrial development tools,[89] however, have not been strong enough to make a *significant* dent in South Africa's hegemony in the Common Customs Area and foreign dominance in commerce and industry. Finally, some scholars and development practitioners may consider the lack of industrial-commercial skills and entrepreneurship at independence and today as domestic and traditional barriers to economic development. This chapter clearly shows that the roots of these barriers are anything but domestic or traditional. Despite its liberal economic ideology and constraints imposed on it by the colonial legacy, Botswana systematically confronted the problem of industrial development. It has also judiciously used its diamond revenues to loosen South Africa's grip.

NOTES

[1] World Bank, *Adjustment in Africa: Reforms, Results, and the Road Ahead* (Oxford: Oxford University Press, 1994). Also World Bank, *Sub-Saharan Africa: From Crisis to Sustainable Development* (Oxford: Oxford University Press, 1989).

[2] Sepehri Ardeshir, "Back to the Future? A Critical Review of 'Adjustment in Africa': Reforms, Results and the Road Ahead," *Review of African Political Economy* 62 (1994): 559–568. The World Bank, characteristically populist in its public relations, claims that traditional culture needs to be considered a boon for development. This is standard rhetoric of the bank; it appeases some of its critics without fundamentally restructuring its development program and seriously taking account of the tremendous negative impact of its policies and those of the international system.

[3] Ibid., 559. In its 1994 report, the bank reversed its position by suggesting that the interventionist South East Asian model is of little relevance for Africa. The reader should know that the East Asian model means greater autonomy for the African state from institutions like the bank.

[4] Dennis McNamara, *The Colonial Origins of Korean Enterprises, 1910–1945* (New York: Cambridge University Press, 1990).

[5] Robert Wade, *Governing the Market: Economic Theory and the Role of Government in East Asian Industrialization* (Princeton, NJ: Princeton University Press, 1990), 108 and 73–74.

[6] McNamara, *The Colonial Origins of Korean Enterprises*, 47.

[7] Ibid. Thomas Gold, *State and Society in the Taiwan Miracle* (Armonk, NY: M. E. Sharpe, 1986). Wade, *Governing the Market*.

[8] Bruce Cumings, "The Legacy of Japanese Colonialism in Korea," in Roman Myers and Mark Peattie, eds., *The Japanese Colonial Empire* (Princeton, NJ: Princeton University Press, 1984), 478–496; Atul Kohli, "Where Do High-Growth Political Economies Come From? The Japaneese Lineage of Korea's 'Development State,' " *World Development* 22, 2 (1994): 1269–1293.

[9] Peter Evans, "The State as Problem and Solution: Predation, Embedded Autonomy, and Structural Change," in Stephan Haggard and Robert Kaufman, eds., *The Politics of Economic Adjustment: International Constraints, Distributive Conflicts and the State* (Princeton, NJ: Princeton University Press, 1992), 139–181. See Evans's most recent work on this subject: *Embedded Autonomy: States and Industrial Transformation* (Princeton, NJ: Princeton University Press, 1995).

[10] Alice Amsden, *Asia's Next Giant: South Korea and Late Industrialization* (New York: Oxford University Press, 1989).

[11] Arthur Lewis quoted in Wade, *Governing the Market*, 78.

[12] Neil Q. Parsons, "'Khama and Co.' and the Jousse Trouble, 1910–1916," *Journal of African History* 14, 3 (1975): 383–408.

[13] Ibid., 389–390.

[14] The story of the campaign is narrated by Parsons in the article just cited.

[15] Elvyen Jones-Dube, "Indigenous and Nonindigenous Entrepreneurs in Botswana: Historical, Cultural and Educational Factors in Their Emergence," Ph.D. diss., University of Massachusetts-Amherst, 1984, chapter 5.

[16] Ibid., Alan Best, "General Trading in Botswana, 1980–1968," *Economic Geography* (1970): 598–611.

[17] Jones-Dube, "Indigenous and Nonindigenous Entrepreneurs in Botswana," 115–116.

[18] Republic of Botswana, *National Development Plan, 1973-78* (Gaborone: Government Printer, 1973–78), 243.

[19] Republic of Botswana, *Transitional Plan for Social and Economic Development* (Gaborone: Government Printer, 1966), 7.

[20] Most indigenous Batswana use this term.

[21] Republic of Botswana, *Transitional Plan for Social and Economic Development*, 7.

[22] Jan Isaksen, *Macroeconomic Management and Bureaucracy: The Case of Botswana* (Uppsala: Scandinavian Institute of African Studies, Research Report No. 59, 1981). For sustained discussions of the benefits and costs of Botswana's membership in the Customs Union, see Ita Mannathoko, "Botswana and the Southern African Customs Union," paper delivered at the 1993 meeting of the Botswana Society, Gaborone; Peter Landell-Mills, "The Southern African Customs Union Agreement," *Journal of Modern African Studies* 9, 2 (1971): 263–281; A. Turner, "A Fresh Start for the Southern African Customs Union," *African Affairs* 70 (1971): 269–276; Steve Ettinger, "The Economics of the Customs Union Between Botswana, Lesotho, Swaziland, and South Africa," Ph.D. diss., University of Michigan, 1973; Paul Mosley, "The Southern African Customs Union: A Reappraisal," *World Development* 6, 1 (1978): 31–34.; Clark Leith, "The Static Welfare Economics of a Small Developing Country's Membership in a Customs Union: Botswana in the Southern African Customs Union," *World Development* 20, 7 (1992); James H. Cobbe, "Integration Among Unequals: The Southern African Customs Union and Development," *World Development* 8 (1980): 329–336. It must be noted that the Government of Botswana draws substantial revenues from the Customs Unions and seems hesitant to risk such income even when the structure of the union may impose tremendous obstacles to its economic diversification program.

[23] Quill Hermans, "Toward Budgetary Independence: A Review of Botswana's Financial History, 1900 to 1973," *Botswana Notes and Records* 6 (1974): 89–115. Also Landell-Mills, "The 1969 Southern African Customs Union."

[24] Republic of Botswana, *Industrial Development Policy: Government Paper No. 2 of 1984* (Gaborone: Government Printer, 1984). See also World Bank, *Opportunities for Industrial Development in Botswana: An Economy in Transition, Report No. 1126-81* (Washington, DC: 1993). The term formally is used here to note that government already shifted its strategy by 1982, when it introduced the Financial Assistance Policy.

[25] Republic of Botswana, *National Development Plan, 1973–78* (Gaborone, 1973), 57. At this time, the Botswana Meat Commission dominated the industrial sector and continued to do so until the late 1970s.

[26] Ibid., 60.

[27] Republic of Botswana, *National Development Plan, 1973–78*, 246. The Company Tax Rate has been further reduced to 25 percent, while a further 10 percent is earmarked for manufacturing firms. See Republic of Botswana, *Budget Speech, 1995* (Gaborone: Government Printer, February 13, 1995): 25.

[28] Republic of Botswana, *National Development Plan, 1973–78*, 241.

[29] Ibid., 248.

[30] Republic of Botswana, *National Development Plan, 1979–85* (Gaborone: Government Printer, 1979), 206.

[31] Ibid., 206.

[32] Republic of Botswana, *National Development Plan, 1985–91* (Gaborone: Government Printer, 1985), 238.

[33] Republic of Botswana, *National Development Plan, 1979–85*, 212.

[34] Stephen Lewis, Jr., and Jennifer Sharply, *Botswana's Industrialisation: Discussion Paper 245* (Brighton, UK: Institute of Development Studies, 1988), 8.

[35] Tsie argues that one of the reasons for relatively low levels of industrial employment in established industries is due to the capital intensive nature of these enterprises: *The Political Economy of Botswana in SADCC* (Harare: SAPES Books, 1995), 247.

[36] Government of Botswana, *Report of the Presidential Commission on Economic Opportunities* (Gaborone: Government Printer, 1982).

[37] Ibid., 1.

[38] Republic of Botswana, *National Development Plan, 1976-81* (Gaborone: Government Printer, 1976).

[39] FGU-Kronberg Untennehmensberatung GMBH Consulting, *Industrialisation Study, Republic of Botswana* (Eschborn, April 1978).

[40] Michael Lipton (Commission of the European Communities/Republic of Botswana), *Botswana: Employment and Labour Use in Botswana. Final Report, Vol. 1.* (Gaborone: Government Printer, 1978), 243.

[41] FGU-Kronberg Untennehmens beratung GMBH Consulting, *Industrialisation Study*, chapters 4, 5, and 6.

[42] Baledzi Gaolathe, interview, Gaborone, December 15, 1994; Gladson Kayira, interview, Gaborone, July 6, 1995.

[43] Republic of Botswana, *Financial Assistance Policy: Government Paper No. 1 of 1982* (Gaborone: Government Printer, 1982).

[44] Ibid., 1. For a careful assessment of the neoliberal thrust of FAP and the severe constraints this created for the industrial project, see Raphael Kaplinsky, "Industrialization in Botswana: How Getting the Prices Right Helped the Wrong People," in C. Colclough and J. Manor, eds., *States or Markets? Neoliberalism and the Development Policy Debate* (Oxford: Clarendon Press, 1991), 148–172.

[45] Ibid.

[46] Ibid., 2.

[47] Ibid., 10. Large-scale projects must demonstrate an economic rate of return of at least 6 percent to qualify for FAP support.

[48] Ibid., 2.

[49] The value of initial capital required for all project scales has been increased at regular intervals; in 1989, for example, these were 900,000, 25,000–900,000, and 25,000, respectively. Republic of Botswana, *Financial Assistance Policy Revised, 1989* (Gaborone: Government Printer, 1989).

[50] Ibid., 5.

[51] Republic of Botswana, *Financial Assistance Policy, 1982*, 2.

[52] Ibid., 3.

[53] Ibid., 39.

[54] Ibid., 115.

[55] Ibid., 54–56.

[56] Ibid., 131.

[57] Cameron L. Smith, Raphael Kaplinsky, John Menz, and Babutsi Beauty Selabe, *Evaluation of the Financial Assistance Policy: FAP and Its Role in Botswana Business Development* (Gaborone: Government Printer, 1988), Tables E-10 and E-11.

[58] Kaplinsky argues that the FAP strategy that opened medium and large-scale enterprises to foreigners has blocked avenues for emergent indigenous entrepreneurs ("Industrialization in Botswana," 167).

[59] World Bank, *Opportunities for Industrial Development in Botswana*, 19–21. The estimate of the bank is slightly higher than my calculation from government figures.

[60] The economic recession (some say depression) in the early to mid 1990s caused havoc in the employment sector as formal unemployment was said to have declined by over 20 percent in the summer of 1995.

[61] Republic of Botswana, *Statistical Bulletin* 18, 2 (1993): 11–12.

[62] Kaplinsky, in "Industrialization in Botswana," calls this group "free-riders" (159).

[63] Some of the firms I interviewed in 1993–94 moved to South Africa in early 1995. This seems to support the claims of some Batswana that if South Africa remains stable, many more firms will move from Botswana to the former country. Such firms will ship their products to be sold in the Botswana market.

[64] The presentation of BDC's contributions to the industrial project is preceded by that of FAP since BDC's activities are not confined to industry but rather on all profitable opportunities.

[65] Republic of Botswana, *National Development Plan, 1970–75*, 61.

[66] Republic of Botswana, *Memorandum and Articles of Association of Botswana Development Corporation* (Gaborone: 1983), 1.

[67] Ibid., 1.

[68] Such conflict was avoided until very recently, and the losses generated by "development projects" were covered by profitable operations from elsewhere. M. O. Molefane, interview, Gaborone, July 14, 1994.

[69] Republic of Botswana, *Memorandum and Articles of Association of Botswana Development Corporation* (1983), 14–21.

[70] Over the years the managing director's authority has increased. For example, the funds that he can disburse without prior approval of the board is now P500,000. Molefane, interview.

[71] Botswana Development Corporation, *Annual Report, 1979*, 3.

[72] Republic of Botswana, *National Development Plan, 1970–75*.

[73] Bank of Botswana, *Annual Report, 1994* (Gaborone: 1994), S37. The fund introduced a two-tier interest rate in 1991. The higher rate applies to nonfinancial parastatals like BDC.

[74] Botswana Development Corporation, *The First Fifteen Years*.

[75] Botswana Development Corporation, *Annual Report, 1993* (Gaborone: 1993), 7.

[76] The figures given here are for the corporation, not the group of companies in which it is involved. The profit rate of the group has been much higher than those of the corporation since the late 1970s. See Botswana Development Corporation, *Annual Report, 1994* (Gaborone: 1994), 17.

[77] The Government of Botswana has finally instructed its parastatal not to look to it for unlimited access to its funds. Consequently BDC embarked on a vigorous strategy to streamline its investment. As the managing director noted, "As we go into accelerated disinvestment, and simultaneously begin to reduce our heavy dependence on state funding, it is inevitable that we must, as a matter of urgency, brutally review and eliminate all nonperformers or enterprises yielding a noncommercial rate of return on capital employed—no matter how otherwise noble their cause may be" (Botswana Development Corporation, *Annual Report, 1994*, 16). For a discussion of BDC's divestment strategy, see Deloitte Touche Tohmatsu (for Botswana Development Corporation), *Divestiture Study: Final Report, April 1995* (Gaborone: 1994). This new strategy does not only call for divesting from unprofitable firms but also mature ones. The case of the Breweries and Sefalana are examples of the latter.

[78] This supervisory role is not always effective, as a few of the managers—almost always whites from South Africa—misappropriated business resources and ran firms to the ground (e.g., Kwena Concrete and Botswana Furniture) and escaped with the loot.

[79] Botswana Development Corporation, Memo (1994?).

[80] Botswana Development Corporation, *Annual Reports, 1972–93* and *1996*.

[81] It has come to the attention of this researcher that many of the firms sold by BDC end up in nonindigenous hands. The most ironic case is that of the Botswanacraft. Botswanacraft is one of the oldest firms established and supported by BDC to develop, enhance, and market traditional handicraft. Batswana produce traditional baskets and other crafts of exceptional quality. The firm has been successful. The BDC sold it to a white entrepreneur. Many of my informants reported that BDC made no serious attempt to find an indigenous buyer. Another example of a privatized firm was the successful Sugar Industries, which was sold to white Zimbabweans.

[82] Anonymous interview, Gaborone, August 1994. I heard the same concern of this citizen from many others, including firms partially owned by BDC. For instance, a brick manufacturer was astounded when it failed to win a government contract to supply brick for the expansion of the House of Parliament. The contract was apparently awarded to a white South African producer. This happened before the formal liberation of South Africa. The irony of a racist white South African firm supplying the construction materials for the parliament of nonracist and democratic Botswana escaped members of the tender board, which simply selected the lowest bidder that met its standards even if that undermines government policy, which is designed to encourage and help local producers to become competitive over time. See also the recent critical remarks by Mr. L. Nchindo, the managing director of Debswana. Nchindo criticized the government for not doing enough to economically empower citizens (*Business Day*, September 22, 1997), 4.

[83] Kaplinsky notes in "Industrialization in Botswana" (163) that Botswana's failure, particularly through FAP, to promote and nurture indigenous entrepreneurs is due to the ideological commitment of policy makers to use the market as a tool for this purpose. He claims that without strategy, government intervention in the market will not deliver on this.

[84] I want to thank H.N.M. for helping in collecting some of this data.

[85] This shows that if the state was more strategically interventionist, it could have played a more activist role in the leather industry.

[86] Textile exports have been praised both by the national development plan and scholars. The NDP and scholars have not acknowledged the role Batswana play in this sector. Batswana are often relegated to tasks that do not require skills. Moreover these exports are taking advantage of FAP and other government supports. Many of them told us that they will move their plants to greener pastures when the FAP and other drinking holes dry up.

[87] Batswana in surrounding villages talk of going shopping to Bombay (Lobatse) in reference to the predominance of Indian shop owners.

[88] Some Asians confided in me, after realizing that I was both a Muslim and a foreigner, that their network in South Africa is very important in maintaining their dominance in the market.

[89] The government also uses its influences to attract foreign investment beyond the purview of BDC. This effort yielded tremendous dividends when Botswana outcompeted South Africa and other countries in the region to attract Owens Corning and the Hyundai Motor Company. Hyundai cars are assembled in Gaborone.

6

MINDING THE MERITS OF THE MIRACLE: THE STATE AND COLLECTIVE INTEREST

INTRODUCTION

[C]urrent [development] advice offered to developing countries, and the thinking that underlies it, is misguided. The advice ignores a substantial body of evidence about the conditions under which [public] organizations perform well. Those who formulate the advice have not been curious enough about the evidence embedded in the instances of good government in the countries being advised . . . that government can be a remarkably strong moral presence in creating an imagery [and reality] of calling around public service—in the eyes of the public and of public workers themselves. With this moral force . . . government can get citizens to monitor its workers. With the same rhetoric and publicity, moreover, it can enlist the public to help protect its own workers from meddling by politicians and others with power in [and out of] government itself.[1]

The literature on African political economy and the state is useful in explicating the class basis of the postcolonial state. However, it is relatively weak in explaining the differential performance of various states in serving the dominant classes and systemic capitalist accumulation. This framework's explanatory power is weakened because of its failure to systematically explain how the nature of the dominant social groups, its leadership, the subaltern classes, and the international and regional context shape the internal coherence of the state apparatus and its ability to consistently and methodically pursue a development program.

By contrast, recent liberal literature on state–civil society relations suffers from two major weaknesses. First, eliminating class and related concepts from its analytical framework, it sidelines forces that are fundamental to the very reality it intends to explain.[2] Second, the liberal literature treats the effects of the international political economic context on African development as a peripheral matter. However, the liberal paradigm's rediscovery of the importance of civil society as a potential source of African political and economic revitalization adds a critical element to the development debate. The reintroduction of civil society into the debate, nevertheless, created more intellectual and political confusion given the absence of ways of differentiating key actors who might be critical to the development project from the plethora of groups in civil society. The populist thrust of this vein of liberalism coincided with the rise of the democratic bandwagon in the West and the collapse of authoritarian regimes. Consequently, strengthening the state by increasing its relative autonomy as a transformative development institution does not figure prominently in the liberal agenda. The populist illusion reaches its summit in Goran Hyden's outrageous claim "with the state literally vanishing in much of Africa, scholarly interest is likely to be elsewhere, if not on regimes at least on institutions and the many informal ways in which cultural phenomena in Africa influence institutions."[3] Other strands of liberalism that recognized the state's centrality felt that African civil societies were fragmented in fundamental ways that disabled the state. As such, this brand of liberalism's principal thrust adds little to the neoliberal prescription for the African state.

The Botswana state's operation since independence defies many liberal assumptions about African social structure, civil society's disabling role, and the postcolonial state's characteristic ineptitude. Botswana's experience also *partially* refutes African political economic analysis of the state. Although Botswana inherited a neocolonial economy in the shadow of apartheid South Africa, it nevertheless plans and manages its affairs in ways that are characteristically superior to all other postcolonial regimes. Political economists writing on Botswana differed with the orthodoxy. They noted the social arrangement among the state, mining capital, and passive-civil society. This arrangement facilitated the emergence of both strong state and liberal democratic polity. The dominant class and its leaders insured that the relatively high degree of autonomy that the BDP government constructed was used to define the country's development strategy along lines primarily beneficial to their class interest. It is not surprising that the dominant class used the state to enhance its accumulation. What is astonishing is that they managed to do this without pervasive rent seeking or corruption.[4] Furthermore, the dominant class recognized that it did not need to resort to authoritarian rule.

This final chapter has three purposes. First, it encapsulates the meaning of the Botswana experience and highlights the critical role of the state in its development. Second, it underscores the positive and negative lessons that concerned groups and institutions in Africa can draw from the Botswana development experience. Third, it elucidates the critical theoretical as well as practical and policy relevance of Botswana's experience to the ways in which we rethink about the African state as a development institution.

THE STATE AND DEVELOPMENT IN BOTSWANA

One main source of state weakness in Africa is said to be the powerful provincial forces rooted in the fragmented ethnic and political fabric of African societies. According to this argument, these centrifugal forces have overwhelmed the postcolonial state's economic and political concoction. These forces, premised on tribal and traditional patron-client ties, undermine the national authority's ability to systematically develop modern state institutions capable of addressing their societies' economic problems. Joel Migdal's book captures the thrust of this vein of scholarship, and Botswana's precolonial and colonial history *seem* to approximate the "weblike" social map of his thesis.

Chapter 2 demonstrated the ability of the strong Tswana chiefs to thwart many colonial administration initiatives. They obstructed Bechuanaland's incorporation into South Africa, as well as the administrations' attempt to reform the chiefs' hegemonic role in the "tribes'" management. These territorially based monarchs had their own ideas about how the British colonial state should act and what matters should fall under its purview. On the one hand, the chiefs went over the head of the Bechuanaland administration when they felt administrative edicts jeopardized their authority or their societies' integrity. On the other hand, the chiefs prodded a reluctant and parsimonious colonial administration when they thought their own and their subjects' interests were best served by an activist state. This multidimensional character of traditional authority goes against the claims of the theory that canonizes the chiefs' provincial nature. This interpretation of the chiefs is taken as a timeless truth and then is projected into these societies' postcolonial future. Consequently, the chiefs' provincial concerns frustrate the agenda of Africa's postindependence leaders.

Migdal's "weblike" thesis has at least five major weaknesses in relation to Botswana. First, the thesis fails to examine the dynamics of tradition in the context of colonial and capitalist domination. It simply turns traditional authority into unchanging and reactionary structures. Second, Migdal assumed that class division and interest did *not* play a critical role in the reproduction of social life in traditional societies under colonialism. Moreover, this classless characterization of traditional order, a historic inaccuracy that presumes traditional leaders did not attempt to induce social transformation that further enhanced their and their communities' interest. Third, this theory treated traditional authority as a monolithic group that retained provincial ambitions. The history of activist chiefs, such as Tshekedi and Bathoen, belies such postulates. These chiefs had their eyes on the national theater; they could not push the British colonial administration fast enough to introduce a territorial legislative council to administer Bechuanaland. Not all chiefs were involved in the movement, but the strongest took the initiative. Fourth, this theory and associated literature assume away the emergence of contemporary African leaders who were committed to the establishment and development of the nation-state and who possessed impeccable traditional credentials. Finally, the "weblike" thesis negates the common class interest shared by traditional and nontraditional leaders.

The rise of a leadership that commanded traditional and nontraditional legitimacy should not be a fiction of one's theoretical imagination if one starts from the reasonable premise that colonialism and capitalism commoditized and restructured access to resources, transformed the internal dynamics of society, and changed the leadership's preoccupation. Traditional leaders were in a privileged position in the colonial society; their children thus had preferential access to schools. Given these factors, it makes sense that the possibility existed that some children trained in secular schools could develop ideas and political ambitions beyond those the colonialists envisioned for them. For example, Tshekedi Khama was not the usual imagined or real supplicant traditional leader.[5] He not only aggravated colonial administrators, but he also had different hopes for his nephew, Seretse Khama, the future king of the Bangwato. When the colonial administrators suggested the young prince attend an industrial school in Southern Rhodesia, Tshekedi rejected this. He preferred more scholarly training to prepare Seretse to govern his people.[6] He quoted the Phelps Stokes Commission report to support his position: "The experience of history, the wisdom of science and the inspiration of literature and art will be required by native leadership to guide and direct their people through the perplexing process of evolution from primitive stages of life to those of civilization now forced upon them by overwhelming forces both kind and unkind."[7]

Tshekedi Khama, the chief of the Bangwato, the largest Tswana group in the Protectorate demonstrated that some chiefs were not narrow-minded creatures of tradition. He confirmed this in two ways. He insured that the future king was liberally educated. Tshekedi vigorously agitated for the creation of a Protectorate legislative assembly and ultimately independence. His vision paid off in Seretse Khama, whose political party, the BDP, brought together a coalition of nontraditionalist and traditional leaders. This coalition led to the formation of a Botswana nation-state unfettered by the provincial elements of chiefly tradition. Seretse and the Young Turks around him in the BDP rushed forward and formed a secular state encompassing all Protectorate Tswana and non-Tswana communities. Meanwhile, this new BDP leadership granted traditional authority a subordinate role in the new political dispensation. Although Seretse formally renounced his claim to the Bangwato throne, his royal pedigree gave his regime added legitimacy.

Serete's party consolidated its grip on power without tremendous and divisive resistance from traditional forces. First, the new government's economic policy did not rock the boat by protecting the well-being of the dominant class, including the chiefs. As a result, no class-based division existed between the young men of the BDP and the chiefs. Second, the new regime presented the chiefs with a dilemma. They enshrined the chiefs' privilege in the constitution, in effect saying retain the prestige of chieftainship, get paid for your services,[8] and stay out of politics, or risk, as one author aptly put it, "the political wilderness." Only one chief ever took up this challenge and threw his lot in politics. Bathoen's challenge was not about protecting provincial interests, but insuring his place and that of the chieftainship in national affairs.[9] In fact, he was driven by the realization that the new political dispensation was trying to lock chiefs into dealing with provincial affairs.

Consequently, the BDP government, even long after Seretse was gone, never faced a fundamental challenge from the chiefs. The BDP's leadership and the opposition parties insured that chiefs-based "tribalistic" politics never crept in from the back door. The chiefs' supposed inability to invoke their provincial magic and undermine the Botswana state attests to the weakness of the "weblike" thesis. Moreover, this argument highlights the salience of social and economic transformation and the centrality of the common economic interest the chiefs and the BDP leadership shared. The social contract consummated preserved this common interest.

The new regime, unencumbered by the burden of provincialism, nevertheless confronted a devastating colonial legacy. The British colonial state failed to develop human resources or physical, industrial, and administrative infrastructure. The government literally had to start from scratch to construct buildings for its rudimentary administration in the new capital of Gaborone under financial duress. The Botswana government was not dismayed by the daunting task of building everything. In fact, the leadership considered such a dearth of development as an opportunity to tailor-make its institutions. The fundamental advantage the new regime had and recognized was the unity of the elite and the unchallenged presidency of Seretse Khama and his government. The BDP leadership was committed to developing a capitalist economy. Their concern was how to firmly root such a system without reproducing the Bantustan they inherited from the British. President Khama and his ministers recognized that an accountable and effective public service was essential for the development of this economy. They regarded technically skilled and relatively autonomous bureaucracy, within the confines of the policy framework set by the government, as a prerequisite to translate their plans into reality. Furthermore, they understood that they needed to protect the state machinery and that its purse needed to be protected from particularistic interests of individual members of the dominant class. These precepts guided how the government developed and managed new state institutions.

The argument in chapter 3 is not that the leadership had an Aladdin's magic lamp to imagine its wishes and then miraculously bring about their realization. Rather it resulted from the BDP leadership's recognition of two prerequisites for creating effective public institutions: dominant class unity, and accountable and technically competent state apparatus insulated from particularistic rent-seeking tendencies of its members. Two factors rooted the dominant class's unity: shared educational experience, mostly in African schools in South Africa, and their common economic base in the cattle, petty trade and the civil service. The dominant class's material and ideological unity was necessary but not sufficient to keep them from engaging in internecine and fractious struggles to determine the prevailing agenda. It required unchallenged leadership that had legitimacy with the elite and the general population. This leadership then defined and nurtured the collective project of the dominant strata. Such was the leadership of Seretse Khama and the group around him. President Khama and Vice President Quett Masire strictly defined and defended the integrity of the collective project. Members of BDP followed suit, and a serious debate about the thrust and integrity of the government's development strategy never existed. The dominant class's unity, the leadership's legitimacy, consciousness, and discipline were sufficient to give the state a high degree of autonomy and potential capacity.

The government did not have a proven formula to translate this potential into coherent, coordinated, and effective state institutions. A trial-and-error planning process ensued. Fortunately the government's first major project to be planned and developed was the Shashe (copper/nickel) Project in Selebi Phikwe. The economic activity the project generated was larger than the country's GNP. The Shashe Project's complexity and economic magnitude required the young republic's undivided attention. The government also wanted to insure that the exploitation of its copper/nickel resources induced development beyond that sector and region. Consequently, it devoted its human resources to planning and directing the Shashe project. This planning exercise required all government ministries to coordinate their resources. The success and effectiveness of the Shashe planning process were not lost on the government. Critical lessons of Shashe included the importance of resources coordination, the need for skilled but expatriate labor, the necessity of national planning. The coordination and planning functions of the Shahse Project were moved to the Ministry of Finance and Development, making it the lead development agency of the government.

The Southern African Customs Union's successful renegotiation and the Shashe Project's success emboldened the leadership to further consolidate its strategy. The donor community's appreciation of the government's effec-

Photo 6.1. President Mogae.   Here he presents his campaign (1994) message to a kgotla. Mogae succeeded Masire in March 1997.

tive and timely use of resources and community's willingness to be more generous encouraged the government. The MFDP, under Quett Masire's leadership, became the government's brain center. Once this institutional framework was established, strengthening state institutions and simultaneously developing the economy moved in tandem. The discovery and exploitation of huge diamond resources and subsequent increasing revenues in the late 1970s and early 1980s did not fundamentally alter the thrust and effective management of the country's development program. Moreover, President Khama's death in 1980 created initial doubt about the vice president's ability to command the same respect and legitimacy as the former president. However, the BDP government, under the tutelage of Quett Masire, maintained its course. Similar reservations have been voiced about the current vice president's political skills to keep the ship of state in even keel with Masire's retirement in March 1998.

Botswana's traditional social structure did not cripple the independent republic. Instead, this traditional order provided an appropriate and firm basis from which to launch a state-directed development program.[10] Accountable, autonomous, and effective state institutions enabled Botswana to do in a decade what the British colonial state was unwilling and unable to accomplish in nearly eighty years of colonial rule.

A major thesis in Africanist literature argues that the continent's disastrous development experience is due to two obstacles to capitalist transformation. These obstacles are supposedly indigenous in nature and origin. The first bundle of obstacles include the absence of entrepreneurship, traditional rural ways of life that subvert capitalist transformation and differentiation, tribal politics and precapitalist patrimonial ties. Obstacles such as these overwhelm the fragile, shallow, and tiny islands of modernity. The second set of forces undermining and distorting economic growth emanates from the excessive and dominant role parastatals play in the economy. This scholarship has not provided a coherent and historically realistic explanation of how Botswana escaped from the supposedly ruinous effects of these traditional forces.

Chapters 2 and 3 demonstrate that Botswana traditional culture did not shackle the state's development efforts. Chapter 4 negates the firmly held belief that African states in general and public enterprises in particular are ineffective and inappropriate development instruments. Botswana developed several parastatals that dominated their respective sectors of the economy and avoided excessive expansion of the state apparatus as many others have done. Such a strategic utilization of public enterprises advanced the development agenda. One such effective public enterprise is the BMC. The BMC, since its nationalization in 1966, has delivered timely and effective service to the livestock industry. Despite being the sole and legal export marketing agency of Botswana livestock, the BMC has not alienated producers by extracting high rents and providing poor or inappropriate services.

The secret of the BMC success cannot be explained by the competence of the agency's management alone. Good management is certainly necessary, but not a sufficient condition to account for the success of any parastatal. Similar African agencies with good management still failed. To operate effectively competent management requires a clearly delineated mandate, a stable and predictable political context and administrative autonomy. Creating these preconditions is beyond the purview of agency management. This is the task of political leadership. Government leaders from the BDP created these conditions because of the dominant class's unity and the leaders' strength and legitimacy. The BDP government concluded that the nation's (elite) interest in the livestock sector or other sectors can be served best if public monopolies operate on a commercial basis, returning their profits to producers, in the case of livestock, or to its main shareholder, the government of Botswana. The leadership also recognized that for BMC and other similar institutions to function according to their mandate they needed to be protected from particularistic interventions by individual members of the elite. This recognition meant that the government rigorously enforced its policies governing public enterprises and acted effectively and decisively when anyone violated the spirit and the letter of these conventions. This recognition also meant that the government was willing to spend all the energies necessary to enable the agency to bring its mandate to fruition.

The government's ability to protect the nation's collective interest meant holding the dominant class together. It was not difficult to maintain this group's unity when it came to the country's development strategy in general and the livestock industry's in particular. This was so in the latter case as the majority of the elite who were in government were large or medium-sized cattle producers. The BMC livestock development strategy entailed modernizing the industry by improving its economic and physical health. This required increased public investment in infrastructural development, such as veterinary service through the ministry of agriculture, establishment of new abattoirs, and a vigorous campaign to attain and maintain access to the lucrative EEC now EU market. The BMC's mandate to return profits to producers meant increasing returns to producers with large and medium-sized herds.

The industry remained lucrative because of public infrastructural investments and EEC/EU price subsidies. The livestock industry's continued profitability benefited the old cattle aristocracy and attracted senior professionals in the civil service whose salaries were high enough to allow them to invest in livestock. The state acted as the livestock industry's guardian, and its successful management of the BMC bonded the two major elements of the dominant class. Because investment opportunities were for anyone who had money to invest, segments of the dominant class had no social basis to challenge the BMC and livestock industry strategy. The cattle elite support the livestock strategy and an efficiently run BMC. It also acts as a watchdog to insure that BMC and the state do not deviate from the established order. Without a challenge from the dominant class regarding livestock development strategy, the government built the BMC's managerial capacity, and gave its management a relatively high degree of administrative autonomy while holding it accountable to its mandate.

The only other possible opposition to the dominant strategy was the majority of small rural producers and noncattle owners. This potential opposition to the government's livestock development strategy has not materialized. These groups are disorganized and trapped in a patron-client relation with the wealthy. The absence of a credible national political opposition party, at least until very recently, that could articulate the rural poor's concerns reinforced this group's weakness. Moreover, the state and BMC had a degree of legitimacy with this group because they, or other arms of the state, delivered social services to this group, such as water, schools, and drought relief. These three factors—dominant class unity, the availability of opportunities for the disorganized rural poor, and a determined political leadership interested in sustaining the integrity of the collective project—helped the manufacture of effective and successful public enterprises, such as the BMC.

I argued in chapter 1 that scholars need to consider domestic and international forces simultaneously when assessing the degree of state's autonomy. Rather than uncritically assuming these forces constrain the state's latitude, scholars needs to unpack them to know the potential and actual effects of each on the state. Since the social geography and developmental predisposition of different domestic or international forces can vary, their respective impacts on the state will also differ.

In Botswana's case, the dominant elite did not hinder the state's autonomy to establish and nurture an effective parastatal to foster and sustain livestock industry development. Although the Botswana leaders were members of the cattle aristocracy, they did not depend on the support of their class alone. Under the Seretse leadership, they also had a wider mandate from the population. This popular legitimacy gave the government sufficient degree of freedom from the dominant class to pursue its collective interest through systematic accumulation rather than particularistic and predatory forms.

Botswana leaders recognized that systemic accumulation required institutions with the capacity to plan and effectively manage the industry. The BMC is a product of this process. The development and operations of an effective parastatal served the interests of the hegemonic domestic force. Consequently, the BMC experience points out that general arguments which portray domestic forces as barriers to development are inaccurate. Scholars need to carefully unpack domestic forces to show which segments are having what exact effects on the state's ability to mobilize resources for development. The BMC's and the government's autonomy from the particularistic interests of the members of the cattle aristocracy does not mean that the state could chart a course that fundamentally negates the group's hegemony. This partly explains why the government never seriously considered a capitalist agrarian reform program based on a smallholder strategy.

External forces can also limit or enhance the state's autonomy. The literature tends to disregard the relevancy and restrictive role of such forces, or it assumes their negative impacts on state autonomy. Actually, external forces have positively affected the government's systematic accumulation strategy, in the BMC case. First, the protected and heavily subsidized EU market has given the BMC a secure and profitable market for its products since the early 1970s. Second, EU's stringent animal health standards required the Botswana government rigorously to enforce necessary rules if it wanted to maintain continued access to this lucrative market. The BMC also has to employ skilled people and appropriate technology to insure its beef exports' quality. These conditions the EU market demanded minimally reinforced the government's livestock development strategy.[11] Finally, the BMC's success is seen as a result of conscious leaders building and guiding an autonomous state to access and exploit a favorable international context.

By contrast, the autonomous Botswana state has not been able to overcome the disadvantages created by British colonial policy, pertaining to entrepreneurial development and Botswana's integration, as a Bantustan, into the orbit of semiindustrial and subimperial racist South Africa. Chapter 5 showed that Botswana faced daunting problems in every facet of development when it became independent in 1966. Chief among these obstacles was the lack of basic physical infrastructure and human capital, such as roads, government building, communications, water and energy, skilled labor, schools, and hospitals.

The dearth of financial resources compounded this lack of physical infrastructure and human capital. Financial resources were so limited the government considered balancing its annual budget, without British subsidy, as its major goal after independence. Under these adverse conditions, the government could not embark on major development projects, particularly in industry where it lacked both basic resources as well as experience. Consequently, although the government considered industrialization critical to its development strategy, it recognized that its best option was to roll out the red carpet for potential foreign investors and to tout its membership in the Southern African Customs Union and its business-friendly climate.

Despite its commitment to a liberal economic strategy, the government was not certain that foreign investors would see this approach's merits and the opportunities available in the country. In addition, it was also concerned that only noncitizens would receive development benefits with substantial foreign investment. As a result, it established its own BDC to entice investors and promote development. When investors were not forthcoming, the BDC was to use its own resources to insure that development opportunities were exploited. As has been the government's custom, the BDC, as a parastatal, was mandated to operate on a commercial basis. The BDC had managerial autonomy while the government held it accountable to its mandate.

This liberal investment policy and mild state intervention served Botswana well during the tight fiscal years of the 1970s. As increasing revenues from diamond exports stimulated the economy—industrial employment and production grew steadily. However, the pace of employment growth, and the economy's industrial diversification and indigenization did not move fast enough to absorb the growing population and reduce dependency on cattle and diamonds. Likewise, these factors were not providing Batswana with an increasing stake in the new wealth quickly enough. Revenues from diamond exports expanded significantly in the late 1970s and the early 1980s just when the mildly interventionist strategy was experiencing serious problems. To induce further industrial production, the government introduced FAP in 1982. The FAP has been the most important element of the government's new Industrial Development Policy, which was enacted into law in 1984; FAP and the government's new industrial policy did not replace the old strategy but built on it.

The FAP was a package of subsidies targeted primarily to attract new productive investment or to *assist* in expanding existing industrial enterprises.[12] The five main purposes of the FAP were to (a) move the economy away from its dependency on two primary products; (b) induce new employment-generating sectors; (c) decentralize production away from the main towns; (d) increase import substitution of industrial products; and (e) improve indigenization and feminization of the economy. The FAP has been successful in generating a large number of new and small enterprises, expanding established ones, increasing unskilled employment substantially, and expanding opportunities for women in these sectors. Although the majority of FAP recipients were small indigenous producers, the bulk of allocated funds went to a few large enterprises owned by foreign or nonindigenous interests. Moreover, FAP-induced industrial production failed to replace industrial imports and did not enhance backward and foreword linkages in the economy. The inability of the FAP to induce such linkages testifies to South Africa's hegemonic role in the region. Finally, large foreign or nonindigenous firms dominate the industrial and commercial sector.

Three external forces circumscribed the efficacy of Botswana's industrial strategy: its social and physical infrastructural legacy, its integration into South Africa's industrial web, and its diamond revenues. The first two forces had unmistakable detrimental effects on the country's industrial effort. Diamonds and the revenues they generate have been a boon for the country. They have substantially enhanced Botswana's political and economic latitude. Diamonds are part of the external forces for two reasons. First, they are marketed overseas. Second, the state had to negotiate with the De Beers cartel. Contrary to what a senior American official in Botswana told me, De Beers was not generous to Botswana in terms of the proportional division of diamond profits between itself and the government. The government of Botswana fielded a strong and well-informed team to bargain with De Beers, particularly during the second set of negotiations. Consequently, Botswana extracted more favorable terms. As such, the exact effect of this external force was significantly contingent on the strength of De Beers as an international cartel; the quality and quantity of Botswana's diamond resources; and the ability of the state to field a skilled and prepared negotiating team with a clear mandate.

The previous four chapters show that Botswana's ability to partially transform its economy is due to several key factors. First, there existed a small and united dominant class whose legitimacy was unchallenged. Second, this class's leaders knew of the long history of independent and strong African leadership. This African leadership had its own agenda, despite British colonialism and racist South African intentions to swallow Botswana. Third, the Khama-Masire combination created an unchallenged, legitimate, and purposive leadership. They understood the importance of strong and effective public institutions to economic development. Moreover, they fully understood the need to protect such institutions and public resources from individualist and particularistic elements within and outside the dominant class. A fundamental tenet of their agenda was to nurture existing accumulation patterns while diversifying the economy.

Without this social structure and conscious and disciplined leadership, no amount of diamond revenues would have been sufficient to make Botswana an African miracle.[13] Conscious, determined leaders with a legitimate power base and autonomous, but accountable public institutions are absolutely the essential internal conditions necessary to give an African society a minimal chance to protect itself from the predations of the international order and predatory elements of the elite. This is also necessary for an African society to take advantage of whatever opportunities the global order has to offer. Still these conditions may not be enough to overcome the legacy of the past.

Botswana's relative success directly contradicts the current debate on African political economic restructuring. First, the state, rather than the romanticized market, has directed the most successful African economy, said to be a model for others. Despite the economy's capitalist nature, the Botswana state is, proportionally, the largest owner of assets and enterprises in the continent. For instance, the Botswana Housing Corporation, a state parastatal, owns more than 70 percent of all urban housing in the country. The issue is not the level of government ownership per se, rather how well public resources are managed.

Second, Botswana's experience shows that the country's success in inducing development is contingent on the autonomy, legitimacy, and discipline of its leaders and institutions. The task of creating political and social infrastructure is more complex than the West's standard prescription of good governance and liberal democracy. It means that the African state needs to be autonomous from the dictates of international financial institutions and imperial states. This is essential if the state is to define a legitimate strategy grounded on a society's needs, rather than on the idealized image of a free-market economy.

Third, Botswana's inability to overcome the legacy of British colonialism and induce successful industrialization, despite effective government, points to the external forces' importance in the postcolonial context and African development. This contradicts the neoliberal characterization of the postcolonial context as an inconsequential peripheral factor. Consequently, the neoliberal project fortifies industrial underdevelopment in the absence of an autonomous state to support such a project.

Fourth, despite the tremendous growth of wealth, Botswana is one of the most socially unjust countries in the world. The leadership's inability or unwillingness to chart a development strategy that progressively reduces such "radical inequality" and maintains economic growth and effective state institution is/was primarily due to the leaders' social inclinations. In part, it is also due to their attempt to avoid being labeled as "radicals or socialists." Labels like these could antagonize Western donors and investors, particularly in early years. They could have also invited the wrath of South Africa. The dominant class's ideological predisposition and the risk of violent South African intervention caused the government to miss a great opportunity to induce growth while minding equity. Growth with equity need not have challenged the leadership's autonomy and legitimacy. Nor would it have necessarily interfered with their effort to establish effective public institutions. Nor did a growth- and equity-oriented strategy *immediately* compromise the dominant class's position in the short term, particularly if the state created opportunities for the rural poor to access productive assets, such as cattle, land, and water resources. This type of strategy would have encouraged the growth of small- and medium-sized farmers, rather than the protection of large traditional and commercial farmers.

A progressive policy in the urban areas would have produced a smaller gap between high- and low-income groups. It also would have produced greater and more coordinated support for promising local entrepreneurs without sickening them with subsidies and protection. Moreover, a growth-oriented, but progressive development program, would not have antagonized social and liberal democrats in the West. This strategy would not have frontally and grossly attacked capitalist economy nor electoral democratic polity.

Fifth, the dominant class–biased Botswana project is a warning that the emerging patterns in the continent, under the tutelage of international financial institutions,[14] may mean that African societies may, at best, emulate elements of Botswana's socially unjust model without state leadership that can advance a more moderate path. Dominant class–biased patterns of development will not have legitimacy with the majority of the population, whose well-being is increasingly marginalized. The illegitimacy of such states will perpetuate political instability and economic lethargy.

Sixth, Botswana, which is blessed with diamonds and has a relatively effective state, has had tremendous difficulty overcoming problems inherited from the past. It also had difficulties embarking on industrialization. Without diamonds and an effective state, other African countries will have greater difficulties in modeling themselves after the African miracle. As such, an African strategy geared toward growth and social justices will entail qualitatively greater state intervention, not less.[15] Furthermore, heightened and effective state involvement will need to coordinate and guide this strategy, particularly in dealing with international forces.

DOMESTIC AND REGIONAL REALIGNMENT: THE BASIS OF AN AFRICAN SOCIAL CONTRACT

The Botswana miracle confirms the critical relationship that distinguishes a developmental state from a predatory one: embedded autonomy. It goes beyond the articulated perimeter of this concept. Botswana's technical capacity to implement its plans and judiciously use public resources is the result of public institutions with autonomy and meticulously enforced coherent and professional code of conduct. This aspect of Botswana's experience supports the notion that bureaucratizing public institutions is a vital part of what capacity building is all about. Such capacity building, however, is only one aspect of creating a public-private alliance that will jointly manufacture development. The absence of entrepreneurial social groups that the state could embed with and Botswana's subsequent inability to induce industrialism indicates that bureaucratizing the state apparatus alone will not deliver a productive and dynamic economy. In other words, technically proficient public institutions and dynamic elements of civil society who share a common development project (industrialization) must join forces to break with the past. In fact, the Botswana state, by playing a complementary role failed to go into a true partnership with the indigenous local entrepreneurs it helped create.

The immensely valuable concept of embedded autonomy assumes two issues that are central to the manufacture of an embedded relationship. First, Evans's book does not fully address the social processes that facilitate or impede the emergence of state leadership that is mindful of the professional bureaucratization of public institutions. I presume that the value of the concept is not only to show the architecture of existing developmentalist states, but to point out what needs to be done and how to achieve that goal. If that is the case, then we need more context specific analysis of the internal political economic dynamics of particular societies. It is out of such context that particular dominant social groups and leaders emerge. The interplay between such dominant groups, the leaders of the state and subaltern classes shape the domestic terrain in which autonomy, legitimacy, and development orientation unfold. The Botswana experience demonstrates that it is possible to bureaucratize the state apparatus given the presence of three factors: a weak and dependent subaltern class, a small and united dominant class, unchallenged and legitimate leaders conscious of the importance of effective, insulated, and accountable institutions.

In other societies, such as Somalia, Uganda, Sudan, Ethiopia, and former Zaire, where the social equation and historical context were different, the institutional outcome was anything but professional bureaucracies. In Somalia, for example, the rural population was relatively powerless and disorganized. Consequently, it did not exert much pressure on the dominant petty bourgeoisie. Unlike Botswana's hegemonic dominant class, the Somali petty bourgeoisie was not united. Nor did it have disciplined leaderships who recognized the importance of bureaucratization[16] in conjunction with systemic accumulation and the protection of the collective project. The disunity of this group and rural people's passivity meant that no social anchor existed that gave the political order any degree of stability. The constant shifting of political alliances among the elite created conditions in which long-term investment in institution building became impossible. In the absence of such institutions, little systematic development took place. The state apparatus, sustained by the largesse of the cold war, disintegrated with that support's termination.

Second, Evans's analysis underestimates the important roles that international forces play in creating and sustaining a political system that can induce developmental or predatory states. A consortium of Western countries brought into power the clique who *owned* the former Zairean state, Evans's archetypal predatory state. This consortium has defended the Mobutu regime until near its collapse. Evans used Zaire as an archetypal predatory state to show the state's nonbureaucratic internal structure.[17] Such a view of the predatory versus developmental state is too narrow. This book's purpose is to understand how developmental or predatory states come into being. From the Zairean vantage point, the Mobutu-led military overthrow, with the full support of the West, of Patrice Lumumba's government created an illegitimate regime. Thanks to the military and material support of the West, the Mobutu regime remained in power from 1965 to 1997 through repression. This regime turned the population against the West, realizing the regime's and the West's mutual dependence and vulnerability. This mutual dependence, unhinged to a productive economic program, virtually created an environment where bureaucratic institutions' logic was counterproductive. Consequently, one cannot understand the genesis of the hell that has been Zaire without appreciating the unholy alliance between a cannibalistic local elite and an opportunistic Western order. This combination jointly produced the archetypal Zairean predatory state.

The critical question in the post–cold war world is: how conducive are local and international conditions for developmental states to rise out of the ashes of predatory ones? Africa tragically lost its autonomy twice with disastrous results and it is currently going through another phase that has deepened its vulnerability. The first loss came with colonization—some may legitimately say with slavery—when African societies lost their collective capacity to govern their affairs. The second catastrophic loss of autonomy occurred when the emergent dominant classes, in collusion with international forces, hijacked the "independent" state. These instances induced conditions that literally and figuratively devastated African life. The destruction of state capacity and the erosion of its legitimacy in the second instance reinvented neocolonial forces as new sovereigns without military presence on the ground. Neoliberal institutions, such as the International Monetary Fund and the World Bank, have usurped public policy-making prerogatives and promise to turn the current crisis into a permanent disaster.

Rejuvenating neocolonial politics and a dependent dominant class will only tighten the grip of these forces. What is needed is a careful redefinition of a collective project such that its central objective is growth *and* social justice.[18] These two fundamental features of the new social contract will circumscribe the state's policy latitude. A growth and social justice project presupposes an alliance of political forces. These political forces must include small rural producers, urban working people, and segments of the business class predisposed to engaging in productive industrial investment. Creating leadership with legitimacy, discipline, commitment to this new social contract, and building the necessary state apparatus and productive and progressive public-private network are key to Africa's resurrection.

A knowledgeable and well-respected senior World Bank official noted in Gaborone that "Batswana business leaders must discipline the state bureaucracy to make it more business friendly." The leaders this World Banker described are nearly all attached to the big, nonindigenous enterprises who have marginalized Batswana.[19] This advice may be counterproductive as many of these businessmen are short-term oriented and therefore concerned about immediate gains. What needs to be done is for a younger group of leaders to take over the policy-making process and to prioritize and nurture certain industries or sectors. The purpose of this exercise is not to have a uniform and blanket policy, but to create a selective method of supporting (midwifing and husbanding) and disciplining promising and transformative business enterprises.

An African-centered reconstruction program minimally has two prerequisites. Building appropriate African state institutions is a necessary but insufficient step for political and economic renewal. The design and architecture of this type of a developmental state machinery will, by nature, be different from those inspired by neoliberal reforms. This is not to say that some elements of the neoliberal program, such as, rationalizing state bureaucracy, will not be part of the strategy for renewal. However, the agenda for renewal goes well beyond bureaucratic reform. It must also reclaim political and policy autonomy so that African societies may choose their priorities.

A second prerequisite for an African-centered reconstruction program is a domestic and regional reorganization of alliances. In the domestic sphere, this will mean a triple alliance of the state, productive domestic capital, and urban and rural working people. The purpose of the domestic alliance is fivefold: (a) to rejuvenate existing but dilapidated assets; (b) to invest in new enterprises; (c) to nurture public-private relations that will induce social justice and growth; (d) to increase productive employment; and (e) hold the state accountable and discipline private enterprises. At the regional level, the strategy has two requirements: building and developing economic complementarities; investing in joint industrial projects and sharing benefits equitably. These domestic and regional programs must be coordinated to avoid unnecessary overlaps and one undermining the other.

As noted earlier, the state's primary domestic objectives are to invest in sectors that may lead to new areas of excellence and capitalize on existing comparative advantage in the short term. These single country–based projects will not succeed, given most African societies' vulnerability and weakness in the fierce and globally competitive market. These circumstances make the need for new types of regional cooperation and integration obvious. Alliances such as these will require novel and formal regional institutions with the authority to negotiate with international forces. The exhaustion of the post-colonial state and inter-state institutions is an opportunity to invent regionally embedded institutions. The future is going to be harsh even with effective state and regional institutions. Without them, the prognosis is too painful to contemplate.[20]

This two-tiered strategy is not a call for autarchy. The strategy emphasizes the need for pragmatic and historically relevant programs to change the continent's fortunes. Finally, the most vital lesson of the Botswana experience is that three factors short-circuited the state's accomplishments. These were: (a) the unjust inclination of the dominant class; (b) the endurance of conditions inherited from colonialism; and (c) unfriendly regional context. Effectively coordinated internal and regional strategies will take account of the full meaning of *An African Miracle*.

NOTES

[1] Judith Tendler, *Good Government in the Tropics* (Baltimore, MD: Johns Hopkins University Press, 1997), 135 and 142.

[2] Some liberal scholars are so ensconced in their worldview that they do not accept "neoliberalism" as a commonly accepted conceptual framework and development strategy. This further blinds them from seeing realities in Africa.

[3] Goran Hyden, "Rethinking Theories of the State: An Africanist Perspective," *Africa Insight* 26, 1 (1996): 34.

[4] Although recent reports by the government and scholarly literature point to increased *corruption* by members of the elite, the level and magnitude of corruption in Botswana is still far less significant than all others in the continent. Furthermore, in Botswana there is at least an attempt to openly debate this problem as well as trying to control its impact on public institutions. Kenneth Good, "Corruption and Mismanagement in Botswana: A Best-Case Example?" *Journal of Modern African Studies* 32, 3 (1994): 499–521. Misappropriation of public resources by the elite in Botswana seems negligible in comparison to the titanic corruption in South Korea, where it was discovered in 1996 that the last military ruler of South Korea embezzled several hundred million dollars.

[5] See the brilliant narration by Michael Crowder, *The Flogging of Phinehas McIntosh: A Tale of Colonial Folly and Injustice, Bechuanaland, 1933* (New Haven, CT: Yale University Press, 1988).

[6] N. Parsons, W. Henderson, and T. Tlou, *Seretse Khama, 1921–1980* (Gaborone: Macmillan, 1995), 30.

[7] Ibid., 30.

[8] Jack Parson, "Succession, Legitimacy, and Political Change in Botswana," in his *Succession to High Office in Botswana* (Athens: Ohio University Center for International Studies, 1990), 98.

[9] Several knowledgeable Batswana told me that had Tshekedi lived long enough, he would have joined and supported the national project rather than nurture provincial hopes. This suggestion is supported by Tshekedi's own view of the need for an educated African leader.

[10] This relationship highlights what Evans and Tendler term social capital. This, however, was not used by the state to vigorously enhance citizens' stake in the economy. For a discussion of social capital and development, see Evans, "Government Action, Social Capital and Development: Reviewing the Evidence on Synergy," *World Development* 24, 6 (1996): 1119–1132. For a sustained discussion of this subject, see Robert Putnam, *Making Democracy Work: Civic Traditions in Modern Italy* (Princeton, NJ: Princeton University Press, 1993). Traditional Botswana patron-client relations facilitated this phase of liberal democracy contrary to the prediction of Putnam's theory. The Botswana case supports Tendler's recent arguments about the importance of the quality of central state institutions and leadership. The paradox is that the same state that has done so much to induce development also hinders the evolution of vibrant society-wide civic culture that can give greater momentum to economic development. As such, I feel that the state and political and business leaders can act as catalysts and substantially speed up the formation of civic culture. This may indeed mean that society does not have to wait but for a generation to get this process under way. Currently dominant neoliberal policies promote individualism and greater inequality at the expense of social cohesion and the development of civic culture.

[11] It has been reported that another condition demanded by the EU was that BMC pass on its profits to producers. J. Solway, personal communication, November 15, 1994. This might have been the case, but such a rule was already an important and enforced tenet of BMC's mandate.

[12] This clearly shows that the state plays the role described by Evans (1996) as "complementary" rather than embedding with local entrepreneurs in synergistic fashion. The aloofness of public officials also underscores this relationship. Some of this aloofness is justified, given the predominance of foreigners in the sector. It is, however, tragic that genuine citizen entrepreneurs get the same or worse treatment.

[13] President Masire stepped down from the presidency in March 1998. Vice President and Minister of Finance and Development Planning F. G. Mogae became president. It is an open question as to whether President Mogae will be able to hold together the two factions of his party (similar statements were about Masire's leadership abilities when he took over the presidency after Seretse's death. Moreover, the party may at best hang on to a substantially reduced majority in parliament after the next general election. Some observers claim that the Botswana National Front, the main opposition party, may in fact defeat the BDP in the next elections, recent internal splits notwithstanding. In either case, this may mean that the unity of the ruling party and the unchallenged leadership of Presidents Khama and Masire may be a thing of the past. What such uncertainty and possible leadership instability may mean for state autonomy and capacity is open to speculation. I will leave this matter to be sorted out by long-term scholars of Botswana.

[14] Note the recent shift in South Africa from the reconstruction and development broadly supported by the population to the Ministry of Finance and international financial institutions–designed and inspired Growth, Employment, and Redistribution (GEAR).

[15] This is also supported by Evans's book, *Embedded Autonomy: States and Industrial Transformation* (Princeton, NJ: Princeton University Press, 1995), chapter 1.

[16] The exception was the second prime minister, Abdirazaq H. Hussein, who seriously attempted to streamline and professionalize the bureaucracy from 1964 to 1967. His government left office after President Osman, who appointed him prime minister, was defeated. There has not been a similar attempt since 1967. For a more detailed comparison, see Abdi Samatar, "Leadership and Ethnicity in the Making of African State Models: Botswana Versus Somalia," *Third World Quarterly* 18, 4 (1997): 687–707.

[17] Evans, *Embedded Autonomy*, 45.

[18] Social justice is critical to rebuilding social cohesion, an essential ingredient for recovery and reconstruction. Social capital and cohesion was destroyed by predatory states and the dynamics set in motion by neoliberalism.

[19] Mr. L. Nchindo, the government-appointed managing director of Debswana, recently criticized the government for marginalizing Batswana in the economy in *Business Day*, "Botswana Not Doing Enough to Empower Citizens," (Johannesburg, September 22, 1997): 4.

[20] For an accessible discussion of the global forces at work and their social and economic impacts, see H. Martin and H. Schumann, *The Global Trap: Globalization and the Assault on Democracy and Prosperity* (Pretoria: Human Sciences Research Council, 1997.) For a different reading of the state in the new global context, see Linda Weiss, *The Myth of the Powerless State* (Ithaca: Cornell University Press, 1998).

GLOSSARY

Basamane	commoner head man
Batswana	citizens of Botswana
Bihari	client families
Bogale	female age regiment
Bogwera	male age regiment
Kgamelo or Mafisa	loaned cattle
Kgosane	headman
Kgosi	king
Kgotla	community meeting ground, also group of related families residing in the same area of a village
Matimela	stray cattle
Mephato	age regiment
Morafe	nation
Motswana	individual citizen of Botswana

BIBLIOGRAPHY

Ake, Claude. *Democracy and Development in Africa*. Washington, DC: Brookings Institution, 1996.

Alavi, Hamza. "The State in Post-colonial Societies: Pakistan and Bangladesh." *New Left Review* 74 (1972): 59–82.

Amsden, Alice. *Asia's Next Giant: South Korea and Late Industrialization*. New York: Oxford University Press, 1989.

———. "Why Isn't the Whole World Experimenting with the East Asian Model? Review of the World Bank's *The East Asian Miracle: Economic Growth and Public Policy*." Working Paper Series, no. 47. New School for Social Research, n.d.

Ardeshir, Sepehri. "Back to the Future? A Critical Review of 'Adjustment in Africa': Reforms, Results and the Road." *Review of African Political Economy* 62 (1994): 559–568.

Bank of Botswana. *Annual Report, 1993*. Gaborone, 1993.

———. *Annual Report, 1994*. Gaborone, 1994.

———. *Annual Report, 1996*. Gaborone, 1996.

———. *Economic Review 1996*. Gaborone, 1996.

———. *Report of the Rural Economic Survey, 1986*. Gaborone, 1986.

Bardhan, Parnab. *The Political Economy of Development in India*. London: Basil Blackwell, 1984.

Barkan, J. McNulty, and P. M. Ayeni. "Hometown Voluntary Associations, Local Development, and the Emergence of Civil Society in Western Nigeria." *Journal of Modern African Studies* 29, 3 (1991): 457–480.

Barkar, Jonathan. *Rural Communities Under Stress*. New York: Cambridge University Press, 1989.

Bates, Robert. *Beyond the Miracle of the Market: The Political Economy of Agrarian Development in Kenya*. New York: Cambridge University Press, 1989.

Bayart, Jean-François. *The State in Africa: The Politics of the Belly*. London: Longman, 1993.

Bechuanaland Protectorate. *Annual Report*. London: HMSO, 1964.

———. *Proclamation and Subsidiary Legislation*, 39, no. 61 of 1954: 20–62.

———. *Proclamation and Subsidiary Legislation,* 42, no. 57 of 1957: 111–114.

———. *The Chieftainship Law, Law No. 29 of 1965.* Supplement to the Bechuanaland Government Gazette. Gaborone, December 31, 1965.

———. *The Local Government (District Council) Law No. 35 of 1965.* Supplement to the Bechuanaland Government Gazette. Gaborone, December 31, 1965.

———. *Development Plan.* Gaborone, 1963.

Beckman, Bjorn. "Imperialism and Capitalist Transformation: Critique of a Kenya Debate." Review of African Political Economy 19 (1980): 48–62.

———. "Imperialism and the National Bourgeoisie." *Review of African Political Economy* 22 (1981): 5–19.

———. "The Post-colonial State: Crisis and Reconstruction." *IDS Bulletin* 19 (1988): 26–34.

———. "Whose State? State and Capitalist Transformation in Nigeria." *Review of African Political Economy* 23 (1982): 37–51.

Beckman, B. and G. Andrea. *The Wheat Trap: Bread and Underdevelopment in Nigeria.* London: Zed Books, 1985.

Benson, Mary. *Tshekedi Khama.* London: Faber and Faber, 1960.

Berman, B., and J. Lonsdale. "Coping with the Contradictions: The Development of the Colonial State in Kenya, 1895–1914." *Journal of African History* 20 (1979): 488–505.

Berry, Sara. *Fathers for Their Sons: Accumulation, Mobility, and Class Formation in an Extended Yoruba Family.* Berkeley: University of California Press, 1983.

———. "Social Institutions and Access to Resources in African Agriculture," *Africa* 59, 1 (1989): 41–55.

Best, Alan. "General Trading in Botswana, 1980–1968." *Economic Geography* (1970): 598–611.

Biersteker, Thomas. *Multinationals, the State and Control of the Nigerian Economy.* Princeton, N.J.: Princeton University Press, 1987.

Boone, C. *Merchant Capital and the Roots of State Power in Senegal.* Cambridge: Cambridge University Press, 1992.

Booth, David. "Alternative in the Restructuring of State-Society Relations: Research Issues for Tropical Africa." *IDS Bulletin* 18, 4 (1987): 23–30.

Botswana Development Corporation. *Annual Reports.* Gaborone: 1972–96.

———. *The First Fifteen Years, 1970–1985.* Gaborone, 1985.

Botswana Development Corporation, Memo [1994?].

Botswana Meat Commission. *Annual Reports.* Gaborone, 1966–1994.

Bratton, Michael. "Beyond the State: Civil Society and Associational Life in Africa." *World Politics* 41, 3 (1989): 407–430.

Burawoy, Michael. *The Politics of Productions: Factory Regimes Under Capitalism and Socialism.* London: Verso, 1985.

Business Day. "Botswana Not Doing Enough to Empower Citizens." (Johannesburg, September 22, 1997): 4.

Cabral, Amical. *Revolution in Guinea: An African People's Struggle.* New York: Monthly Review Press, 1974.

Central Statistical Office. *Employment Survey* (Gaborone: Government Printer: September 1985).

———. *Statistical Bulletin,* vol. 21, no. 4 and vol. 22, no. 1. Gaborone: 1997.

———. *Population Census Data.* Gaborone: Government Printer, 1991.

———. *Labour Force Statistics.* Gaborone: Government Printer, 1991–92.

Charlton, R. "Bureaucrats and Politicians in Botswana's Policy-making Process: a Re-interpretation." *Journal of Commonwealth & Comparative Politics* 29, 3 (1991): 265–282.

Charney, Craig. "Political Power and Social Classes in Neocolonial African State." *Review of African Political Economy* 38 (1987): 48–65.

Cheru, Fantu. *The Silent Revolution in Africa: Debt, Development and Democracy.* London: Zed Books, 1989.

Cobbe, James H. "Integration Among Unequals: The Southern African Customs Union and Development." *World Development* 8 (1980): 329–336.

———. "Minerals in Botswana." In J. H. Cobbe, ed., *Government and Mining in Developing Countries* (Boulder, CO: Westview Press, 1979).

Cohen, D. L. "The Botswana Political Elite: Evidence from the 1974 General Election." *Journal of Southern African Affairs* 4 (1979): 347–372.

Colclough, C., and S. McCarthy. *The Political Economy of Botswana: A Study of Growth and Income Distribution.* Oxford: Oxford University Press, 1980.

Comaroff, John. "Class and Culture in a Peasant Economy: The Transformation of Land Tenure in Barolong." In R. P. Webner, ed. *Land Reform in the Making.* London: Rex Collings, 1982.

Crook, R. "State Capacity and Economic Development: The Case of Cote d'Ivoire." *IDS Bulletin* 19 (1988): 19–24.

———. "State Capacity and Political Institutions in Cote d'Ivoire and Ghana." *IDS Bulletin* 21, 4 (1990): 24–34.

Crowder, M. *The Flogging of Phinehas McIntosh: A Tale of Colonial Folly and Injustice, Bechuanaland, 1933.* New Haven: Yale University Press, 1988.

———. "Tshekedi Khama and Opposition to the British Administration of the Bechuanaland Protectorate, 1926–1936." *Journal of African History* 26 (1985): 193–214.

———. "Tshekedi Khama, Smuts, and South West Africa." *Journal of Modern African Studies* 25, 1 (1987): 25–42.

Cruise O'Brien, D. *Saints and Politicians: Essays in the Organization of a Senegalese Peasant Society.* Cambridge: Cambridge University Press, 1975.

Cumings, Bruce. "The Legacy of Japanese Colonialism in Korea." In Ramon Myers and Mark Peattie, eds., *The Japanese Colonial Empire.* Princeton, NJ: Princeton University Press, 1984.

———. "The Origins and Development of Northeast Asian Political Economy: Industrial Sectors, Product Cycles, and Political Consequences." In F. Deyo, ed., *The Political Economy of New Asian Industrialism.* Ithaca, NY: Cornell University Press, 1987.

———. *The Origins of the Korean War.* Princeton, NJ: Princeton University Press, 1981.

Currey, Robert L. "Poverty and Mass Unemployment in Mineral-Rich Botswana." *American Journal of Economics and Sociology* 46, 1 (1987): 71–87.

Danevad, Andreas. *Development Planning and the Importance of Democratic Institutions in Botswana: Report 7.* Bergen, Norway: Chr. Michelsen Institute, 1993.

Deloitte Touche Tohmatsu (for Botswana Development Corporation). *Divesture Study: Final Report, April 1995* (Gaborone).

Diop, M. C., ed. *Senegal: Essays in Statecraft.* (Dakar: CODESRIA, 1993).

Diop, M. C. and M. Diouf. *Le Senegal sous Abdou Diuof: Etat et societé.* (Paris: Karthala, 1990).

Dukiewics, Piotr, and Gavin Williams. "All the King's Horses and All the King's Men Couldn't Put Humpty-Dumpty Together Again." *IDS Bulletin* 18 (1987): 39–44.

Ettinger, S. "The Economics of the Customs Union Between Botswana, Lesotho, Swaziland and South Africa." Ph.D. diss., University of Michigan, 1973.

Evans, Peter. "Class, State, and Dependence in East Asia: Lessons for Latin Americanists." in F. Deyo, ed. *The Political Economy of New Asian Industrialism.* Ithaca, NY: Cornell University Press, 1987.

———. *Embedded Autonomy: States and Industrial Transformation.* Princeton, NJ: Princeton University Press, 1995.

———. "Government Action, Social Capital and Development: Reviewing the Evidence on Synergy." *World Development* 24, 6 (1996): 1119–1132.

———. *Dependent Development: The Alliance of Multinationals, State and Local Capital in Brazil.* (Princeton, NJ: Princeton University Press, 1979).

———. "The State as a Problem and Solution; Predation, Embedded Autonomy and Structural Change." In S. Haggard and R. Kaufman, eds., *The Politics of Economic Adjustment: International Constraints, Distributive Conflicts and the State.* Princeton, NJ: Princeton University Press, 1992.

Evans, Peter, D. Rueschemeyer, and T. Skocpol, eds. *Bringing the State Back In.* New York: Cambridge University Press, 1985.

Eyoh, Dickson. "From Economic Crisis to Political Liberalization: Pitfalls of the New Political Sociology for Africa." *African Studies Review* 39, 3 (1996): 43–80.

FGU-Kronberg Untennehmensberatung GMBH Consulting. *Industrialisation Study, Republic of Botswana.* Eschborn, 1978.

Fidzani, N. H. "Understanding Cattle Off-take Rates in Botswana." Ph.D. diss., Boston University, 1993.

Finlay, David. Interview (Ramatswa, November 22, 1993, and January 18, 1994).

Frank, L. "Khama and Jonathan: Leadership Strategies in Contemporary Southern Africa." *Journal of Developing Areas* 15 (1981): 173–198.

Galborone, Harry. "The Problem of the State in Backward Capitalist Societies." *African Development* 6, 1 (1981): 45–70.

Gaolathe, Beledzi. Interview (Gaborone, December 15, 1994).

Gillett, Simon. "The Survival of the Chieftainship in Botswana." *Botswana Notes and Records* 7 (1975): 103–108.

Glassman, Jim, and Abdi I. Samatar. "Development Geography and the Third World State." *Progress in Human Geography* 21, 2 (1997): 164–198.

Gold, Thomas. *State and Society in the Taiwan Miracle.* Armonk, NY: M. E. Sharpe, 1986.

Good, Kenneth. "At the Ends of the Ladder: Radical Inequalities in Botswana." *Journal of Modern African Studies* 31, 2 (1993); 203–230.

———. "Corruption and Mismanagement in Botswana: A Best-Case Example?" *Journal of Modern African Studies* 32, 3 (1994): 499–521.

———. "Interpreting the Exceptionality of Botswana." *Journal of Modern African Studies* 30, 1 (1992): 69–95.

Gossett, C. W. "The Civil Service in Botswana: Personnel Policies in Comparative Perspective." Ph.D. diss., Stanford University, 1986.

Government of Botswana. *The Laws of Botswana: Vol. X, Chapter 74:04*, rev. ed. Gaborone: Government Printer, 1987.

———. *The Rural Income Distribution Survey in Botswana, 1974–75.* Gaborone: Government Printer, 1975.

———. *Report of the Presidential Commission of Inquiry into the Operation of the Botswana Housing Corporation.* Gaborone: Government Printer, 1992.

———. *Report of the Presidential Commission on the Inquiry into the Land Problems in Mogodishane and Other Peri-Urban Villages.* Gaborone: Government Printer, 1991.

———. *National Policy on Tribal Grazing Land: Paper No. 2 of 1975.* Gaborone: Government Printer, 1975.

———. *Report of the Presidential Commission on Economic Opportunities.* Gaborone: Government Printer, 1982.

Great Britain. *Bechuanaland Annual Report, 1959.* London HMSO, 1959.

Grotpeter, P.J.J. "Political Leadership and Political Development in the High Commission Territories." St. Louis: Ph.D. diss., Washington University, 1965.

Gulhati, R. "Who Makes Economic Policy in Africa and How." *World Development* 18, 8 (1990): 1147–1161.

Gunderson, G. L. "Nation Building and the Administrative State: The Case of Botswana." Berkeley: Ph.D. diss., University of California, 1970.

Hailey, L. *Native Administration in the British African Territories. Part V. The High Commission Territories.* London: HMSO, 1953.

———. *The Republic of South Africa and the High Commission Territories.* Oxford: Oxford University Press, 1961.

Harland-Thunberg, P. *Botswana: An African Growth Economy.* Boulder, CO: Westview Press, 1978.

Harvey, C. *Botswana: Is the Economic Miracle Over?* Brighton, UK: IDS Discussion Paper 298, 1992.

———, ed. *Papers on the Economy of Botswana.* London: Macmillan, 1981.

———. "Successful Adjustment in Botswana." *IDS Bulletin* 16, 3 (1985): 47–61.

Harvey, C., and S. Lewis, Jr. *Policy Choice and Development Performance in Botswana.* London; Macmillan, 1990.

Henderson, W. "Seretse Khama: A Personal Appreciation." *African Affairs* 89 (1990): 27–56.

Hermans, Quill. Interview (Gaborone: June 6, 1994).

———. "Toward Budgetary Independence: A Review of Botswana's Financial History, 1900 to 1973." *Botswana Notes and Records* 6 (1974): 89–115.

Hitchcock, R. H. "Comment." *Botswana Notes and Records* 19 (1987): 173.

———. "Tradition, Social Justice and Land Reform in Central Botswana." *Journal of African Law* 24, 1 (1980): 1–34.

Hubbard, Michael. *Agricultural Exports and Economic Growth: A Study of the Botswana Beef Industry.* London: Routledge, 1986.

———. "Botswana and the International Beef Trade 1900–1981." Ph.D. diss., Sussex University, 1981.

Hudson, D. J. "The Taxation of Income from Cattle Farming." In Charles Harvey, ed., *Papers on the Economy of Botswana* (London: Macmillan, 1981).

Hyden, Goran. *Beyond Ujamaa in Tanzania: Underdevelopment and an Uncaptured Peasantry.* Berkeley: University of California Press, 1980.

———. *No Shortcuts to Progress: African Development Management in Perspective.* Berkeley: University of California Press, 1983.

———. "Rethinking Theories of the State: An Africanist Perspective." *Africa Insight* 26, 1 (1996): 26–35.

Iliffe, John. *The Emergence of African Capitalism.* London: Macmillan, 1983.

Isaksen, Jan. *Macroeconomic Management and Bureaucracy: The Case of Botswana, Research Report No. 59.* Uppsala: Scandinavian Institute of African Studies, 1981.

Jacqz, Jan W. *Report of a Conference on United States Assistance to Botswana & Lesotho.* New York: The African-American Institute, 1967.

Jefferies, Keith. "Public Enterprises and Privatization in Botswana." In Thomas Clarke, ed., *International Privatization Strategies and Practices.* New York: Walter De Gruyter, 1994.

Jefferies, K. R. and C. Harvey. "Botswana's Exchange Controls: Abolition or Liberalization." *Development Policy Review* 13, 3 (1995): 277–305.

Jessop, Bob. *State Theory: Putting Capitalist States in Their Place.* University Park: Pennsylvania State University Press, 1990.

Johnson, Chalmers. *MITI and the Japanese Miracle: The Growth of Industrial Policy, 1925–1975.* Palo Alto, CA: Stanford University Press, 1982.

Jones, D. *Aid and Development in Southern Africa: British Aid to Botswana, Lesotho and Swaziland.* London: Croom Helm, 1977.

Jones-Dube, Elvyen. "Indigenous and Non-Indigenous Entrepreneurs in Botswana: Historical, Cultural and Education Factors in their Emergence." Ph.D. diss., University of Massachusetts, Amherst, 1984.

Kaplinsky, Raphael. "Capitalist Accumulation in the Periphery—The Kenyan Case Reexamined." *Review of African Political Economy* 17 (1980): 83–105.

———. "Industrialization in Botswana: How Getting the Prices Right Helped the Wrong People." In C. Colclough, and J. Manor, eds. *States or Markets? Neoliberalism and the Development Policy Debate.* Oxford: Clarendon Press, 1991.

Khama, Tshekedi. "Chieftainship Under Indirect Rule." *Journal of the Royal African Society* 34, no. 136 (1935): 251–261.

———. "Developing Representative Government in a Changing Africa: Problems of Political Advance in Backward Territories." *Africa World*, September 1956.

———. "The Principles of African Tribal Administration." Address at the Chatham House, April 11, 1951.

Kim, Kwan S. "The Korean Miracle (1962–80) Revisited: Myths and Realities in Strategies and Development." In H. Stein, ed., *Asian Industrialization and Africa: Studies in Policy Alternatives to Structural Adjustment* (New York: St. Martin's Press, 1995).

Kohli Atul. "Where Do High-Growth Political Economies Come From? The Japanese Lineage of Korea's 'Development State,'" *World Development* 22, 2 (1994): 1269–1293.

Landell-Mills, P. Interview (Gaborone, October 19, 1993).

———. "The Southern African Customs Union Agreement." *Journal of Modern African Studies* 9, 1 (1971): 263–281.

Langdon, Steven. "The State and Capitalism in Kenya." *Review of African Political Economy* 8 (1977): 90–97.

Leith, Clark. "The Static Welfare Economics of a Small Developing Country's Membership in a Customs Union: Botswana in the Southern African Customs Union." *World Development* 20, 7 (1992): 1021–1028.

Lewis, Steven Jr., and Jennifer Sharply. *Botswana's Industrialisation: Discussion Paper 245.* Brighton, UK: Institute of Development Studies, 1988.

Leys, Colin. "Capital Accumulation, Class Formation and Dependency—The Signifi- cance of the Kenyan Case." *Socialist Register* (1978): 241–266.

———. "The Overdeveloped Post-colonial State: A Reevaluation." *Review of African Political Economy* 5 (1976): 39–49.

Lipton, Michael (Commission of the European Communities/Republic of Botswana). *Botswana: Employment and Labour Use in Botswana. Final Report, Vol. 1.* Gaborone: Government Printer, 1978.

Luke, T. (Government of Bechuanaland). *Report on Localization and Training.* Gaborone, 1964.

Mamdani, Mahmood. *Politics and Class Formation in Uganda.* New York: Monthly Review Press, 1976.

Martin, H., and H. Schumann. *The Global Trap: Globalization and the Assault on De- mocracy and Prosperity.* Pretoria: Human Sciences Research Council, 1997.

Maylam, P. *Rhodes, the Tswana and the British, 1885–1899.* Westport, CT: Greenwood, 1980.

Mazonde, Isaac N. *Ranching and Enterprise in Eastern Botswana: A Case Study of Black and White Farmers.* London: Edinburgh University Press, 1994.

McDonald, I. *Report on Cattle Marketing in Botswana.* Gaborone, 1982.

McNamara, Dennis L. *The Colonial Origins of Korean Enterprises, 1910–1945.* New York: Cambridge University Press, 1990.

Meillassoux, Claude. "A Class Analysis of Bureaucratic Process in Mali." *Journal of Development Studies* 6, 2 (1970): 91–110.

Migdal, Joel. *Strong Societies and Weak States: State and Society Relations and State Capabilities in the Third World.* Princeton, NJ: Princeton University Press, 1988.

Ministry of Agriculture. *Annual Agricultural Statistics.* Gaborone, 1979, 1984, 1990, 1993.

Ministry of Commerce and Industry. Personal Communication. September 21, 1994.

Ministry of Finance and Development Planning. *Keynote Policy Paper.* Gaborone, 1989.

———. *The Third Evaluation of Financial Assistance Policy (FAP).* Draft Report Sub- mitted by Phaleng Consultancies (Pty) Ltd, March 1995.

Mkandawire, Thandika. "The Social Sciences in Africa: Breaking Local Barriers and Nego- tiating International Presence." *African Studies Review* 40, 2 (1997): 1–22.

Mkandawire, Thandika, and Naceur Bourenane, eds. *The State and Agriculture in Af- rica.* Dakar: CODESRIA Book Series, 1987.

Molutsi, P. P. "The Ruling Class and Democracy in Botswana." In J. Holm and P. P. Molutsi, eds., *Democracy in Botswana.* Gaborone: Macmillan, 1989.

———. "Social Stratification and Inequality in Botswana: Issues in Development, 1950– 1985." Ph.D. diss., Oxford University, 1986.

Molutsi, P.P., and J. Holm. "Developing Democracy When Civil Society Is Weak; The Botswana Case." *African Affairs* 89, 356 (1990): 323–340.

Morrison, John Stephen. "Botswana's Formative Late Colonial Experience." In S. J. Stedman, ed., *Botswana: The Political Economy of Democratic Development.* Boulder, CO: Lynn Rienner, 1994.

———. "Development Optimism and State Failure in Africa: How to Understand Botswana's Relative Success." Ph.D. diss., University of Wisconsin, Madison, 1988.

Mosley, Paul. "The Southern African Customs Union: A Reappraisal." *World Develop- ment* 6, 1 (1978): 31–43.

Munro, William. "Power, Peasants and Political Development: Reconsidering State Construction in Africa." *Society for Comparative Study of Society and History* 38, 1 (1996): 112–148.

Murray, R. "Second Thoughts on Ghana." *New Left Review* 42 (1967): 25–39.

Natural Resources Institute. *National Resources Sector Review, Botswana: A Strategy for ODA Technical Assistance.* Chatham, UK: Natural Resources Institute, 1993.

Nielson, O. K. *Memo.* London: Botswana Meat Commission, October 15, 1990.

Nwako, M.P.K. Interview (Gaborone, March 22, 1994).

Obondo-Okoyo, T., ed. *Botswana 1966–1986: Twenty Years of Progress.* Gaborone: Department of Information and Broadcasting, 1986.

Oden, Bertil. *The Macroeconomic Position of Botswana: Research Report No. 60.* Uppsala: Scandinavian Institute of African Studies, 1981.

Onimode, Bade. *Imperialism and Underdevelopment in Nigeria.* London: Zed Books, 1982.

Oyugi, A. Odhiambo, M. Chege, and A. K. Gitonga, eds. *Democratic Theory—Practice in Africa.* London: James Currey, 1988.

Parson, Jack. *Botswana: Liberal Democracy and the Labor Reserve in Southern Africa.* Boulder, CO: Westview, 1984.

———. "Cattle, Class and the State in Rural Botswana." *Journal of Southern African Studies* 7, 2 (1981): 236–255.

———. "The Political Economy of Botswana: A Case in the Study of Politics and Social Change in Post-Colonial Botswana." Ph.D. diss., Sussex University, 1979.

———, ed. *Succession to High Office in Botswana: Three Case Studies.* Athens: Ohio University Center for International Studies, 1990.

———. "Succession, Legitimacy, and Political Change in Botswana." In Jack Parson, ed. *Succession to High Office in Botswana: Three Case Studies.* (Athens, OH: University Center for International Studies, 1990).

Parsons, N. W. Henderson, and T. Tlou. *Seretse Khama 1921–1980.* Gaborone: Macmillan, 1995.

Parsons, N. Q. "The Economic History of Khama's Country in Botswana, 1884–1930." In R. Palmer and N. Parsons, eds. *The Roots of Rural Poverty in Central and Southern Africa* (Berkeley: University of California Press, 1977).

———. "The Evolution of Modern Botswana: Historical Revision." In Louis Picard, ed., *The Evolution of Modern Botswana.* Lincoln: University of Nebraska Press, 1985.

———. "'Khama and Co.' and the Jousse Trouble, 1910–1916." *Journal of African History* 14, 3 (1975): 383–408.

Peters, Pauline. *Dividing the Commons: Politics, Policy, and Culture in Botswana.* Charlottesville: University Press of Virginia, 1994.

———. "Cattlemen, Borehole Syndicates, and Privatization in Kgatleng District of Botswana: An Anthropological History of a Commons." Ph.D. diss., Boston University, 1983.

Picard, L. *The Politics of Development in Botswana: A Model of Success?* Boulder, CO: Lynn Rienner, 1987.

Pim, A., Sir. *Financial and Economic Position of the Bechuanaland Protectorate: Command Paper 4368.* London: HMSO, 1933.

Proctor, J. H. "The House of Chiefs and Political Development of Botswana." *Journal of Modern African Studies* 6, 1 (1968): 59–79.

Putnam, R. *Making Democracy Work: Civic Traditions in Modern Italy.* Princeton, NJ: Princeton University Press, 1993.

Raikes, Philip. *Modernizing Hunger: Famine, Food Surplus and Farm Policy in the EEC and Africa.* London: James Currey, 1988.

Raphaeli, N., J. Roumanu, and A. C. MacKeller. *Public Sector Management in Botswana: Lessons in Pragmatism.* Washington, DC: World Bank, 1985.

Republic of Botswana. *Budget Speech 1995.* Gaborone: Government Printer, 1995.

———. *The Development of Bechuanaland Economy: Report of the Ministry of Overseas Development: Economic Survey Mission.* Gaborone: Government Printer, 1966.

———. *Financial Assistance Policy: Government Paper no. 1 of 1982.* Gaborone: Government Printer, 1982.

———. *Financial Assistance Policy Revised, 1989.* Gaborone: Government Printer, 1989.

———. *Government Paper no. 1 of 1973.* Gaborone: Government Printer, 1973.

———. *Industrial Development Policy: Government Paper no. 2 of 1984.* Gaborone: Government Printer, 1984.

———. *Memorandum and Articles of Association of Botswana Development Corporation.* Gaborone: Government Printer, 1983.

———. *National Assembly Official Report (Hansard 22): Part 2.* Gaborone: Government Printer, 1987.

———. *National Development Plan, 1970–75.* Gaborone: Government Printer, 1970.

———. *National Development Plan, 1973–78.* Gaborone: Government Printer, 1973.

———. *National Development Plan, 1975–80.* Gaborone: Government Printer, 1975.

———. *National Development Plan, 1976–81.* Gaborone: Government Printer, 1976.

———. *National Development Plan, 1979–85.* Gaborone: Government Printer, 1979.

———. *National Development Plan, 1985–91.* Gaborone: Government Printer, 1985.

———. *National Policy on Incomes, Employment, Prices and Profits: Government Paper No. 2.* Gaborone: Government Printer, 1972.

———. *Planning Officers Manual.* Gaborone: Government Printer, 1986.

———. *Report of the Ministry of Overseas Development.* Gaborone: Government Printer, 1966.

———. *Statistical Bulletin* 16, 3 (1993).

———. *Statistical Bulletin* 18, 2 (1993): 11–12.

———. *Statistical Bulletin* 21, 2 (1996) and 22, 1 (1997).

———. *Transitional Plan for Social and Economic Development.* Gaborone: Government Printer, 1966.

Robertson, Harold. "From Protectorate to Republic: The Political History of Botswana, 1926–1966." Ph.D. diss., Dalhousie University, 1979.

Rothchild, D., and N. Chazan, eds. *The Precarious Balance: State and Civil Society in Africa* (Boulder, CO: Westview Press, 1988).

Rudolph, I., and S. Rudolph. *In Pursuit of Lakshami: The Political Economy of the Indian State.* Chicago: University of Chicago Press, 1987.

Samatar, Abdi. "Leadership and Ethnicity in the Making of African State Models: Botswana and Somalia." *Third World Quarterly* 18, 4 (1997): 687–707.

———. *The State and Rural Transformation in Northern Somalia, 1884–1986.* Madison: University of Wisconsin Press, 1989.

———. "Structural Adjustment as Development Strategy? Bananas, Boom and Poverty in Somalia." *Economic Geography* 69, 1 (1993): 25–43.

Samatar, Ahmed. *Socialist Somalia: Rhetoric or Reality?* London: Zed Books, 1988.

———, ed. *The Somali Challenge: From Catastrophe to Renewal?* Boulder, CO: Lynne Rienner, 1994.

Sandbrook, Richard. *The Politics of Africa's Economic Recovery.* New York: Cambridge University Press, 1993.

———. *The Politics of Africa's Economic Stagnation.* New York: Cambridge University Press, 1985.

Saul, John. "The State in Post-colonial Societies: Tanzania." *Socialist Register* (1974): 349–372.

———. "The Unsteady State: Uganda, Obote and General Amin." *Review of African Political Economy* 5 (1976): 12–28.

Schapera, I. *A Handbook of Tswana Law and Custom.* London: Oxford University Press, 1938.

———. *Tribal Innovators: Tswana Chiefs and Social Change, 1795–1940.* London: Athlone Press, 1970.

Sekyi-otu, Ato. *Fanon's Dialectic of Experience.* Cambridge: Harvard University Press, 1996.

Shaw, Timothy. "Towards a Political Economy of the African Crisis: Diplomacy, Debates and Dialectics." In M. Glantz, ed., *Drought and Hunger in Africa: Denying Famine a Future.* New York: Cambridge University Press, 1987.

Shivji, Issa. *Class Struggle in Tanzania.* New York: Monthly Review Press, 1976.

Sklar, R. "Developmental Democracy." *Society for Comparative Study of Society and History* 29, 4 (1987): 686–714.

Smith, L. Cameron, Raphael Kaplinsky, John Menz, and Babutsi Beauty Selabe. *Evaluation of the Financial Assistance Policy: FAP and Its Role in Botswana Business Development.* Gaborone: Government Printer, 1988.

Solway, Jacqueline. "Commercialization and Social Differentiation in a Kalahari Village, Botswana." Ph.D. diss., University of Toronto, 1986.

———. Personal communication (March 15, 1995).

Steenkamp, Philip. "Cinderella of Empire?: Development Policy in Bechuanaland in the 1930s." *Journal of Southern African Studies* 17, 2 (1991): 293–308.

Steenkamp, P. Interview (Gaborone: November 15, 1994).

Stein, Howard. "Theories of Institutions and Economic Reform in Africa." *World Development* 22, 12 (1994): 1833–1849.

———, ed. *Asian Industrialization and Africa: Studies in Policy Alternatives to Structural Adjustment.* New York: St. Martin's Press, 1995.

Stevenson, M. "Aid Management in Botswana: From One to Many Donors." In C. Harvey, ed., *Papers on the Botswana Economy.* Gaborone: Macmillan, 1981.

Strokke, Kristian. "Authoritarianism in the Age of Market Liberalism in Sri Lanka." *Antipode* (forthcoming).

———. "The Postcolonial African State and Development Geography." *Norsk Geografish Tidsskrift* 48 (1994): 123–131.

Swainson, N. *The Development of Corporate Capitalism in Kenya, 1918–1977.* Berkeley: University of California Press, 1980.

Swainson, Nicola. "The Rise of a National Bourgeoisie in Kenya." *Review of African Political Economy* 4 (1977): 39–55.

Tendler, Judith. *Good Government in the Tropics.* Baltimore, MD: Johns Hopkins University Press, 1997.

Tlou, T. "The Nature of Batswana States: Towards a Theory of Batswana Traditional Government—The Batswana Case." *Botswana Notes and Records* 6 (1974): 57–75.

Tlou, Thomas. "A Political History of Northwest Botswana to 1906." Ph.D. diss., University of Wisconsin, 1972.

Tsie, Balefi. *The Political Economy of Botswana in SADCC.* Harare: SAPES Books, 1995.

Turner, A. "A Fresh Start for the Southern African Customs Union." *African Affairs* 70 (1971): 269–276.

Turner, Terisa. "Multinational Corporation and the Instability of the Nigerian State." *Review of African Political Economy* 5 (1976): 63–79.

UNDP, UNICEF, and Republic of Botswana. *Planning for People: A Strategy for Accelerated Human Development in Botswana.* Gaborone: Sygma Publishing, 1993.

Von Freyhold, Michaela. *Ujamaa Villages in Tanzania: Analysis of a Social Experiment.* New York: Monthly Review Press, 1979.

Wade, Robert. *Governing the Market: Economic Theory and the Role of Government in East Asian Industrialization.* Princeton, NJ: Princeton University Press, 1990.

———. "The World Bank and the Art of Paradigm Maintenance: The East Asian Miracle in Political Perspective." *New Left Review* 217 (1996): 3–36.

Watts, M. "The Agrarian Question in Africa." *Progress in Human Geography* 13 (1989): 1–44.

———. *Silent Violence: Food, Famine and Peasantry in Northern Nigeria.* Berkeley: University of California Press, 1983.

Watts, M., ed. *The State, Oil and Agriculture in Nigeria.* Berkeley, CA: Institute of International Studies, 1987.

Watts, M., and T. Bassett. "Politics, the State and Agrarian Development: A Comparative Study of Nigeria and the Ivory Coast." *Political Geography Quarterly* 5, 2 (1986): 103–125.

Weiss, Linda. *The Myth of the Powerless State.* Ithaca: Cornell University Press, 1998.

White, Gordon. *Developmental States in Asia.* London: Macmillan, 1988.

World Bank. *Accelerated Development in Sub-Saharan Africa: An Agenda for Action.* Washington, DC: World Bank, 1981.

———. *Adjustment in Africa: Reforms, Results and the Road Ahead.* New York: Oxford University Press, 1994.

———. *Botswana: Development Strategy in a Mineral-led Economy, Basic Economic Report, Volume 1, Report No. 735-BT.* Nairobi: Eastern Africa Regional Office, 1975.

———. *The East Asian Miracle: Economic Growth and Public Policy a World Bank Research Report.* New York: Oxford University Press, 1993.

———. *Opportunities for Industrial Development in Botswana: An Economy in Transition, Report No. 1126-81.* Washington, DC: World Bank, 1993.

———. *Sub-Saharan Africa: From Crisis to Sustainable Growth.* Washington, DC: World Bank, 1989.

Wylie, Diana. *A Little God: The Twilight of Patriarchy in a Southern African Chiefdom.* Johannesburg: Witwatersrand University Press, 1990.

Ziemann, W., and M. Lazendorfer. "The State in Peripheral Societies." *Socialist Register* (1977): 143–177.

INDEX

ABOUT THE AUTHOR

ABDI ISMAIL SAMATAR is Associate Professor of Geography and member of the MacArthur Program for International Peace and Cooperation at the University of Minnesota. He is also chief research affiliate at the Human Sciences Research Council, Pretoria, South Africa.

ISBN 0-325-00069-7

HARDCOVER BAR CODE